The Paradox of
Fiscal Austerity

The Paradox of Fiscal Austerity

Justin Vélez-Hagan

LEXINGTON BOOKS
Lanham • Boulder • New York • London

Published by Lexington Books
An imprint of The Rowman & Littlefield Publishing Group, Inc.
4501 Forbes Boulevard, Suite 200, Lanham, Maryland 20706
www.rowman.com

6 Tinworth Street, London SE11 5AL, United Kingdom

British Library Cataloguing in Publication Information Available

Library of Congress Cataloging-in-Publication Data Available

ISBN 978-1-4985-7193-7 (cloth)
ISBN 978-1-4985-7194-4 (electronic)

Contents

Introduction

The Paradox Explained

"It's time to tighten the family's belt." If you grew up in a typical American household, you probably heard this once or twice in your lifetime. My own family's belt seemed to be ever-tightening (unless it was preoccupied with correcting my behavior), a memory I don't mind passing on to my own children, whether or not it is financially necessary. Thrift used to be heralded as a useful characteristic for family heads to maintain, especially in times that required putting the budget on the chopping block. Ben Franklin, for instance, wasn't just one of America's Founding Fathers; he was the first Cheapskate-in-Chief. Despite being quite wealthy, he advocated frugality by choosing to eat economically, and leveraged his fame to make his famous hobo-chic manner of dress a worldwide trend.

Certainly, there are generationally learned traits that our ancestors tried to send along as a "gift" with their other finer attributes. My grandparents mastered the art of penny-pinching during the Great Depression, as did everyone else alive in the 1930s. They mock us for going to Starbucks when we can easily plant a coffee tree in a nearby mountain range and, in only five years or so, have unlimited free arabica for life. Despite being free-loving hippies, their kids couldn't shed the guilt of parsimony either. My wife thanks them for creating the food hoarder that I am today.

In the United States, it's difficult to see how these philosophies have translated into upward trending consumer, or household, debt, and a downward trend in our personal savings. Figure 0.1, *U.S. Personal Savings*, demonstrates the former. Look at the nominal rate of household savings (using 1959 as the benchmark rate), and you can clearly feel a downward vibe. Those large, seemingly out of nowhere, spikes are when we hoarded like the end of the world was coming (which we probably thought it was) just after a period

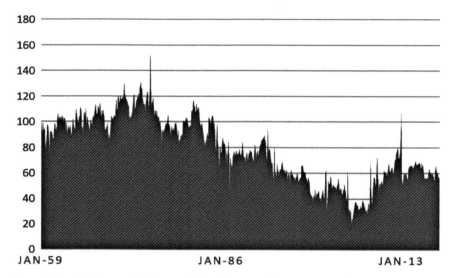

Figure 0.1 US Personal Savings. Author Generated from "Personal Saving Rate," U.S. Bureau of Economic Analysis, Accessed July 22, 2019, https://fred.stlouisfed.org/series/ PSAVERT.

of economic contraction. While these data don't take us far enough back to see the conditions right after the Great Depression of the 1930s and World War II in the 1940s, it does show the lagging effects that continued through the 1960s and 1970s, before a long nosedive that troughed before the housing crisis and Great Recession of 2006–2007 began. Figure 0.2 presents more dramatic results. Whereas household savings in the United States have dipped to almost half of what it used to be, our debt has gone through the roof. Consider the indexed time period of 1959, when personal savings were set equal to 100; as of late 2018, we're butting up against about half that level. Consumer debt, on the other hand, increased eighty times over the same time period, to nearly $4 trillion today.

Worldwide savings rates have remained remarkably stagnant since 1977, increasing to a peak of 27 percent of GDP just before the global economic shock that developed on the heels of the U.S. Great Recession (henceforth known as the 2008 global crisis or Global Crisis of 2008), only to return to recent historical averages of close to 24 percent (see figure 0.3). On the other hand, a slew of research—attempting to find something to blame after the most recent worldwide crises—has begun to point the finger at rising private consumer debt. In 1900, household debt equated to around 40 percent of GDP, passing total public debt in 1960-ish and growing far beyond 100 percent of GDP since the recent Global Crisis of 2008.[1] Clearly, our global belt has been loosened.

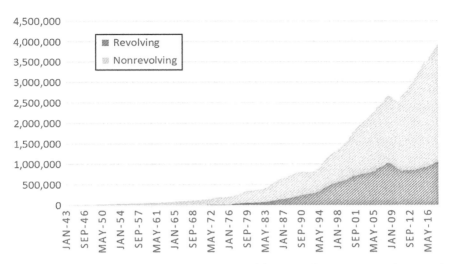

Figure 0.2 US Consumer Debt. Author Generated from "Total Consumer Credit Owned and Securitized, Outstanding," Board of Governors of the Federal Reserve System, Accessed July 22, 2019, https://fred.stlouisfed.org/series/TOTALSL.

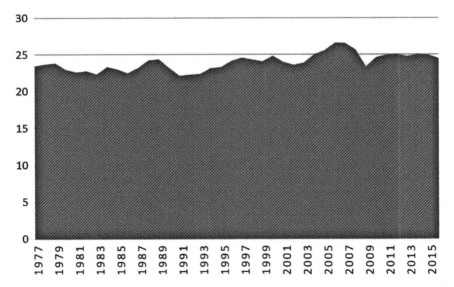

Figure 0.3 World Gross Savings. Author Generated from "Gross National Savings (% of GDP)," International Monetary Fund, Accessed November 18, 2018, https://www.imf.org/external/pubs/ft/weo/2019/01/.

But, if we look at pure correlation, you may assume that debt is necessarily good. After all, over the period from 1990 to 2010—the same period in which consumer debt seems to have begun an exponential acceleration—the world's poverty rate was also cut in half.[2] Clearly our lives have improved: educational attainment has increased, GDP per capita has increased, equal rights have expanded, literacy has improved, life expectancy is up, and when I'm tasked with the household chore of grocery shopping, I literally only have to lift a finger and that's just to hit the "re-order last delivery" button (though I still complain). The ease and comfort at which we conduct our daily lives, along with unparalleled access to modern conveniences and entertainment, means that we live in a time in which our daily lives are far easier with the opportunity to be far more productive (if we choose to not be distracted by our devices) than ever in history.

Whether we finance our chosen lifestyles on personal credit cards is our own business, but when governments do it, it's everyone's business. In our own households, we are generally aware of the maximum debt load we can withstand. While too often you hear about the McMansion financed by maxed-out credit cards, most of us live within a particular set of well-defined means: we make an income, we spend more than we take in because, well, we can, and we eventually find a way to pay off the chunk of debt we built up or file bankruptcy and wait out the consequences. Governments, on the other hand, have a lot more at stake.

If governments followed the "optimal" fiscal policy path, budget surpluses during economic expansions would counter deficits that arise as a result of increases in government spending during contractions, leading to balanced budgets in perpetuity (with an average of zero public debt outstanding). That sounds nice and sweet, doesn't it? But, when was the last time we (or any country) followed what has now become a fairy-tale philosophy?

Adam Smith advanced his belief that what is good for wholesome family fiscal management practices should be applied to nations as a whole when he wrote "what is prudence in the conduct of every private family, can scarce be folly in that of a great kingdom."[3] Though Smith's profound impact on the economic system of the United States is undisputable, America has maintained a nice balance on its revolving credit line ever since the country's inception. Alexander Hamilton was a staunch advocate of a national debt—a consolidation of all of the states' debts acquired during the Revolutionary War at the time—as a means of ensuring national unity.[4] It worked; we've been united in our indebtedness ever since.[5]

It hasn't been a straight uphill climb, however. For much of the country's history, the United States has maintained some level of fiscal prudency, or at least a tendency toward and a desire to retreat to a balanced budget. While running deficits when necessary—during wars and other crises, we realized the importance of doing whatever we had to do to the national bottom line to get out alive—we also had a number of surpluses that Adam Smith, Ben Franklin, and the shrinking cadre of surviving Grandmothers who lived through the Great Depression would be proud of. Most living today will be surprised to know how often twentieth-century U.S. policymakers followed what Buchanan and Wagner deemed that "old-time fiscal religion,"[6] confining deficits to only the neediest of bad times. In the 1920s, the United States ran a surplus for an entire decade. We took a break from all of that money-saving during the Depression and World War II, but surpluses made a resurgence in the late 1940s, 1950s, 1969, and as recently as 1998–2001. For most of the twentieth century, however, we took a decided turn in another direction. Since World War II, with the few noted exceptions, fiscal deficits haven't been viewed as so desperately reckless to the well-being of future generations as they once were. Though again, considering pure correlation, one can argue that it hasn't been all bad, as the United States has simultaneously developed the world's most prosperous economy.

Chapter 1 will delve more deeply into where *public debt* (henceforth, all references to debt will mean a nation's aggregate public or government debt) has taken us in this country, along with a comparison across the countries of the Organization for Economic Co-operation and Development (OECD), which is generally considered to comprise the developed world. What has allowed for the proliferation of what some may define as "a lot of debt" is better understood as a positive relationship between a country's growth rate and the interest rate on its outstanding public debt balances. Yes, just like a typical household, a country has to pay interest on its debt as well. It makes logical sense then that if the interest rate that a country has on its growing pool of debt outpaces expected economic growth rates, there will eventually (if not immediately) be a problem. On the other hand, if this is true, some suggest the opposite may also be true: as long as growth rates exceed interest rates, we should be able to borrow in perpetuity. There has been a substantial body of recent literature that has developed to study these effects (see *Modern Monetary Theory* discussion in chapter 4), along with some controversial forays into the exact levels of debt that are considered *too much*.

Outside of the grand question of what level of debt will eventually cross a country into danger territory, there is less controversy over the fact that excessive government spending is unsustainable in the long run, in most circumstances. For example, consider the Great Recession in the United States that started around 2007, which eventually led to a global shock that affected the world in 2008. As the economy of the United States, and those of a number of other countries, began to contract, a typical response is to either maintain spending levels or increase them in order to counter contractionary effects leading to increased deficits. Deficits can't be sustained forever (or can they be? We'll get into this more in chapter 1), so your elected legislators or your friendly local dictator will get together to decide which fiscal policies they should enact—or whose land they should confiscate—in order to reverse the trend. Such policies that attempt to reduce the deficit in order to allow for long-run sustainability of a nation's economy are known by several names. *Austerity* is the word you'll more commonly hear across the news media, but it is too often used as a term of disparagement today, making it hard for policymakers to apply it without having to explain the potential positive outcomes of fiscal discipline. Some prefer *fiscal austerity*, *austere fiscal policy*, *cutting like there's no tomorrow*, and *austere measures*, but I'm partial to the sweeter sounding, and more poetic, *fiscal consolidations*, or FCs, which I will use throughout the rest of this book (though I will often interchange it with some of the other versions, just to make sure you are paying attention). The effects of FCs will be a major point of focus and the theme that is woven into the remaining chapters.

But here's the paradox: despite the insistence of technocrats, academics, and other experts regarding an optimal fiscal policy regime, we tend to want to implement FC measures the least when we may need them the most. As debt gets out of control and economic growth begins to wane, elected and appointed leaders often shun the policies that help control deficits for those that expand them in order to do what they perceive as "best" for today's economy. Perhaps they are right to not want to cut back on spending in a time that the populace needs more help, but we'll talk more about that later.

Doubling down on the paradox: what is really needed to help a country grow again is too often the opposite of what our intuition and inner gut tell us to do. Nudged by classical Keynesian economic theory, policymakers tend to assume that only more spending will drag us out of a recessionary hole, while cutting back often leads to better outcomes. FCs are important and necessary in many cases, and in lots of those cases actually help an economy.

Part One of this book will begin with a history of public debt crises, furthering some of the concepts mentioned above. There have been a million books written on the history of such crises, considering both public and private debt, but this section will lay out the context for the additional discussions after. Despite the vast number of attempts to describe and understand crises of yore, the fascinating part is that we are constantly learning more about history, with updated facts, figures, and fun. Even considering the most recent Great Recession in the United States—and subsequent impact across the world—few of us remember what really happened just a few short years ago. Forgiving our short memories, the issue may always be that we generally fail to grasp the entire context of a crisis, relying instead on contemporary news reports and the first books to hit the market as foundations for our understanding of those crises. Unfortunately, only time gives us a consistently better frame of reference and an increasing ability to understand. Throughout Part One I try to provide an overview of the most updated knowledge on our favorite times of economic peril.

Chapter 2 discusses the various policy solutions that have been drawn from legislators' tool belts in response to crises. Here I will touch on the monetary policies (those that are enacted by central banks) that succeed economic crises, but will focus more on the fiscal side of things (those implemented by elected legislators, appointed officials, and other bureaucrats), while chapter 3 kicks off what you really wanted to learn: How do these solutions compare? Here I'll get into the weeds and discuss some of the nitty-gritty results that researchers have discovered over a period up until around 2008, or so (warning: statistics may be involved). If you want to know what the data says—because you've already decided that my opinion or that of others is meaningless—focus your attention here.

Since we're all wrong once or twice in our lives, chapter 4—and a bit in chapter 6—will be dedicated to our historical wrongness. Since the worldwide economic shock of 2008, a substantial subset of research has been dedicated to updating, sidestepping, explaining, and overturning everything we ever said in the past. Here we get into some of the more prominent findings since this time period by famous researchers who *actually* know what they are doing. For the most part, studies tend to build upon past studies and generally offer updates, twists, and minor corrections. However, occasionally a mass of rebuttals negate prior findings faster than a politician's actions counter his own words, allowing us to better understand why we were getting it so wrong before.

The problem, however, is that the powers that enact policies suffer from what I'll deem *politicitis*: a dangerous, highly contagious, and (to date) incurable disease that inhibits logic and any sense of fiduciary duty in favor of an intense, insatiable desire to be elected into a position of leadership and influence. (I might be a bit cynical about politics.) Chapter 5 opens the discussion of the ever-present influence of politics in the world of policymaking. While most of the world's population admits to a desire for economic policies that impact us in the long term, our short attention spans have allowed for the proliferation of so much *politicitis* that legislators often focus on short-term solutions that don't always allow for long-term prosperity. This chapter gets into the why of politics and how the political world relates to fiscal policy, attempting to provide some evidence of the impact of austerity on political success. The evidence may not be as clear-cut as you might have once thought.

Part Two of the book contains a series of case studies, providing a deeper insight into the root causes of public debt crises in a few selected countries, the FC or other fiscal and monetary policies that were subsequently enacted, and how they all fared in the end. If you have the attention span of a normal human,[7] feel free to pick a section and study a particular country. The last section will provide some contextual discussion, including my general thoughts on the world, as well as your daily horoscope for the following year (if you don't find the last part, blame my editor).

NOTES

1. Oscar Jordà, Maritz Schularick, and Alan M. Taylor. "Sovereigns Versus Banks: Credit, Crises, and Consequences," *Journal of the European Economic Association* 14, no. 1 (2016): 45.

2. "Poverty," World Bank, accessed February 13, 2019, from https://www.worldbank.org/en/topic/poverty/overview.

3. Adam Smith, *An Inquiry Into the Nature and Causes of the Wealth of Nations* (London: Printed for A. Strahan and T. Cadell, 1784), Volume 1.

4. Vélez-Hagan, J. (2015). *The Common Sense Behind Basic Economics*. Lanham: Lexington Books.

5. We actually paid off our entire national debt once in 1835. President Andrew "penny-pinching miser" Jackson was the culprit.

6. James A. Buchanan and Richard E. Wagner, *Democracy in Deficit: The Political Legacy of Lord Keynes* (New York: Academic Press, 1977).

7. It is interesting to note that some scientists have found goldfish to have longer attention spans than us humans. Kevin McSpadden, "You Now Have a Shorter Attention Span Than a Goldfish," *Time Magazine*, May, 2015.

Part One

WHAT IS AND WHAT IS TO COME

Chapter 1

Disaster and Debt

There are as many different types of financial crises as there are lattes at Starbucks. Most are categorized as one of the following: domestic banking crises, external debt crises, domestic debt crises, asset price bubble-bursting crises, crises of crises, crises that deal with inflation and currency fluctuations (depreciation or debasement of currencies are included here), or some other exogenous shock crisis—such as a war or financial crisis in another part of the world—that leads to one of the above crises. Within each category there are a million ways in which a financial crisis can occur, while oftentimes one type of crisis impacts or leads to another. For example, in the United States, the asset price bubble that burst in 2007 created a subprime financial crisis (or vice versa, depending on who you ask) that begat a banking crisis. Not all such crises lead to a fiscal crisis—the focus of this book—which we will define as the inability of a government to close the gap between its spending and income (if public spending is greater than income in a given period, we define this as a *budget deficit*; income that exceeds spending is a *budget surplus*) sufficiently enough to sustain its existence in the long run. The concept of long-run sustainability will be defined later.

It sounds like a simple concept, but not everyone understands what a *fiscal crisis* means to a government and even fewer recognize when we are in the midst of one. (Common answers: "It's definitely bad" and "I know it when the news tells me so.") Nor, do we—as very normal humans—remember all the facts that surrounded the financial crises of yesteryear, that often lead to fiscal crises. What perhaps is most concerning, however, is that we generally fail to have a grasp of the facts surrounding the events that led to crises in the very recent past. While it's easy to dismiss our lack of understanding as due to a lack of data or hindsight, it's even easier to just simply forget, especially if you are a non-expert who doesn't study economic history all day long. Yet,

11

without this basic understanding of concepts and a surface-level knowledge of national crises, we are quite surely doomed to repeating our mistakes.

I won't delve too deeply into the many examples of financial crises and their causes in this book. However, a bit more about the subprime housing crisis in the United States (which led to the Great Recession, global shocks, and pure terror around the world) will serve as an example of how a crisis of one sort may intersect with others and will be useful in understanding how fiscal issues develop.

HOW ONE CRISIS LEADS TO ANOTHER

Beginning in the early 2000s, home lending standards in the United States began to shift, substantially. There are a number of reasons for why this may have happened: some point to policies in the late 1990s that led to more lenient standards, while others note technological innovations. While the truth is likely a perfect combination of the two unanticipated by regulators and legislators (what's new?), it's easier to point to the proliferation of new technologies that allowed lenders to pool riskier borrowers that had a hard time getting a loan in the past.

While it is a simple decision to deny a single borrower based on specified credit standards, lenders also knew that not all borrowers with poor credit profiles would default. As they were able to more finely differentiate factors that led to default and pool together borrowers in order to reduce overall risk, leveraging new-fangled technologies, lenders got a little loose with their dollars and began lending to those considered "subprime." Since the new technological advances allowed banks to mitigate various concerns and spread the risk, most lenders felt as though they were still maintaining the same standard of risk that they were previously comfortable with. As evidence, the rate of new borrowers required to present full loan documentation fell from nearly 80 percent in 2000, to about 60 percent in 2006. Simultaneously, loan-to-value ratios rose from close to 75 percent in the late 1990s to an average of close to 90 percent in 2006.[1] There was essentially little wiggle room between the amount someone borrowed and the value of the home, meaning that it wouldn't take much of a fall in prices for homeowners to incite a run on snorkel store inventories.

The perfect confluence of events that led to a housing "crisis," therefore, often follows this narrative: official policies that intended to increase homeownership led to an incentive for banks to lend more broadly (some say the government-supported guarantees created a *moral hazard*, where lenders didn't feel the need to protect against their own risk, since they were protected from the consequences), which were amplified by unscrupulous brokers (or outright fraud) and historically low lending rates driven by central banking policies, providing just the right combination of explosive material for a big housing bang. As lending became overextended and markets started to sway, housing prices started to fall, while the economy also veered from the rainbow and lollipop phase of the business cycle. It didn't take much veering to put people under, leading to a ripple effect of budding new home foreclosures.

But the party didn't just stop with homeowners and local bankers, instead spreading to the financial markets through more intricate, less understood, and oft-blamed processes. As mentioned earlier, big-moneybag lenders and their sophisticated tech had more than a few borrowers to service, as they maintained vast pools of diverse borrowers (prime, subprime, and everything in between) to moderate risk within a larger portfolio. Large banking institutions would buy up and package these pools of mortgages to create an asset-backed security that could be sold to investors. They were known as *mortgage-backed securities* (MBS) because their value was intrinsically based on the ability and expectation of future mortgage payments from the original pool of mortgages. As long as everyone paid their mortgages, the banks weren't the only ones to win, but the larger investment banks and purchasers of the MBSs got their money and were happy too. It should be noted that not all MBSs were alike. These securities were broken into "tranches," or various levels of risk, where lower tranches had higher rates of return, but more risk. Higher tranches had greater guarantees but lower returns.

However, as defaults began, those in the lower tranches of MBSs (the riskiest group) began receiving "insufficient funds" notices in the mail. They weren't happy, but for the most part, the financial markets would live on, or so they thought. In comes the now well-known *derivative*, a product whose value was based on these MBSs. You may remember derivatives for being endlessly referred to by talking heads on TV as one of the evil culprits that instigated the economic apocalypse of the day, but unless one is a finance graduate, works in finance, or manages one's household's financial investments, most don't know what one is. A derivative is essentially any contract between two parties based on an underlying asset. Options contracts, for example, are investment tools that stock investors often use to hedge against certain risks. They are considered derivatives because they are a contract between two parties which allows a party to buy or sell the underlying asset by a certain date in the future and are based on an underlying asset: a share of stock in a company (or generally hundreds of shares of stocks).

Derivatives that were based on MBSs were known as collateralized debt obligations (CDOs). CDOs were pools of the pools. Since not all lower tranches of MBSs were affected the same way, savvy investors had a great idea: Why not gather together MBSs in the same way MBSs pooled mortgages and create a new, bright, and shiny security that reduced an investor's overall risk (but, mostly because it will make us a lot more dough)? *What could go wrong?*

CDOs were essentially investment tools (a tranched security) based on other investment tools (a tranched MBS) based on an original investment (pools of mortgages), multiplying the amount of investments in the financial sector that were all tied to mortgages (the original asset). The difference between an MBS and a CDO is that an entire CDO could be based on the riskiest, lowest tranche of an MBS. When only the lower tranches of the MBSs defaulted, therefore, entire groups of CDOs that were based on these lower-tranched MBSs would also default, leaving poor multinational conglomerate investment banks empty-handed (insert sad face). By taking a small slice of more poorly rated, riskier MBSs and turning it into an additional security called CDOs, the original risk was replicated and amplified—many times over.

And the intricate web of lending and borrowing extended well beyond even these more detailed nuances of the finance world. International financial and regulatory bodies began complying with new standards set forth in the 1980s (see the *Basel Accords*) which forced banks operating internationally to maintain certain minimum capitalization standards. In other words, they had to have enough actual money in the bank to cover any unexpected losses, as well as expected obligations. Banks, being the profit-seeking corporations that they are, are pretty good at finding alternative paths to profitability. What helped spread the contagion of the financial crisis was the fact that most banks had developed elaborate *shadow banking* networks that helped them keep loans off the balance sheets and avoid oversight by international financial regulators, thereby allowing them to circumvent the need to maintain the required capital that they would have if said loans were overt. It has taken years for the Fed, government authorities, and researchers to fully understand how banks opted for regulatory arbitrage instead of abiding by the wishes of well-intentioned regulators, a story better told by many others.[2] Yet, many contribute the crux of the financial crisis that launched the Great Recession to the development of this shadow banking industry. Regulators just looking to prevent such a catastrophic event from happening helped cause the very crisis they were hoping to avoid (a theme oh so common over time).

Before you get all teary-eyed and concerned for what happened to our nation's richest investment bankers, remember that these big banks all lent to each other and to major corporations (some for super short-term, overnight-style lending operations, some for longer terms) to help grease the wheels that keep the economy churning. Though it was clear that more and more individuals were defaulting on mortgages, what wasn't clear was who owned assets that were based on these mortgages. Given this lack of clarity, lending began to cease, which trickled to other lenders and investors, which affected smaller banks and local lenders, and made it harder for large companies to operate efficiently, employers to hire, families to get a mortgage, and entrepreneurs to entreprenuerize (that's a word, right?).

Vast amounts of uncertainty—regarding where the housing market was going as well as the balance sheets of major corporations and lenders—are what stalled economic activity and led to our Great Recession in the United States. Since the United States' economy and financial system was in the middle of a period of increased integration into world markets, the implications of our financial system's follies spread far and wide. A number of institutions halted their funding to money markets, which impacted multinational corporations, bankers, and more. The lack of liquidity in the U.S. financial system led to a lack of liquidity in other parts of the world and slowed economic activity everywhere.

While the U.S. Federal Reserve took it upon itself to coordinate a monetary policy attack, partly by buying up distressed assets, the fiscal policy response is what helped drive America's debt. *The Emergency Economic Stabilization Relief Act of 2008* allowed for the creation of what is more commonly known as the *Troubled Asset Relief Program* (TARP), which permitted the U.S. Treasury to spend $700 billion to assuage the crisis through various means (though in the end, this limit was reduced significantly). Most attribute the nation's huge increases in public debt to this program. However, the nation's deficit (the amount of governmental spending above its income) was already on the rise due to effects of the concurrent recession (see figure 1.1, *U.S. Surplus/Deficit*). Even without additional spending, reduced tax revenues inherent in economic contractions generally combine with level government spending (at a minimum, though spending usually increases) to create growing deficits in recessions. The U.S. Great Recession wasn't immune to this phenomena, as total public debt went from 60 percent of GDP in 2006 to 90 percent of GDP in 2010 (see figure 1.2, *Total Public Debt*), a trend that continues today.

What initially started as a mere subprime housing crisis created a full-blown financial crisis that sparked the beginnings of what many now consider a long-term fiscal and debt crisis.

THE PANDEMIC BEGINS

The rest of the world, and all its wondrous global economic integration, wasn't immune to the debt disease, though the underlying reasons for its proliferation were a bit more complicated. While European countries may not have had the same subprime housing crisis as the United States, they did have their own borrowing addiction. And, like any good addict, no one wanted to take the blame for their own problems.

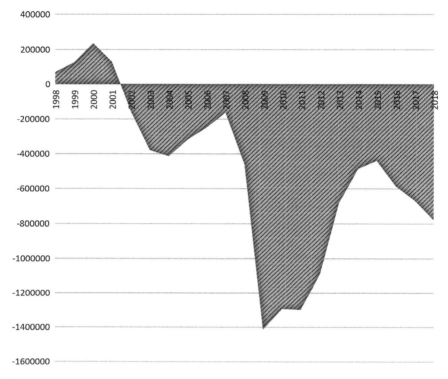

Figure 1.1   US Surplus/Deficit. Author Generated from "Federal Surplus or Deficit," U.S. Office of Management and Budget, Accessed July 22, 2019, https://fred.stlouisfed.org/se ries/FYFSD.

Good intentions in Europe very likely contributed to their eventual fall, not too different from those in the United States. After the formation of the Economic and Monetary Union (EMU), which was created in part to stabilize risk and rates across the continent in the late 1990s, bond rates began falling precipitously. As you will see, this seemingly great benefit eventually added to an even greater debt load.

Prior to the formation of the EMU, every member country had its own monetary policy, developed by a country's central bank according to the needs of that particular country. However, the EMU was developed to further integrate the economies of Europe. Despite the many headline-creating complaints from a wide range of European leaders at the time, most thought that the EU would have a net positive benefit in both the short and the long term. Yet, after its formation, interest rates (the cost of borrowing) converged across the new economic unit, an advantage that eventually became Europe's own moral hazard. Governmental borrowers that were historically considered

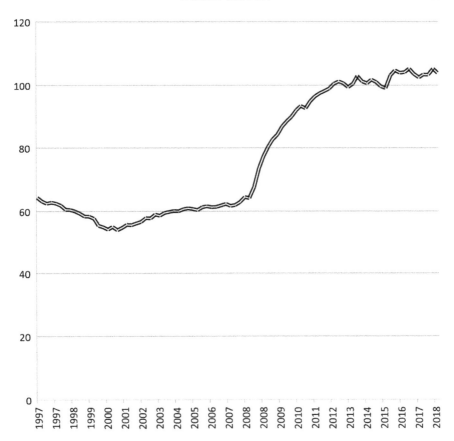

Figure 1.2 Total Public Debt. Author Generated from "Total Public Debt," U.S. Department of the Treasury, Accessed July 22, 2019, https://fred.stlouisfed.org/series/GFDEBTN.

to be of high risk were suddenly allotted an opportunity to borrow at the same, or similar, rates as those that were known as Europe's pillars of fiscal prudence. The rate at which a borrowing government was required to pay in order to borrow from lenders (through the sale of bonds) was suddenly on par with the rest of Europe, and all were lumped together into the same basket of responsible citizens.

The periphery states of Portugal, Italy, Greece, and Spain (these countries have been previously known by the acronym PIGS, but many protested that they aren't actually pigs; now we call them GIIPS, with the addition of the iffy fiscal house of Ireland) were facing lending rates as high as 20 percent before the EMU formed. Their economies were already suffering, so they had to rely on the kind benefactors of the bond market to supply the funds they required to sustain spending at the levels promised to its citizens. It was difficult to sustain the kind of borrowing needed to rebuild an economy (or, under more corrupt circumstances, to lose enough in "accounting errors" to fund a friend's business in perpetuity) while having to pay 20 percent in interest, so borrowing caps impeded indebtedness before the newly formed EMU. Theoretically, such impediments imposed by the open market allowed for a system of checks, balances, and budget restraint, regardless of whether a country wanted it or not. Interest rates on debt have the inherent purpose of enacting discipline by restricting overly ambitious fiscal policies. If you can't pay the interest on your loans in the near term, you just can't borrow as much as you might otherwise.

For the most part, more successful countries such as Germany and France anticipated the changes, understanding the inevitable response by and opportunities to the periphery states. Instead of providing lump-sum cash, or even lending directly to these states, it was seen as a "least bad" investment opportunity. Successful countries hoped that the new European economic unit would help to improve trade and other economic and social opportunities for the entire EMU if periphery countries could borrow, invest in their economies, and stymie the concerns of foreign and domestic lenders. Initially, the direct cost to the more advanced economies was very little: they merely became guarantors of debt. Yet, the potential for returns became quite the carrot. If fiscal and monetary policy stabilized and leveled across the EMU, it should lead to successful economic outcomes in periphery countries, or newly developed wealth that will demand goods and services from those advanced economies. The new-found success in these countries would then reduce the need for the direct and indirect social support from richer countries. For example, if Greece became a more economically successful country, it would need to borrow less from the likes of the International Monetary Fund (IMF) while also ensuring that needy Greeks are less likely to migrate to other parts of Europe.[3] Life should be much better behind the veil of a more general and inclusive monetary unit such as the EMU.

But, when economic tides turned—most were impacted by worldwide economic shock effects that occurred around 2008—borrowing was let loose, especially in the periphery countries (see figure 1.3, *GIIPS Public Debt*). Greece borrowed to expand a growing public sector, Ireland supported its own housing crisis, Spain's private sector borrowed to get itself over the hump and invest more, Italy borrowed at low rates to stave its longer term debt issues, and most had to finance trade deficits brought on by uncompetitive economies.

A lot of spending and borrowing during poor economic conditions led to high deficits and even higher public debt in the periphery states of the EMU, which produced some of the worst fiscal crises the region (or world) has seen.

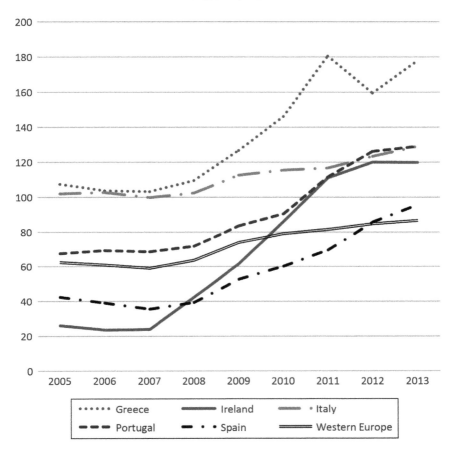

Figure 1.3 GIIPS Public Debt. Author Generated from "Debt (% of GDP)," International Monetary Fund, Accessed July 22, 2019, https://www.imf.org/external/datamapper/DEBT1@DEBT/OEMDC/ADVEC/WEOWORLD.

WILL THIS TIME BE DIFFERENT?

Knowing what we know now, it's easy to see how growing consumer debt led to a housing and mortgage crisis, which led to a more full-blown financial crisis, which spread across the globe, affected markets worldwide, and impacted government finances as well. While household debt wasn't the only reason for the recent crisis, the overarching point is that one type of financial or economic crisis can easily lead to another. Given our global integration today, the benefits of globalization tend to favor worldwide economic expansion, yet also create the opportunity for crises to spread everywhere. Regardless of the culprit and origin of any particular crisis, most will inevitably and eventually catch policymakers off-guard once again, leading to the tragedy that is a fiscal crisis.

For the rest of Part One, I will put aside a discussion of the root causes of such crises. It is, however, important to further investigate this idea of "too much" debt, since no one seems to really know the point at which it's absolutely necessary to take some significant and serious debt and deficit action.

How Much Is Really Too Much?

Sometimes I eat too much chocolate cake in a single sitting. I'll admit it, because I love chocolate cake and there shouldn't be shame in admitting your love for another. But, how do I really know when I've had too much? Is it the building headache, onset of the sweats, or the overall feeling of unease?

A country with a growing, and seemingly uncontrollable, public debt isn't much different. Though the country's leaders begin with their own stress-induced headaches, which leads to a line of uncomfortable confirmations to its citizens, the overall dis-ease in the national conversation creates some sweaty-palmed discussions, leaving elected officials to wonder whether they should just take a pension and get out of Dodge.[4]

As the economic theory goes, public debt can generally increase until the rate you pay on that debt outpaces the growth rate of an economy. The equation that explains this interaction adds the primary deficit to the interest rate on debt divided by the growth rate of the economy, then subtracts the growth of the money supply to find the long-term debt-to-GDP,[5] or: see figure 1.4.

Simple, right? Well, if you're not a Nobel Prize economist, let's break it down into more understandable terms. As the deficit (the *primary deficit* = government spending, g, plus old-age benefits, h, minus taxes, τ) increases, so does the public debt. This should be obvious as the amount you spend above your own personal income must be financed by debt (unless you are a Kardashian or a Kennedy, in which case you just have money and don't know how or why, nor what everyone is complaining about), which is also the case for a country or government. As the money supply, or m, grows, the debt-to-GDP ratio falls because more money dilutes and depreciates the existing stock of currency and debt (all else equal), so it should be subtracted. However, the term that describes the relationship between the interest rate on debt, i, and the economic growth rate, η, may be the most interesting one. Whereas a country can quickly reverse a deficit (in theory, and all things

$$b_t = g_t + h_t - \tau_t + \frac{1+i}{1+\eta}\, b_{t-1} - \lambda m_t$$

Figure 1.4   Author Generated. Olivier Blanchard, "Suggestions for a New Set of Fiscal Indicators," in *The New Political Economy of Government Debt*, eds. H.A.A. Verbon and F.A.A.M. van Winden (Amsterdam: Elsevier Science Publishers, 1993).

from equal, a government can immediately cut spending, raise taxes, or a combination thereof, to eliminate a deficit) as well as has the tools to change the money supply (normally through central banking policies, but sometimes through dictatorial fiat—looking at you Venezuela), it is much more difficult to improve the growth rate or reduce the rate of interest on outstanding debt. If the interest rate surpasses the growth rate, therefore, debt can theoretically grow in perpetuity (or at least until an economy implodes), but will more likely lead to a rapid state of insolvency. Conversely, if the growth rate of an economy remains higher than the rate of interest on its debt obligations, it should be able to cover the bills, at least until someone else comes along to mess it all up.

Put another way, if a country cannot enact policy that adjusts the ratio of interest to growth, it will have to make major adjustments in the other two terms. Heard of the term *easy money* when referring to central bank policy (aka *quantitative easing*, or "QE")? That's the central bank's (e.g. the Federal Reserve is the central bank of the United States; the European Central Bank [ECB] is that of Europe) way of expanding the money supply. These types of policies are especially prevalent when inflation isn't a worry and economies are flailing. In the case of a country that has rising interest rates on debt and falling growth rates, some assert that QE-type policies help to ameliorate long-term growth. The other term referring to the primary deficit is the *fiscal policy variable*—that which concerns government spending and taxes—and will be discussed shortly.

But, why do interest rates on debt increase in the first place? It's really not much different than when you're out hunting for a car loan to get that new Lamborghini Veneno Roadster you've been waiting for (since you're smart enough to read this book, I'll assume you are incredibly talented and successful enough to go big). If you have poor credit, the rate of interest you are likely to get on your new $3 million supercar is going to be a bit higher than you may like. The factors that go into your own credit rating are similar to the ones Moody's, Standard & Poor's, and Fitch use to establish credit ratings for countries. If your income has recently trended downward (maybe your hedge fund isn't performing as well as last year?), your credit may drop from an 850 to an 837, leaving auto lenders to cap you at a $2 million loan, forcing you to front cash for the other million.[6] The logic is, if your debt to income ratio is too high, the risk that you will default on any one of those debts is higher. A country with a slowing growth rate is going to also have problems producing an income. As it accumulates more debt, its ratio of debt to income increases, causing the big credit rating agencies to drop ratings like they're hot. Ratings among the big three agencies typically range from AAA down to the depths of "junk" status in the B's and C's (Mozambique is holding steady at a strong D) and are inversely related to yields on initial bond offerings. If a country's debt trends upwards, combined with little future income potential, a country will eventually have credit ratings low enough and bond yields high enough that it will be priced out of the market. If a country has little fiscal sense—or simply plans to default at some point in the future—it can decide to pull a Venezuela and borrow as much as humanly possible, then ask your dictator in chief to pass a decree that you owe nothing. Hey, it's turning out well for them, right?[7]

The very same situation happened to Puerto Rico in the mid-2010s. As its debt increased and income wobbled (especially after the Great Recession in the United States, which exacerbated Puerto Rico's own depression), debtors asked for more interest to cover the increased risk on new loans. Rates increased at virtually the same time and in a similar magnitude that growth rates fell (historically, this situation is not that unusual for countries in similar predicaments), and they were eventually unable to sustain payments, which led to default, lack of credit rating agency confidence, and the eventual inability to obtain financing from anyone . . . except Uncle Sam. The unusual case of Puerto Rico will be discussed in Part Two.

After the global economic shock that impacted the world in 2008, a lot of important people (at least we all think they are important) began writing a lot of important papers about the various degrees of public indebtedness and the importance that those levels of debt will have on future economic growth. Since the temptation for regulators and legislators is biased toward borrowing before vetting alternative means of improving a government's income (to be fair, after the Great Recession and succeeding global shock, most complained that they lacked the tools to incentivize growth), the biggest question on their minds was *How much is too much?*. Reinhart and Rogoff attempted to answer this question in their famous works of 2010 and 2012.[8]

The answer to the question of how much debt is too much debt is quite the contentious conundrum for a number of reasons—some political, some reasonable (notice the distinction). The results of research, or the interpretation of those results, point to various fiscal policies as solutions that may or may not align with one's particular political tastes, leading to tremendous debate surrounding the new and growing body of research during Reinhart's time (which extends to today). Reinhart and Rogoff set out to discover how historically high levels of public debt impacted economic growth, which was especially interesting and relative in a world that just came off, or was still in the middle of, the global crisis that started in 2008. However, when their results pointed to specific policy solutions that countered those of the political powers that be, one may feel compelled to doubt their scientific wherewithal. You don't agree with me? Then *you* must be wrong.

In their 2012 paper, for example, the economists investigated the postcrisis landscape by considering the correlation between public debt and GDP growth. There are many kinds of debt that can have an impact on GDP, including private consumer debt (previously described), debt in national pension and medical programs (Social Security and Medicare in the United States), and external debt (which is often a combination of both private and government-owned debt that is owed to foreigners). All have important implications for a macroeconomy, but for the most part researchers have focused on the total public debt of a country.

In order to study the growth rates of countries and how they are associated with different interest rates and debt levels, Reinhart observed historical data for countries that at some point had debt-to-GDP ratios in excess of 90 percent for at least five years, episodes they called "debt overhangs."[9] By compiling data going back to 1800, they were able to distinguish twenty-six such debt overhangs across a number of advanced economies, including Australia, Canada, France, Japan, the United States, and more.[10]

Within this group, and their respective debt overhangs, they found an interesting correlation: in twenty-three of the twenty-six identified debt overhands, average growth was 1.2 percentage points lower (for an average of 2.3 percent year-over-year growth) than in periods where debt was below this threshold (which averaged 3.5 percent). This was a significant and important finding at the time, especially considering the rising debt-to-GDP ratios after 2008. Japan's debt, for instance, had already surpassed 180 percent of its GDP, while Italy and Greece were close to 120 percent.[11] Not long after, in 2010, the United States crossed that magical 90 percent level. The implications could be read that, if your ratios were above the 90 percent level, your country better start finding a way to get things under control and fast, or there may be no turning back.

However, contrary to the recent case of Puerto Rico, most of the countries in the study didn't have trouble accessing capital markets. For the most part, they were able to continue borrowing more (and then a bit more, and then some more on top of that). How so? Countries with high amounts of debt have historically continued to comply with their obligations without default, providing an incentive to creditors to continue to offer reasonable rates of interest. Some debt overhangs have even correlated with decreased real interest rates.[12]

While an economics textbook might have predicted a big jump in short-term costs via higher interest rates, alongside increasingly limited access to credit markets, expectations didn't always meet reality. The IMF released a paper in 2018 that showed how interest rates in some countries (especially highly advanced countries) have been able to float below the growth rate for quite some time, leading the paper to even suggest that "maximum sustainable debts [in some cases] are unbounded,"[13] while famous macroeconomist Olivier Blanchard gave a speech showing how a number of countries, specifically the United States and UK, were able to keep interest rates far below growth rates for quite some time, leading them to borrow without bound at "no fiscal cost."[14] Without those disincentives to more borrowing, debt has continued to increase to unprecedented levels. With little visible impact on the lives of the contemporary electorate, policymakers solidified the momentum with a kick the can down the road philosophy—which is some cases has grown to a 50-gallon drum—that became the pervasive policy across the advanced world. Especially during an economic crisis, the potential long-term costs of debt are easy to ignore in the face of short-term relief. But, what if, according to some and in some cases, there is not a long-term cost at all? We'll dig a bit more into that further down the road (yes, I'm also a pretty good can kicker).

Reinhart & Co. certainly didn't have the last word, especially given the politics involved. Once their fame (or infamy) was solidified, ambitious opponents brought the research heat. The next generation of researchers forged ahead with rebuttals citing methodological malfeasance and uncited alternate explanations.[15] Harsh critiques noted spreadsheets and calculation errors—*whoops!*—but, most impressive to the typically reclusive world of academia was the public attention given to the work; Reinhart and Rogoff were among the first researchers to be mentioned in the late-night world (or anywhere on TV). Despite all the hubbub, few found errors substantial enough to invalidate the entirety of their findings.[16]

Embarrassing Excel errors by inexperienced research assistants aside, Reinhart and Rogoff's work exposed an irrefutable fact: research that has significant bearing on public policy will inevitably be caught up in *The Octagon* of politics. The potential weight of the suggestion that governments may need to adjust primary fiscal balances to assuage long-term economic concerns was faulted for having political biases. Reinhart and Rogoff's results pointed to the need for policies that increased taxes or cut government spending. Those who believed that opposite policies were the solution to a nation's grief were quick to claim that Reinhart and friends must have had a political slant that infiltrated their work, whether they knew it or not. The political world's influence on policy is a factor that can't be ignored and is considered more in-depth later in this book.

If, however, the results of studies that align with Reinhart's work are correct, one has to consider why high levels of debt might cause such a reaction in economic growth. After all, if interest rates don't necessarily increase when countries cross major debt thresholds, and lenders continue offering bags of money at the bequest of country leaders, what really causes growth to sway?

WHAT CAUSES CONSUMERS TO CONSUME?

To many of us, the field of economics seems unnecessary. Social scientists study the interactions between individuals and groups of individuals, in consideration of how society's scarce resources are allocated. This is the common textbook definition. But, in practice, economic results are better understood in the context of people's behavior. We mere humans react given certain conditions that surround us and the incentives placed before us; quite simply, we act based on what motivates us.

What motivates us—as individuals, companies, institutions, or governments—to consume, that is to purchase or use goods and services, is based on our interest and ability to consume, combined with our incentives to act on those interests and abilities. In your introductory economics course, the intersection of your wants and the goods and services that were available were described as the point where supply and demand curves come together to establish a market price.[17] But, how do policies enacted by our central governments impact our demand for goods and services and ability to consume?

In his famous work, *The General Theory of Employment, Interest, and Money*, John Maynard Keynes made himself known as a famous inventor. You thought he was an economist? Well, yes you may be correct, though you may be surprised to learn that he only attended a single semester of graduate economics lectures. Keynes' aversion to formal economics study may be the reason why he was able to think so far outside of his day's box, eventually inventing macroeconomics. Prior economists had a harder time seeing the forest for the trees, according to Keynes. The missing link in understanding how a country's economy worked was a closer examination of the factors that affect the total demand (hence, the use of the term "general" in his *magnum opus*) across a larger economy, also known as aggregate demand,[18] which is the sum of consumption, investment, and government spending. Prior to *The General Theory*'s 1936 release date, Keynes tended toward the view that central banks should adjust interest rates to stabilize prices and improve an economy. Better said, his view aligned with the more common theory at the time, that after rates were adjusted, the invisible hand of the free market will align itself, sans the help of the many-handed government.

But after sitting through the prolonged period of unusually high unemployment during the 1920s (which reached 20 percent in the UK, at a time when the United States was sitting below 10 percent), Keynes realized something else must be afoot. Something was restricting the natural rebalancing act presumed in previous theories. So began his research, which pointed to an important policy role for governments that is still hotly debated today: in order to achieve full employment, the government needs to spend.

The General Theory supposed that what causes us (a nation as a whole) to consume today can best be described as a function of our income today, combined with incomes we have received in the past. Since the only income information that we can be 100 percent certain of is that related to what we have received in our checking accounts today, or what we have already received in the past, our consumption decisions can only factor in this current information. Consider the decision to buy (consume) a home. On our loan application to purchase a second home in the Poconos (we've overextended a bit on the Veneno and had to cut Vail), we might try to convince the bank that we expect to increase our income by 3000 percent in the coming two months. Few loan officers (outside of those no-doc lenders who've managed to stick around since the housing crisis) are going to bite.

In other words, Keynes' theoretical underpinnings suggest a volatile consumption trend that is sensitive to changes in today's income. Any policy that is expected to have an impact on today's income is immediately reflected in our consumer behavior. Richard Kahn, a fellow economist out of Cambridge in the UK, created the mathematical description of Keynes' theory by noting the relationship between an increase in aggregate government expenditure and a country's aggregate output, more commonly known as the infamous *Keynesian multiplier*. This multiplier captures the magnitudinal effect of a particular fiscal policy on a national economic response. If the multiplier is positive, that is, increased government spending results in more aggregate demand, then Keynes' suggestions are correct and governments should spend more to create more. On the other hand, a negative multiplier, that is, an increase in government spending leads to less aggregate demand, implies that such spending policies are counterproductive. Here is the eye-squinting mathematical model you may find in today's macroeconomics courses:

$$C_t = C_{\$0} + X(\$)$$

The above hieroglyphics attempts to describe how net income today (income today minus taxes today, or the money you can actually spend), expressed as $, combines with the amount you will consume even if you have zero income (you'll find a way to eat, somehow), expressed as $C_{\$0}$, to equate to our aggregate consumption today (the amount we all consume together), C_t. The magic intermediary of interest is that giant X, which you may read elsewhere described as the *marginal propensity to consume*. If data show that we spend at least a portion of the increased income an economy gains from a new round of government spending, then the X will be positive. If the X is large enough, Keynes' theory has pretty strong support and legislators have compelling evidence to bring out the checkbook. If it's small, or negative, well . . . crickets.

How big is *large enough* and how small is *small enough* is another debate altogether. Some will say that anytime X is positive, we benefit as a society. Others argue that it has to be high enough to beat the return that the aggregate economy would yield from those dollars if they just stayed in private sector hands and weren't taxed at all. Others say we should just bury all cash and wait for an orchard of money trees to grow. Yes, the arguments are complicated (and sometimes more unhinged than that money tree lobby).

Even more complicated is how Keynes' own words seem to so staunchly contradict the class of economists and policy analysts that attempt to summarize his findings today. Many take his findings out of context, as some even try to claim that Keynes must have been a socialist, faithfully supportive of government intervention in all economic activity. Keynes, however, might disagree: "Apart from the necessity of central controls to bring about an adjustment between the propensity to consume and the inducement to invest, there is no more reason to socialise economic life than there was before."[19] Keynes seemed to believe that, once fiscal policy was able to put employment back on the path to heaven, the government should step back and let the rest work itself out.

More contemporary research has often contradicted some of Keynes' more prominent suppositions, leading to several new schools of thought. Some of these new lines of thinking include the lazily named *new-Keynesians*, which concedes some of the faults of original Keynesianism, but holds fast to the idea that markets can fail (mostly because prices and wages aren't as flexible as others have assumed) and governments have to intercede; the *neoclassical* and *new classical* economists, which will be touched on in the following section; the *monetarists*, launched by the likes of Milton Friedman and his friends (also briefly discussed in the following); the *Austrians*, not because of their nationality, but because they tend to shuck modern-day formulas and complex calculations in favor of sitting and thinking about the complexities of human nature and behavior, much like the originators of this school of thought (yes, they were actually from Austria); and everything in between.

Of all the known and more mysterious approaches, perhaps the most interesting bond that joins them is the fact that so many are attempts to overcome what are deemed shortcomings of Keynesian thought, to better capture the interaction between a government's fiscal policies and macroeconomic consumption (or have attempted to support the favorite political bent one may hold). Milton Friedman, for example, concocted his own rebuttal with *A Theory of the Consumption Function* in 1957, which kicked off a decades-long study on a new theory of consumption. Though generally more famous for his work in monetary policy—Friedman created the monetarist movement when he claimed that all monetary expansion is inflationary, instead of advocating for central banks to focus on maintaining stable prices—Friedman also made substantial contributions to understanding national consumption. Combining the two, he was awarded the Nobel Prize in economics in 1976.

Less of a worrier about times gone by, Friedman was more of a forward thinker, in the literal sense. His conclusion was that today's aggregate consumption is more accurately depicted as being based on what consumers see as their future, permanent income. Remember the lender that refused to consider the massive raise you promised you were going to get in the future as part of your income profile? A bank charter that gives some credence to Friedman might instead let bygones be bygones, and focus on whatever future income picture we paint for them. *Everyone gets a Veneno!*

The concept of a permanent income, which is the summation of all future expected income, is something that few give much thought. Friedman and others seem to admit that its less of a scientific approach than what they deem common sense: when considering what one can afford to spend disposal income on, consumers put more focus on what they think they will earn in the near- and long-term future, than what they earned yesterday. Keynes may argue that yes, when purchasing a new car you may purposefully think about your expected income in the coming months or years, but all of those anticipations are simply a projection of past occurrences. As a reasonable human being, you probably won't anticipate a 3000 percent increase in income in the coming months if you've only been given inflation adjustments every year since you started your government job. Friedman, on the other hand, surmised that, while true, there are plenty of changes that a rational person can anticipate in the future, and we all incorporate that into our individual consumption decisions.

Per Friedman, any income that is received today that is not considered additional long-term income, rather is viewed as a windfall in the current period, will raise current income by an amount divided by the number of time periods of lifetime income, which is the crux of his now famous *Permanent Income Hypothesis* (PIH). If my crazy Aunt Sally gives me a thousand dollars for Christmas (she meant to give me a cool hundred, but is a bit off her rocker), I won't consider that a substantial addition to my long-time income, under the Friedman assumptions.

The implications for the distinction led to the theory that consumers view their current income as a proportionate fraction of a perceived lifetime's income and will adjust savings and borrowing to maintain it, an idea known as *consumption smoothing* in economic research. As it related to fiscal policy, Friedman rocked the boat significantly. If Friedman was correct, changes to government spending and taxes are entirely irrelevant to short-term movements in the economy.[20] Why did he think so? Friedman realized that spending had to somehow be financed and that the "debt" that arose would somehow have to be paid by taxpayers. These tax-paying consumers, in turn, would incorporate the new information about taxes into their permanent incomes, counteracting any positive incentives or influences brought about by a government stimulus. Regardless of how you may like to spend crazy Aunt Sally's money, you may think twice about blowing it at the casino if you know that her own gambling problem will lead her to ask for it back in the future. Consumers who anticipate that the benefit of government spending today may be outweighed by future taxes may also be a bit more tightfisted with their money; the data just may present an economic wash in the end, with little gain to show.

Robert Hall's famous 1976 paper supported the PIH (which he combined with a life cycle descriptor and called the "life cycle-permanent income hypothesis"; no academics aren't always the most creative) by showing how rational consumers maximize intertemporal *utility* (the sense of well-being they derive from consumption decisions at various points in time), which leads to a stochastically defined marginal utility (the additional utility gained from each unit of consumption is more randomly determined). By applying some statistical modeling techniques—known in economics as *econometrics*, or the application of statistical techniques "for estimating economic relationships, testing economic theories, and evaluating and implementing government and business policy"[21]—he tested the data to find whether past income adjustments had much impact on current consumption. In other words, he was directly testing whether the Keynesian theory that consumption is a function of past and current periods of income holds. "Rational" consumers, in contrast to Keynes' theory, maximize the enjoyment of the fruits of their labor today based on today's income or that in the future, not on the past.

His conclusion empirically supports Friedman and his peers' results by demonstrating how only unexpected policy changes can have an impact on consumption today, as all information about future income is therefore condensed into the consumer's view of a permanent, lifetime income. If true, a short-term stimulus spending package by a government will have little impact on current consumption. Only long-term shifts, such as a permanent decrease in taxes, will change consumers' rational expectations of future income and, hence their spending choices today. Consumers that "smooth" their consumption over time are, therefore, less likely to contemporaneously respond to a fiscal stimulus that a Keynesian will advocate for.

However, the theory of *consumption smoothing* is far from conclusive, as many others have found that various factors, including the availability of and access to credit—known as *liquidity constraints*—may have an impact on current consumption, as many others point out that we just don't always act rationally. While Friedman and Hall may be right that, in the aggregate we all want and try to smooth our consumption over time, if we borrow when and how much we want, it may be difficult to do so. If there are rigidities in the lending processes for portions of the aggregate (for instance, lower income households tend to find it more difficult to borrow), they may not have the capacity to smooth an income. Those who can't borrow may be more sensitive to today's macroeconomic shocks, but also to the short-term fiscal policies intended to give a shot of adrenaline to an economy. Therefore, the ability to affect consumption through tax or spending measures may be limited, or conversely, inadvertently negative depending on the relationship between liquidity constraints and consumption. And, finally, if most of us base our spending whims on the feelings we have in the deep pit of our stomach at this very moment—which may be more impacted by whether we had a tough day at work than whether we are close to spending today's quota based on our income today, or in the future—then who knows what the heck consumers are going to do at any given moment.

If the Keynesians win out in the wonderful world of policy and decide that they're going to give us some nice stimulus for our own good, the debate doesn't end there. In fact, it only gets more intense. If we start or increase government spending, there are a million ways to do so, generally summarized by the questions: Should we just take more of the taxpayers' money to increase governmental revenues that we turn around and spend? Or, should put it all on the credit card, hoping that things bounce back in the future and we're able to pay off our debts then?

The *Ricardian equivalence theory* (named for the now famous David Ricardo of the early 1800s, long before the first economics professor was given a desk at Harvard) took a stab at answering those questions. The results? It really doesn't matter to the consumer, or aggregate consumption, which way you finance government spending. Whether a government adds to the national debt by selling more bonds or takes the citizen's money right now by way of higher taxes makes little difference in the Ricardian world, as the consumer (in the aggregate) will foot the bill either way.

Consumers may purchase government-issued bonds in anticipation of grand future returns on their investments, but they're not stupid (Ricardo puts it a bit more eloquently). In order to pay the interest and eventual principal on those bonds, the government must increase its income, which means it has to raise taxes. To the Ricardian, consumers are either taxed now or taxed later, but they will be taxed in nearly an equivalent fashion either way.

Under the assumptions of the PIH and Ricardian equivalence, household spending will not adjust under policies that cut taxes either, as tax cuts are merely negated by the present value of future tax payments. Neither of these theories have gone uncontested. No, the policy stakes are too high; the debate has proliferated, especially after the more recent buildup of debt since the global economic crisis of 2008. Today, most agree that there isn't really a lot of evidence for Ricardian theory, for instance. It's not because we don't realize the implications of tax and spending policies today on future tax and spending policies and income, but because too many of us don't care (hey, I'd rather live for the moment), don't think too much about it (I'm too busy to think about the future), or have constraints that don't allow us to do anything about it (sounds nice, but I have to live the way I need to live today to keep my family alive and don't have much choice in how and when I'll consume).

While the above discussion demonstrates some of the limitations of the effectiveness of consumption-focused policy measures, alternative lines of research follow the impact of aggregate debt levels on economic output and agree that there is one. The empirical and theoretical conclusions that stem from consumption smoothing research have underlying policy implications parallel to those within the increasingly important field of study related to public debt and its effect on economic output.

DO WE NEED FISCAL POLICY?

With a greater understanding of how a fiscal crisis can develop, as well as how it can spread, it's easy to see the need for some sort of solution, in general. However, knowing when we need to implement a solution is a much more difficult question to answer. Should policymakers start clamoring for action when we have a debt-to-GDP ratio of 90 percent? Or should we just wait to see if economic growth is really affected before taking action? If we wait, will it be too late? Without fully understanding how aggregate demand is impacted by consumer choices and fiscal policy, it's difficult to know when to act. But, one thing is for sure, whether we good citizens of the world's economic powerhouses want to take action or not, action will be had. When our grand leaders have made the decision that our long-term fiscal outlook has taken a turn for the worse and something needs to be done to correct a growing deficit or debt, or both, fiscal policies known as FCs are implemented to constrain the repercussions. How they are executed—and whether they make any real difference in the world—is discussed in the following chapters.

NOTES

1. "Single-Family Loan-to-Value Ratios," Federal Housing Finance Agency, accessed July 22, 2019, https://www.fhfa.gov/DataTools/Downloads/Pages/Public-U se-Databases.aspx.

2. If interested in learning more, consider a search on "structured investment vehicles (SIV)," "conduits," "rehypothecation," or see Viral V. Acharya, Philipp Schnabl, and Gustavo Suarez, "Securitization without Risk Transfer," *Journal of Financial Economics* 107, no. 3 (2013): 515–536.

3. The Schengen Agreement of 1985 allowed for open migration across most of Europe. Given a certain allowance for mobility, individuals and families that are unable to make ends meet in one part of Europe may seek opportunities in more economically vibrant areas, or so goes the theory. However, a number of recent studies have shown that movement is fairly restricted. The impoverished are less likely to move as theory might dictate. Theory ≠ undebated fact.

4. For a more robust discussion on the national debt history of the United States, consider reading Chapter 16 of *The Common Sense behind Basic Economics*, noted in the bibliography.

5. Olivier Blanchard, "Suggestions for a New Set of Fiscal Indicators," in *The New Political Economy of Government Debt*, eds. H.A.A. Verbon and F.A.A.M. van Winden (Amsterdam: Elsevier Science Publishers, 1993).

6. Believe it or not, ultra high net worth individuals don't always have the best credit. According to *Fortune* Magazine, Warren Buffett's credit rating teeters above average.

7. No, it's not. See "Police believe thieves steal Venezuela zoo animals to eat them," dated August 16, 2017, https://www.reuters.com/article/us-venezuela-anima ls/police-believe-thieves-steal-venezuela-zoo-animals-to-eat-them-idUSKCN1A W2NN.

8. Carmen Reinhart and Kenneth Rogoff, "Growth in a Time of Debt," *American Economic Review* 100, no. 2 (2010): 573–578; Carmen Reinhart, Vincent Reinhart, and Kenneth Rogoff, "Public Debt Overhangs: Advanced Economy Episodes Since 1800," *Journal of Economic Perspectives* 26, no. 3 (2012): 69–86.

9. Reinhart, Reinhart, and Rogoff, "Public Debt Overhangs," 70.

10. If you have a hard time understanding the lingo in a 1970s rerun of Hollywood Squares on the Gameshow Network, imagine what it's like to interpret handwritten economic data from the 1800s in an antiquated form of a foreign language.

11. Source: Organization for Economic Co-operation and Development (OECD).

12. Reinhart and Rogoff, "Growth in a Time of Debt," 71.

13. Philip Barrett, "Interest-Growth Differentials and Debt Limits in Advanced Economies," *IMF Working Paper No. 18/82*, Washington: IMF (April 2018).

14. Olivier Blanchard, "Public Debt and Low Interest Rates," Speech given in January 2019 to the American Economic Association.

15. See, for example, Thomas Herndon, Michael Ash, and Robert Pollin, "Does High Public Debt Consistently Stifle Economic Growth? A Critique of Reinhart and Rogoff," *Cambridge Journal of Economics* 38, no. 2 (2014): 257–279. Note, however, that Reinhart and Rogoff's updated work incorporated a response to this critique in their findings.

16. To be clear, everyone believes that—at some point—debt influences growth. The level that causes a country to enter the danger zone is the dispute.

17. If you didn't have an intro to econ course (or prefer to never think about it again), might I suggest a good primer on the matter? It's called *The Common Sense behind Basic Economics: A guide for budding economists, students, and voters*, and is available at most online retailers.

18. While any political pundit will gladly tell you that if Keynes were alive, he'd be a member of party X, you may be surprised at how little he discussed politics in his books. Regardless of your political identity, his work established many of the principles that macroeconomics is based on today.

19. John M. Keynes, *The General Theory of Employment, Interest, and Money* (New York: Palgrave Macmillan, 1936).

20. Tim Congdon, "Milton Friedman on the Ineffectiveness of Fiscal Policy," *Economic Affairs* 31, no. 1 (2011): 62–65.

21. Jeffrey M. Wooldridge, *Introductory Econometrics: A Modern Approach*. 6th ed. (Mason, OH: South-Western Cengage Learning, 2016).

Chapter 2

How Did We Respond?

Even within a crowd of relatively impoverished neighbors, Cameroon can't seem to figure out how to get ahead of the pack. With a GDP per capita near $1,400 USD, the central African country is surprisingly right in the middle of the continent's 50-plus countries. It manages to separate itself from the pack by its take on national finances, however. Over the period from 2010 to 2016, Cameroon doubled its public debt (surprisingly, still not the worst offender in Africa). However, most surprising is what the country's leader has done, repeatedly, in the face of pending doom: the longtime head of state simply packs up and leaves the country. A recent study found that, despite a number of onsetting crises (kidnappings, civil war, lack of potable water, and extreme poverty, just to name a few), President Biya has a propensity to wander over to greener European pastures, spending up to a quarter of his more than thirty years as elected leader in posh hotels overlooking the serene and peaceful (and fiscally responsible) Switzerland.

When facing an ongoing crisis, or multitude crises, governing authorities around the world are faced with the same question: Should I buckle down and try to do something productive, or give up and let everyone learn a lesson from past generations' fiscal negligence? As much as we would all like for some of our elected leaders to take a permanent vacation, "hightail it out of town" is (generally) not a well-received option. When faced with a fiscal crisis, national governments oftentimes have no choice but to enact policies that reduce deficits and regulate the public debt burden. As defined previously, such policies are known as *fiscal consolidations*, also known as measures of *fiscal austerity*, or more simply *austerity*.

THE ROLE OF FISCAL POLICY

Before discussing the need for FCs, along with the various types, it's important to have an understanding of the role of fiscal policy within a government. The role of macroeconomic fiscal policies is generally summarized as having three legs: the creation and management of *automatic stabilizers*, discretionary changes in taxation and spending policies, and planning total expenditures so that public debt never spins out of control. All of these are planning tools used to stabilize output, insulate an economy from major shocks (or disturbances in the economic *Force*), and provide a long-term planning mechanism (or the appearance of such anyway).

Automatic stabilizers are economic stabilizers that activate, well, automatically. While it would be a lot more fun to leave this here, a bit more explanation might be useful. Programs that have been created to adjust the tax and transfer system within a government can help to adjust an economy in the same way in which any discretionary policy can, but generally much more rapidly. Policymakers that want to cool off the economy when it is overheating (generally due to ever-prevalent inflationary concerns, whether appropriate or not) or to provoke economic activity when an economy needs a boost can adjust taxes as well as other economic safety nets in order to provide greater security and stability within an economy. Automatic stabilizers are simply those rules already in place that allow these adjustments to take place without the direct intervention of policymakers.

If the economy is flourishing and incomes are higher or increasing faster than usual, eligibility for government programs that provide benefits to individuals and families will fall. For example, if your cousin Larry's mobile plastic surgery business idea finds a significant investor, the government may be quick to revoke the taxpayer-funded support he was previously offered, in light of his new-found riches (no matter how likely he is to promptly fail and return to poverty). Such automatic responses to benefits eligibility reduce government spending and the boost to economic activity that it might otherwise provide.

On the other hand, if the economy is slumping, incomes fall and spending in similar benefits programs will rise, allowing for a boost to economic activity via the government's hand. If the economy turns so sour that even the unexpectedly successful *#1 Best Mobile Plastic Surgeons, Inc.* has to cut staff and eventually shut down, Larry might be able to once again apply for social welfare benefits to help put food on the table. Since he doesn't have to appeal to his congressman to create a law that provides his family a benefit, it automatically provides economic stability to him and his family. Imagine this scenario amplified across an entire economy and one can see the benefit that an automatically implemented policy may provide to the aggregate economic output during a contracting, or stalling, economy.

Many deem these policies useful in stabilizing the economy and absolutely essential in most economies in the free world given the inability of policymakers to react to economic shocks as quickly as necessary. A side effect is that, since government spending automatically increases when economic activity falls, budget deficits will also increase. On the flip side, as spending decreases during swell times, so does a deficit (all things equal, which all rarely are). The Congressional Budget Office (CBO) in the United States— a non-partisan federal agency tasked with providing budgetary analyses and economic information to Congress—regularly attempts to quantify the impact of automatic stabilizers. During the Great Recession of 2007–2009, the CBO found that economic stimulus from automatic stabilizers came out to more than $300 million each year from 2009 to 2012,[1] an amount equal to at least 2 percent of *potential GDP.*[2]

Fiscal policy rules are often set up by policymakers to keep government finances in check. As previously discussed, perhaps the most important function of fiscal policy is to ensure long-term solvency so that a government can continue to pay for the expenditures that society has deemed necessary. To ensure such long-term fiscal balancing acts are sustained, planners often create rules that establish boundaries within which fiscal policies must operate, in the hopes that FCs will never become necessary. One such rule is the UK government's *Golden Rule*, which attempts to constrict fiscal policy by keeping the government spending deficit (as a share of GDP) to within a range that is no larger than required to finance government investment spending. The logic behind the rule is that government spending should be restricted to that which provides a return on investment, much like you might have demanded (to your current chagrin) if you were a series A round investor in Larry's mobile plastic surgery failure. While such policies attempt to restrict spending to those that are most prudent and beneficial to society's future, one problem is similar to that of those who invested in Larry's idea. There are no guarantees on investments, and which investments are deemed worthy for receiving a round of financing is purely subjective. While most never imagined that Larry could be successful in his venture, a wealthy, supposedly successful and semi-intelligent person thought otherwise. Policymakers are human beings who can also make poor investments—or who can alternatively expand the scope of what is deemed an "investment" beyond the original intention—creating unexpected risks that fail to be constrained by such a fiscal policy rule.

THE ROLE OF MONETARY POLICY

If a country's administrators fall out of favor with its fiscal policy rules, if it chooses to never have them in the first place, or if sheer economic calamity attacks us all, that ratio of debt-to-GDP may start to lean into the "unsustainable" category. At this point, governments have to make a series of decisions, one of which relates to the central bank's monetary policy.

I won't delve too deeply into the world of monetary policy in this book, but a government can technically keep on living the high life and spending to its heart content without ever borrowing money—for a time. Oftentimes monetary policies (generally controlled by an independently operated central bank) are shifted in conjunction with or parallel to fiscal policies (enacted by legislatures), but if fiscal policy is inept or incapable of countering a weak economy, if legislators simply don't want to use fiscal policy tools, or if credit markets have little taste for new bonds from a government at risk of default, a government can finance its bills by printing up more money—what is known in economics as *monetizing the debt*.

Printing more cash doesn't go without its own cost. Yes, a government can continue to spend by increasing the growth rate of its money supply (the value of newly minted money minus the cost of producing it is the government's profit, known as *seigniorage*), but the cost is inflation. Both John Maynard Keynes and Milton Friedman have not so nice things to say about the cost of inflation. Per Keynes, "by a continuing process of inflation, government can confiscate, secretly and unobserved, an important part of the wealth of their citizens."[3] Milton Friedman couldn't help but concede to Keynes' point, suggesting that we should all be wary of inflation, for it is a form of taxation that legislators don't have to include in the tax code.[4] A general increase in prices, known as inflation, will decrease the value of a country's aggregate income. On the flip side, inflation also has the same effect on our debt. The value of our overall debt stock also loses relative value as inflation increases. (The actual value of income or debt, minus the cost of inflation, is usually preceded by the term "real" in economics, for example, *real* wages.)

Which detriment or benefit outweighs the other is a debate for another book, but it likely depends more on the level of inflation than the existence of inflation in and of itself. Many believe that moderate inflation actually helps the economy to chug along, and not just by cutting the real value of debt. For example, a dash of inflation can serve as an extra tool for the employer who is a bit wary of a riot-inducing, across-the-board pay cut. If times are slow and an employer needs to make a few of its own financial adjustments, slashing benefits to your employees doesn't always create the happy-go-lucky work environment that promotes a healthy and productive workforce. Instead, Mr. Bossman can let inflation do the work and simply hold pay steady for a time, until things pick back up again. By keeping nominal wages of employees steady, relative costs will fall for the employer, and the average worker won't know the difference (well, they may not like the lack of a raise, but they're less unhappy than the alternate scenario). What may seem like a pittance in savings for a mom-and-pop shop can add up to substantial cost cutting for a major multinational conglomerate. Thanks inflation!

Another reason for central bankers' desire to keep a moderate level of inflation is that they know they're not very good at it. I know that seems counterintuitive, but this time we should be thankful that they know their flaws. Given how difficult it is to keep inflation at any particular level (imagine trying to create a policy that keeps all prices of everything across an entire country steady), central bankers generally choose to give themselves a bit of a buffer. In the United States, the Federal Reserve has an inflation targeting policy of around 2 percent. Because the Fed knows that it's nearly impossible to consistently hit that target rate,[5] it has to set it high enough to ensure that when it does miss on the downside, real inflation never actually falls below zero. When prices are generally in decline, we are in a state of *deflation*. Many consider this to be worse than high levels of inflation, as once deflation sets in, it's really hard to stimulate your way out of it. Japan is still trying to climb out of its deflationary spiral that started in the early 1990s. The bad news about falling prices is that consumers know things are probably going to be cheaper tomorrow, so why spend today? And the death spiral ensues.

Compared to deflation, low levels of inflation look pretty rosy, though they do have a cost. I'd like to keep piles of cash under my mattress like we used to in the good ol' days. But, I know that inflation is constantly working against my hard-earned dollars. So I make a deposit and hope for returns that keep pace with inflation (given that current APY's on checking accounts average 0.06 percent, this is merely a pipe dream). Or, if I'm ambitious, I put my dough in a money market and day-trade options while taking in *The View*. For businesses, it's not enough to simply grow; money management is just an added bonus to the fun of entrepreneurial/managerial life. All this time spent banking and managing money is a cost to society that inflation has caused. While an astute investor and manager may want to spend a little extra time doing some banking, the requirement to do so just to maintain the real value of a dollar is the price we have to pay to enjoy the "benefit" of increasing prices.

Though there's no clear-cut answer as to whether moderately low levels of inflation are a net positive boost to an economy, the other, flip-side concern is the potential for out-of-control prices. *Hyperinflation*—the general term for high and rapidly increasing price levels within a market—leads to a reduction in the value of your current money and future earnings. Because it's difficult for an employer to accurately compensate you for the real value of your hard work in a state of hyperinflation, and it's nearly impossible to fully understand what anything should cost in a given moment, our motivation to work for a salary or spend money is reduced. Consider Zimbabwe's 2008 inflation rate, which peaked at around 15 *billion* percent (is that a mathematical possibility?). With inflation that high, aggregate income and consumption plummeted.

Moral of the story: monetizing the debt may not be the best choice for a government that wants to continue spending. Fortunately, fiscal policy has a few weapons left in the arsenal.

THE LAST RESORT: AUSTERITY

While there are certainly some leaders who think there's nothing more fun than to sit back, pop a cold one, and watch citizens wheelbarrow around piles of paper money all day, reasonable governments that see the debt writing on the wall may realize that they have no choice but to undergo a period of FC. Consolidating one's finances is never easy. Doing so on behalf of an entire nation is even harder, especially when the term "austerity" has commonly become acquainted with only its pejorative connotation, referring to extreme economization. Austere fiscal measures are simply those that force money to be spent only as necessary, something we've all experienced as our piggy banks begin to rattle with less vigor. What types of austerity measures can a country, or even a larger, multinational economic union, deploy in order to reduce a budget deficit? In general, there are three types of austerity measures: tax increases, spending cuts, or a mix of the two. But, there are many caveats, such as the composition of FCs, the real necessity of austere policies (skeptics abound), the types of structural economic reforms needed and proposed outcomes, how consolidations are measured, whether the proposed and anticipated economic outcomes of FCs are the best for an overall society, as well as the role of cheating cheaters (see discussion on Greece).

Types of Fiscal Consolidations

If a government views its public debt as "too high," it has merely made the decision to start making a series of much more difficult decisions. Confirming that the debt ratio is out of whack, requiring controls to be implemented that lead to a more sustainable version, is a lot like admitting that you have a "problem." While this first step is a prerequisite, there are at least eleven more that need to be thought through and completed over a long period of time, before one can be on the road to recovery.

Somewhere in the middle of these twelve fiscally refined steps, countries get to decide how quickly to implement FCs, whether to impose policies based on spending cuts, tax increases, or a combination thereof (and a million other factors related to the composition of these policies). On top of these discretionary fiscal policies, what some fail to fully consider are the policies that independent agencies enact in conjunction with, or as a result of, newly applied fiscal policies. A central bank such as the Federal Reserve, for instance, may react differently based on the decisions of Washington, D.C. legislators. Policymakers also too often fail to consider the real-life daily implications that policies—no matter how prudent—will have upon citizens across the demographic and socioeconomic spectrum. Yes, policymakers have to be omniscient legislators, benevolent enough to make the effort to do what they think is right for everyone, while also being competent soothsayers. Perhaps that's why so many drop out of the 12-Step program?

Let's remember that, in the long run, it probably matters little the means implemented in order to achieve the end result of "long-run debt sustainability." That is to say that there are a number of ways to adjust a country's finances to get back to a fiscally solvent path, or one that won't eventually lead to debt so high as to seize the normal borrow and spend functions of a government. I'll discuss this a bit more, but that excludes the number of social welfare and distributional effects that policymakers consider beneficial to the long-term well-being of a society. In general, when discussing long-run sustainability in the fiscal sphere, this book will generally refer to the ability to continue borrowing and spending to cover the expenses that a government deems necessary and desirable, and will be able to do so well into the foreseeable future (with all due respect given to the usual "all things equal" caveat).

The speed and depth choices of FC policies, therefore, are generally concerned with the various effects on short-run economic performance, such as the immediate impact on GDP and employment. How these choices affect us all down the road, in the long run, is a much harder question to answer as one has to parse out the potential effects from an even greater number of intertwining factors that combine to influence an economy along the way; therefore, this book will try to focus more on the short-run impact, while I would be remiss to not mention some of what we think are the longer term outcomes.

To many, the argument for which type of FC to implement is similar to the rip the band-aid right off versus slowly soak the bandage and peel it away philosophies. In the former, you'll likely scream and embarrass yourself in front of anyone within earshot, but it will be over quickly and most will forget about how weak you are in relatively quick order; in the latter case, no one will see the relatively little pain that you are in as you begin to allow the bandage's glue to release, but everyone will eventually notice that you've been struggling with something for an unusually long period of time. A country that has to make the decision of whether to yank or dawdle is theoretically in the same situation. Per the common Keynesian macroeconomic theory taught in most economics courses (look up the *IS/LM model*, for instance, which demonstrates the give and take between interest rates and real economic output), the assumption is that either a cut in government spending or a tax increase will cause economic performance to subside and unemployment to jump. Under this assumption, if you rip the fiscal band-aid off by hiking taxes and/or reducing government spending, a country must deal with the immediate impact of a very sad population. Slower growth or a contracting economy could lead to recession, while unemployment could be so high as to force automatic stabilizers to react (increased benefits equals more money the government spends), which will counteract some of the spending reduction measures. Of course, the intention is to quickly get the books back in line, so long-term solvency projections lean toward "more likely than not." If this happens fast enough, as theorized by these fiscal hawks, markets and the economy as a whole will react positively, bringing GDP growth and employment back to where we would like it to be. On the other hand, the slow, steady, and gentle hand of a dawdler nudging deficits toward surpluses may feel the same economic output and employment pain that the band-aid ripping masochists enjoyed, just spread out over a longer period. While still painful, proponents of this method will claim that the constant, yet shallow pain is far more desirable in the long term, hoping that an economy will be more adept at adjusting to this form of FC, eventually overcoming it altogether to get back to the path it theoretically should have been on if administered properly (or if it had not been so unlucky) in the first place.

However, it's also important to note that the time taken to implement an FC is not the only factor that contributes to economic outcomes. Too often we hear the word "austerity" in the news and automatically assume that it means whatever idea of FCs that we have assembled in our own minds. As not all fiscal policies are made equal, neither are all fiscal adjustments, and certainly not all FCs. The words austerity and FC are as general as the word "car." Yes, we gather an overall idea of what someone means when they say they just crashed their new car, but what kind of car was it? A truck? An old beater? No, don't tell me it was the new Veneno you *just* wasted your hard-earned money on. I mean, that you worked so hard to be able to buy?! The difference between an old throw-away 1976 Chevette (*Time* once called the Chevette one of the "Worst Cars of All Time"[6]) and a piece of rolling art that you spent several million dollars on is tremendous. Calling your expensive Veneno a car doesn't give anymore insight into the type of vehicle you drive than the term *fiscal consolidation* or *austerity* provides any more specificity than simply using the term *fiscal policy*. It could be bad, it could be good, it could be necessary or unnecessary in the eyes of the person mouthing the words, but it doesn't shed any light on the matter beyond that fact that it's a governmental policy that is expected to impact a nation's fiscal balance.

To Spend or To Tax

To better understand FCs, one has to delve into their composition. Reducing a deficit through fiscal policy with the intent of getting public debt under control requires, as noted earlier, an increase in taxes, a reduction in spending, or some infinite mix of the two. (While monetary policy—e.g. printing more cash—is an additional tool, I focus on the fiscal policies here.) These limitations are often described in terms of a *government budget identity* (because economists always prefer equations to written words). Government tax revenues, *T*, combine with the proceeds from the sale of new bonds, *B*, to make up the amount of money available that a government can spend on its various expenditure plans, *G*, as well as the required interest it has to pay on the debt that it has currently accumulated, *i*, as shown in the following:

$$T + B = G + i$$

Since one side must always equal the other, if spending goes up because of new spending measures introduced by a government, taxes or borrowing have to increase as well. On the other hand, tax revenues can fall during a recession or by way of new policies that reduce taxes, and something has to give to make up for it. If legislators choose to reduce government spending, it has to do so consistent with the fall in revenues in order to ensure that a deficit is not created and the public debt increased. Or, a government can make up for the difference and choose to maintain a portion or all of the spending variable's current level by increasing the total value of *B*, via more borrowing and bonds. Once it does so, the interest it has to pay, *i*, obviously increases. This tiny, seemingly simplistic equation is a bit more complicated than it might look at first glance.

Yet, even the category labels of taxation and government spending are too broad. Using a term to merely indicate a policy to reduce spending is akin to saying "car" in the analogy above. Generic language can cause one to question whether you are referencing a Chevette, when you mean the refined engineering wonder that is the Veneno, just as it can cause confusion and misunderstanding regarding the type of FC available and applied.

In order to cut spending, there are a ton of options that need to be evaluated. Those with a government-issued AmEx Black Card can reconsider their outlays on goods and services such as toilet paper and customized IT software support, salaries for public sector employees that install the toilet paper or manage the IT systems (including the social insurance contributions often rolled into payroll costs), the public university and other educational costs so we can train the next generation of public toilet paper installation engineers, and public healthcare options so that toilet paper cuts can be treated with the

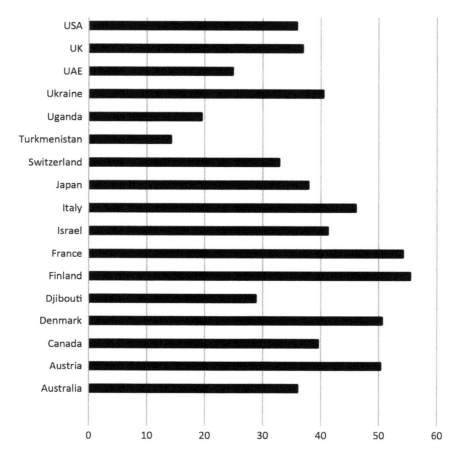

Figure 2.1 Government Expenditures. Author Generated from "Government Finance Statistics," International Monetary Fund, Accessed July 22, 2019, https://data.imf.org/?sk= 3C005430-5FDC-4A07-9474-64D64F1FB3DC.

greatest of alacrity and care. Figure 2.1 offers a glimpse into how much a select few governments spend, as it relates to the country's GDP.

Some non-surprises might include the social democracy of Finland and la République française. But look at Turkmenistan, one of the most command-dominated economies in the world (per the Heritage Foundation/*Wall Street Journal Index of Economic Freedom*), yet its government spends less (as a percentage of its GDP) than half of the government of Switzerland, considered one of the "freest" economies in the world. While this statistic may be interesting, it should leave you to realize that there is a lot more going on in the spending category than meets the eye, and a lot of other contributing factors that support a nation's overall fiscal health and perceived success.

What is often included in the broader list of government expenditures is something referred to as *transfers*. The term simply connotes a payment that a government transfers to a private entity, without expecting anything in return (economists, much like their peers across academia, aren't known for their creative nomenclature). From the perspective of an economist, however, there are reasons why the expense line item dedicated to transfers is studied as a separate category, especially as it relates to the impact on GDP. Because transfer spending—such as welfare, financial aid, subsidies to your congressman's favorite businesses/donors, and social security—doesn't result in a corresponding good or service being returned to the government, transfers aren't direct contributors to aggregate demand, or GDP. It also should be noted that, while we don't count this initial transfer of funds from the government as part of GDP, those dollars are eventually counted when private entities spend the dollars they receive (if they spend the dollars, which often equates to a slightly smaller proportion of the original amount).[7]

Since, for the most part, analysts who aim to study the impact of fiscal policies that fine-tune government spending practices want to see how spending impacts the country's total, final demand, we must consider transfers differently. We at least benefit from breaking out this category to better understand how it is impacted by certain policies and then can study the resulting correlation with movement in the GDP.

It's easy to understand the simple transaction that exchanges taxpayer money for a good or service, but governments often expend monetary resources without expecting anything in return. Well, not an immediate return anyway. Most government expenditures occur a lot like your trip to Amazon: a public employee logs onto a vendor's website, clicks the order button which initiates a flow of money to a government contractor, who then sends a product or begins providing a service. But the government also tries to make investments in the nation's future by spending money that plants the seed for returns in the future. The total of government investments is also sometimes called the *government gross fixed capital formation*, a super-complicated way of leveraging the economics definition of *capital*—an asset that is purchased or invested in as a means of creating other goods or services (oft-confused with the use of capital in finance, which means money that can be invested, as well as the word meaning the most important city in a country; e.g. many consider the capital city of the United States to be the place where other forms of capital go to die).

When governments spend money to improve land, build plants, purchase property and equipment, or to construct bridges and highways, it expects that the return to the country be higher than zero. In other words, the hope is that no one will be justified in suggesting that the government's chosen "investment" was a complete waste of money. These types of expenditures are called investments for the same reason that you hold investments in a retirement account.

Government taxation is a fiscal category that has at least as many accompanying nuances as government spending. But, we all see taxes as an entirely different animal. When the taxman cometh, we tend to pay a lot more attention. Transactions in which the government purchases goods or services, makes investments, or even directly provides a benefit such as a social security check are pretty important to any average citizen; however, most don't understand the extensive role of government expenditures, and even more rarely do we get to see when they occur. When we are taxed, we know it's happening, and we usually know it immediately. The path from taxation to government spending is an easy concept for grade school civics students to grasp and, regardless of ideology, everyone believes the government must have some tax revenues. For example, military protection from roving bands of horseback-laden invaders is a service that we're all fairly willing to pay a bit for. Such a service is *non-excludable* (with its creation, no citizen can opt out of military protection) and *non-rivalrous* (protecting a few citizens doesn't use up the good and prohibit its use by other citizens), to put it in economic terms. If we allowed a person or group to choose to avoid taxes and their right to military service, the service offered to everyone else through their own transactions with the government would create a *positive externality* for everyone who didn't (i.e., despite not paying for it, you're going to get a benefit).[8] No one likes a freeloader, so in situations in which the vast majority agree to the necessity of such a product, societies have generally decided that it's best to make everyone pay a share.[9]

While government expenditures are the clear near-mirror image of citizens' tax dollars and government revenues, many of us mere humans can't help but focus more on the direct impact that taxation policies have on us. When the PIH was introduced in chapter 1, I hinted at some of the psychological aspects involved in consumption behavior, a topic we will broach again later. Given the differences, even the perceived and theorized differences, it makes good sense to consider whether the impact on economic performance from tax-focused FCs significantly differs from the impact of similar policies based on cutting government spending. This book will discuss some of these behavioral and psychological factors that are at play in our consumption behavior a bit more during a more robust discussion of research results. Before discussing behavioral influences, analyses should begin with disaggregating the various types of tax policies to first take a close look at what the data presents. The diverse categories include the more direct and unavoidable taxes on personal income and property (land, cars, etc.), as well as those on corporate and business profit. More indirectly, we have tax categories that result from transactions. When we purchase goods and services, we have sales taxes, some have a value added tax (VAT), there are taxes on imports/exports, duties, and more. Ostensibly, given how different the included parties are in any of the above transactions, tax adjustments that affect one over the other may have very different consequences or benefits to society and economic performance. For example, if a government decides to triple the sales tax on services that only individuals purchase, these services may see a more significant decline than a similar tax on those purchased only by businesses. If one policy has an effect distinct from another, it would be beneficial to know.

Another fun fact about fiscal plans: they are almost never debated, planned, announced, and enacted within and over a single year. If you've ever closely followed the path of a bill introduced in your respective legislature, you won't be surprised to know that many take years to finalize and sign into law. The appropriations process in the United States is no cake walk either. The 1974 Congressional Budget Act requires the president to first submit his own budget proposal, which the two chambers of Congress debate in order to pass their own resolutions (which are, strangely, non-binding) that are supposed to serve as guides for the actual funding bills.[10] While there are target deadlines for this process, Congress has passed its mandated appropriations bills on time just a few times in the last 40-plus years. In the UK, austerity measures were first introduced after years of budget deficits peaked in the cloud left behind by the financial crisis of 2008. Yet, programs didn't officially commence until 2010. On top of the time it takes to actually get something done and working, many FC plans are enacted in such a way as to not take full effect at any given time. For instance, a percentage of cuts to spending or an increase in taxes may take place in year 1, with the meat of the plan taking place in years 2 and 3. Considering, again, the very real and normal human reaction to expected adjustments to future income and expenses and it's easy to see why fiscal plans that go beyond a single year can have varying effects at different points in time. These intertemporal effects have to be considered in any analysis to accurately contribute economic outcomes to fiscal policies.

It would be a whole lot easier to study the impact of FCs on our economy without having to consider the disparate effects of taxes when compared to government spending policies. But, that sort of oversimplification doesn't tell policymakers much. Results in these types of studies are so general as to be, well, generally useless. Breaking down the categories within each group to study the differences in outcomes that have come about from the wide variety of policies that have been attempted enables policymakers to have a larger set of tools available to choose from to create and manage policies that can greatly improve outcomes. Of course, the difference between the theoretically possible and actual reality is what separates a local community college marketing professor from Jeff Bezos. (I mean no offense to you local community college professors who purchased this book. You are awesome people who will do the right thing for your students by making this one required reading.) Consider how you might study the following examples of FC policies that have been implemented.

THE REAL WORLD

If you're anything like me, sometimes it just takes a good example or two to really understand what all of this stuff really means. In the following, I describe two specific instances in which Australia and the UK passed their own FCs. Later in the book, I get into a bit more detail with a few case studies, but to give the reader an idea of how these things work in the real world, it's helpful to know what legislators were thinking, what types of plans they passed, and how they eventually unfolded.

Australia

Ah yes, the Land Down Under.[11] Home to a giant red rock in the middle of nowhere, the didgeridoo (aka the coolest instrument on Earth), and a lovely opera house with a view. Oz isn't just the largest island on Earth; it's also the place where fiscal prudence was developed[12] and is now emulated around the world. Whether your home country has followed the Ozian fiscal path is irrelevant; Australia has still provided us with some excellent examples of FCs that incorporate all of the aforementioned characteristics, and then some.

Much like in the rest of the world, the sixth largest country (by land area) wasn't immune to the effects of a recession in the early 1980s. However, its own recession was exacerbated by a severe drought which reduced farm output by a third, along with a simultaneous positive shift in real wages incited by successful trade union advocates.[13] Higher wages may have been great for employees at first, but if inappropriately or artificially (meaning outside of market forces) advanced, they may be a pain to employers—during economic contractions employers need payroll flexibility as a tool to counter the effects of a down business cycle. As a result of this fierce combination, unemployment leaped from 5.75 percent in 1981 to 10 percent in 1983, while GDP per capita fell from nearly 15 percent above the OECD average to 5 percent below (per the OECD).

Given the combination of automatic stabilizer responses (which increase government spending) and a bit of loosey-goosey discretionary spending, Australia went from a nearly balanced budget to a deficit of nearly 4 percent of GDP in the early 1980s. Compared to the rest of the OECD, Australia has always been a financial prude, substantiated by government debt that equaled 10 percent of GDP in 1980 (the U.S. debt was three times this rate at the time). However, by 1985, it doubled to 20 percent.[14] Though still pretty prudish by the world's standards, Aussie legislators got a bit skittish and proposed FC policies to get its finances out from down under its comfort level. In 1985, its parliament came up with the ominous-sounding *Trilogy*, which was a series of commitments aimed at getting the deficit under control.

The Trilogy provided a framework for budgets that curtailed tax increases and government spending, while also reducing the deficit. Remember the government budget identity, $T + B = G + I$ (excluding monetary policy tools)? If taxes, T, don't go up, and government spending, G, isn't allowed to increase, how can legislators reduce the budget and deficit? Since it can't reduce the amount of new bonds issued, nor can a government reduce the interest on existing bonds (without a default on its obligations), its only option is to reduce spending, and that's exactly what Australia did. In 1985, it announced spending cuts of nearly 1 percent of GDP, spread out over two years (almost half a percent in cuts was introduced in 1985, with another half percent the following fiscal year).

Did the Aussies get the job done? Well, that depends on how you define "done." For now, we'll ignore the wider, societal implications that parallel austere fiscal policy. That being said, a budget deficit of nearly 3.5 percent of GDP in 1983 turned into a 2 percent surplus five years later. Parliament was so thrilled with its own success that it patted itself on the back with another FC of a full percent of GDP in 1986, along with another one in 1987. Both years' cutbacks were based considerably on spending—which were spread across improving entitlement efficiencies, reducing state capital assistance, cuts to defense, education, foreign aid, and public employees—while taxation increases made their debut (with a meager two tenths of a percent increase in each year) that led to surpluses in the late 1980s and significant debt reductions. Taxes were increased on Medicare, business taxes rose, excise taxes increased slightly, and wholesale taxes were bumped up a notch—a broad range of small tax increases.[15]

Golden Wattles bloomed[16] and rainbows became ubiquitous—until the next major hiccup, a recession in the early 1990s.

The UK

The Queen of England—who also happens to be the queen of Australia, Canada, Jamaica, all of the UK, and more, for a total of sixteen sovereign states—is worth a lot of money, and everyone knows it. Though impossible to be precise, some have estimated her net worth to be a cool half billion.[17] Yet, she still tries to relate to the British flare for parsimony. During her annual Christmas address in 2018, the queen decided it was time to reflect on her homeland's values and give a rousing "keep your chin up" speech to encourage the average citizen in the midst of what some have deemed a rough economic patch for the Brits (who are also in the middle of deciding whether to remain fully integrated in the European Union, which will doubtfully be resolved by the publication of this book). While a sweet gesture, some doubted the queen's sincerity and ability to relate. It wasn't for the fact that she was always a royal, becoming the heir apparent at the ripe old age of ten, but rather due to a poor choice of optics. All agree that it's nice to see the queen attempt to lift the spirits of her less fortunate countrymen, but difficult to watch her do so while wearing a flamboyant display of royal family jewels, in front of a piano made of gold.

Despite the deliberately profligate finances of the royal family, the government of the UK has been no stranger to austerity. In fact, they are sometimes quite proud of it. In 2009, with a worldwide economic crisis fresh on the mind, future prime minister David Cameron was quoted as saying, "the age of irresponsibility is giving way to the age of austerity," which became a platform that he ran and won on.[18] He and his "coalition of the skinflints" (my term, not theirs) kept to their word too, proposing to cut the deficit and lower the national debt by introducing spending cuts and tax increases that amounted to more than $100 billion. Down and down the deficit has gone, to today's 1.2 percent of GDP (as of close of the first quarter 2019), which is the lowest the deficit in the UK has been since the golden years of 2001 and 2002 (see figure 2.2).

While unfortunate for the deficit hawks of the UK, the politics and feasibility of the FC scheme hit a major hurdle when the country's electorate voted to leave the European Union in a move famously known as *Brexit*. The prime minister, chancellor, and numerous other budgeteers have now conceded their doubts of the feasibility of reaching budget Nirvana (i.e., a surplus) by 2020.

However unlikely it now seems that the UK will reach its stated goal of having some extra cash in the bank at the end of the fiscal year, it has frequently dabbled in the art of FC in the past. Following a couple of years of GDP shrinkage from 1990 to 1992, the Chancellor of the Exchequer (the head of *Her Majesty's Treasury*) put forth a budget plan that intended to "put the public finances on to a sound basis, so that the economic recovery now under way can be sustained over the medium term."[19] Ostensibly to allow for the economic recovery to do a bit of its own magic, the FC measures weren't implemented until a couple of years after the end of the recession. When they did begin in 1994, the fiscal adjustment policies continued for a few years, right through 1997.

In this case, UK legislators laid out the harsher portion of their austerity plan in the beginning, feathering off in the end. What is interesting with the British case is that consolidations teetered between a plan based on spending to one that relied more on tax increases. In 1994–1995, the country aimed to

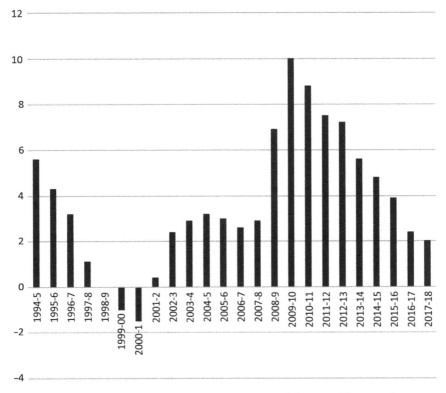

Figure 2.2 UK Government Deficit. Author Generated from "Public Spending," UK. Office for National Statistics, Accessed July 22, 2019, https://www.ons.gov.uk/economy/ governmentpublicsectorandtaxes/publicspending.

cut the deficit by 0.83 percent of GDP over two years, more than three quarters of which was comprised of planned tax increases on households such as a higher income tax, tobacco taxes, and a decreased mortgage relief credit. The 1995–1996 budget called for a similarly arranged consolidation, but to a lesser magnitude, leaning on spending cuts to discretionary spending, specifically within "government departments" in 1996. In the following year, the government decided to go a little bigger, announcing a five-year plan to once and for all knock out the deficit and hit a surplus. The plan was based solidly on tax hikes, with a little bit of increased spending on welfare to offset some of the benefits to budget from the income from tax revenues.[20]

While it is interesting to see the creativity of the minds of the budget artists that come up with FC plans, the reason we want to study them so intently, and from an insider's perspective with insight into all the moving pieces, is that (theoretically) the various types of consolidation measures should have a different effect on a country's economic performance. The textbook Keynesian response is that FCs have a negative effect on economic output, period. In the classical Keynesian function, aggregate demand, Y, is equal to consumption, C, government spending, G, investment, I, and net exports, X-M:

$$Y = C + G + I + (X - M)$$

If this model holds in real life, any negative adjustments to government spending (all else equal) will also negatively affect aggregate demand, meaning that FCs that are based on government spending cuts should be recessionary. Yet, there is a fairly dramatic debate with wide-ranging implications that suggest that the model may not hold for a number of reasons. Some of the theories for why this basic model doesn't apply to the real world include *wealth effects*, which suggests that private sector consumption may actually increase when government consumption goes down. Why? Perhaps individuals realize that they may be off the hook for future tax liabilities if the government doesn't spend so much today, which makes them feel more "wealthy" today. When you feel wealthier, you may be the type that thinks it's okay to let go of a few extra dollars here and there.

Countries also have credibility issues to consider. When making investments in a foreign country, every investor has to consider the country-level risk that is inherent, before getting down to multitude other risk factors. In the case of a country with high debt, there will likely be a higher risk premium and therefore higher interest rates on money lent to domestic investors. If, however, the government sends a strong signal that it's going to make fiscal choices that restrain, contain, and constrain in order to regain its fiscal pride, that risk premium will go down. With a lower risk premium there will be a higher incentive to invest (as more investment options become more profitable pursuits), which can improve total investment, I, and improve aggregate demand more than the Keynesian might predict.

In addition to the types, depth, composition, and timing of FC policies, many will argue that economists are just too simpleminded in their analyses. Sometimes they get too caught up in studying the Y and forget about the *distributional effects*, or other social adjustments that may adversely impact a society. Suppose, for example, an austerity program is put into place that tackles the deficit entirely over a three-year period, but does so in a way that increases taxes on only those earning under $100,000 per year (the majority of the population in any country). What happens to the next generation of workers if youth unemployment bears the brunt of FC pain today (see figure 2.3, which shows that more than half of Greece's population of eighteen- to twenty-four-year olds couldn't find a job in 2013)? Yes, the country on a

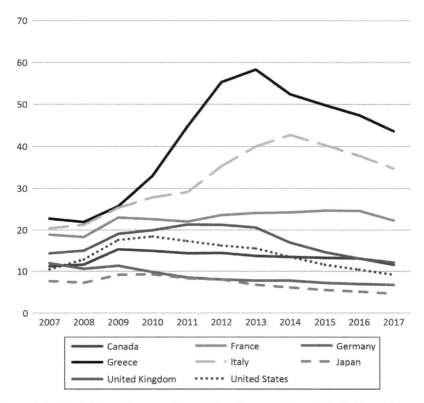

Figure 2.3 Youth Unemployment Rate. Author Generated from "Youth Unemployment Rate," OECD, Accessed July 22, 2019, https://data.oecd.org/unemp/youth-unemploymen t-rate.htm.

whole may be on a better fiscal path, but many will argue that the cost outweighs the benefit. Or, what if austerity measures are implemented to cut the deficit to exactly where policymakers want it to be, but are focused entirely on cuts in the public expense line item that provides for a police force. What good is a solid fiscal outlook if we get robbed everyday on the way to work? These austerity naysayers have become quite the force to be reckoned with, and oftentimes have some good points, especially since the recent global economic shock of 2008.

The following two chapters will take a deeper dive into some of the results of the many studies on the benefits, or detriments, of FC policies, both before and after the breaking point of the most recent global economic crisis, with a constant eye toward the naysayers of the world, along with other influences that may make you want to throw your hands in the air and say "no one really knows, do they?" But, stick with it! Regardless of whether you, or anyone, can be 100 percent correct about any given set of policies, someone is going to make a decision that impacts everyone around you—your educated opinion may be able to influence theirs.

NOTES

1. Congressional Budget Office (CBO), *The Effects of Automatic Stabilizers on the Federal Budget as of 2013* (Washington: CBO, 2013).

2. The term *potential GDP* is oft talked about, but rarely understood. Essentially it is economists' best guess about where a country's GDP would be if nothing too bad or too good were going on. In other words, if aggregate quantity demanded by an economy is equal to the aggregate output produced, an economy is at its maximum sustainable potential GDP. The problem with this concept is that no one really knows where this point is, so it's quite difficult to measure, and even more difficult to develop a concept derived from its definition.

3. John M. Keynes, *The Economic Consequences of the Peace* (New York: Harcourt, Brace and Howe, 1919).

4. Milton Friedman, "Government Revenue from Inflation," *Journal of Political Economy* 79, no. 4 (1971): 846–856.

5. In fact, the latest research shows the Fed maintaining a strong bias below the targeted rate, leaving many to suggest that the Federal Reserve Board undergo a policy shift that is more neutral.

6. Dan Neil, "The 50 Worst Cars of All Time," *Time* (2017), accessed December 13, 2018, from http://time.com/4723114/50-worst-cars-of-all-time/.

7. For you budding economists, it's useful to note that an important economic attribute of transfers is that they don't affect the *marginal rate of substitution* between consumption and leisure.

8. However, there is research that illustrates a negative effect on GDP growth, in both the short and long run, from military spending. Try typing "military spending and economic growth" in Google Scholar. However, I'm not sure those calculations include the alternative scenario in which another, less generous invading country, becomes our new Uncle Sam.

9. In a fairy-tale world, everyone might pay a "fair share," but there is a lot of room for argument about what "fair" means, and very few societies that make everyone pay the same. For example, the Urban-Brookings Tax Policy Center recently estimated that 44 percent of Americans will not pay federal taxes in 2018. "Tax Units with Zero or Negative Income Tax Under Current Law, 2011–2028," *Tax Policy Center*, accessed January 1, 2019, https://www.taxpolicycenter.org/model-estimates/tax-units-zero-or-negative-income-tax-liability-september-2018/t18-0128-tax-units.

10. James Santurno, Bill Heniff, and Megan Lynch, *The Congressional Appropriations Process: An Introduction* (Washington: Congressional Research Service, 2016). https://www.senate.gov/CRSpubs/8013e37d-4a09-46f0-b1e2-c14915d498a6.pdf.

11. This example is partly borrowed from a dataset created by the IMF. Pete Devries, Jaime Guajardo, Daniel Leigh, and Andrea Pescatori, "An Action-Based Analysis of Fiscal Consolidation in OECD Countries," *IMF Working Paper No. 11/128*, Washington: International Monetary Fund (2011): 33.

12. This isn't true at all, but I'm trying to make up for my ignorance of the country with flattery.

13. David Gruen and Amanda Sayegh, "The Evolution of Fiscal Policy in Australia," *Treasury Working Paper 2004–5* (2005). The Treasury of the Australia.

14. All statistics are from the Australian Treasury, found at www.archive.treasury. gov.au.

15. International Monetary Fund (IMF), *IMF Recent Economic Developments* (Washington: International Monetary Fund, 1987): 36–37.

16. The Golden Wattle, or *acacia pycnantha*, has been Australia's national flower since 1988. It's a beautiful flower "with large fluffy, yellow, sweet smelling flower heads." If the Australian government would be so kind as to fly my family and I out for a visit, I'd be happy to include more fascinating facts in my next book.

17. Jennifer Calfas and Alex Langone, "All the Members of the British Royal Family, Ranked by Net Worth," *Time* (2018). Retrieved from http://time.com/mone y/5178274/royal-family-net-worth/.

18. Deborah Summers, "David Cameron Warns of 'new age of austerity,'" *The Guardian* (April 26, 2009), accessed December 13, 2018 from https://www.theguard ian.com/politics/2009/apr/26/david-cameron-conservative-economic-policy1.

19. "United Kingdom Financial Statement and Budget Report (FSBR) of 1994– 95," The National Archives (UK), accessed December 14, 2018 from https://webarch ive.nationalarchives.gov.uk/20130105093314/http://www.official-documents.co.uk/ document/hmt/budget94/budget94.htm.

20. Devries, et al., "An Action-Based Analysis of Fiscal Consolidation," 75–78.

Chapter 3

What We (Think We) Knew, Before We Didn't Know

It probably won't surprise you that politicos and academics disagree—even, and especially, among themselves—on which type of FC policy will win in a fight (even mentioning the word "austerity" in a pub in London has been known to start a brawl). Yes, despite every politician and researcher being 100 percent certain of the accuracy and righteousness of their own efforts and results, there exists quite the variety of conclusions that have come about subsequent to the variegated sea of FC measures. From major institutions like the IMF and the World Bank to high-profile individuals like Paul Krugman, as well as prominent researchers from Boston to Milan, everyone seems to have an opinion, all of which are conclusive. A closer look reveals that—among the hundreds of serious, insightful, and thoughtful studies that were conducted before the global economic crisis of 2008—there are many, many factors that contribute to the study of the impact of various measures of FC on a country's immediate and short-run economic performance, and a budding body of literature that supported different theories as well as the methodologies for testing those theories. Yes, that's a mouthful I know, but even worse: virtually all that we knew, or thought we knew, has been tossed in a blender since 2008, seemingly making every policy imaginable fair game for policymakers and researchers once again.

An early examination of the basket of notable research on FC policies exposes a revelation that went hard against the Keynesian grain, and hence the "intuition" of prominent thinking. Prior to the 1970s, few even questioned the supposition that cutting back on government spending would translate into a similar reduction in a country's GDP, just as they also knew the same response would transpire via tax increases. But studies in the 1980s and 1990s began to find that it is possible, seemingly contrary to everything we had come to know and love, that an economy could cut back and grow at the same time. These paradoxical findings (and the inspiration for the title of this book) led to the development of the theory of expansionary fiscal contraction (*EFC theory*). Of course, given the immense number of inner-working contributors to the macroeconomy, others contradicted the contrarian findings, others jumped on the bandwagon, others argued for the sake of arguing, and then others extended and advanced the work of their peers. It's been a fun ride (aka, vicious research cycle) giving rise to some exciting and interesting policy advances and frameworks, until 2008 threw everyone for a loop.

This chapter will lay the historical foundation for the research behind the policies enacted to stabilize and grow economies in the near term, highlighting the "best" solutions and ideas of the time that were thought to have the highest chance of prosperity, and will constantly note debated points, contradictions, exaggerated concerns, under-discussed themes, and more. If there was such a thing as a "wild ride" in economics, the following will be one.

THE THEORY OF EXPANSIONARY FISCAL CONTRACTIONS

If the ever-stalwart, dominating philosophy that is oh-so Keynesian were true, ratcheting down government spending wouldn't lead to anything good (*ceteris paribus!*). After all, let's remind ourselves of the famous formula:

$$Y = C + G + I + (X - M),$$

where aggregate demand, Y, is equal to consumption, C, government spending, G, investment, I, and net exports (exports minus imports), X-M.

You may not be much of a math whiz, but most people's basic understanding suggests that if government spending falls, that big Y (which captures economic performance) has to fall as well. On the other hand, relying upon tax increases to reduce a deficit should have a similar effect, though the difference in magnitude has always been debated. If taxes are increased, consumption, investment, or net exports may fall, which ends up kicking Y in the pants.

What some researchers have found, however, is that the effects of such FCs on the economy are not so cut and dry. Whereas the standard Keynesian model predicts contractionary effects for short-term economic performance, others found evidence to support the exact opposite. One can only imagine the triple-checking that underpaid research assistants must have undergone in the smoke-filled back offices of academia when the first set of orthodox-busting results began rolling in.

Giavazzi and Pagano (1990) were among the first brave souls to go against the Keynesian grain, as it relates to FC policy research. By publishing their findings that austerity policies may in fact lead to *increased* private consumption in the short span of a couple of years after an FC—a phenomenon known as the previously described EFC theory—they launched a subset of literature in the field that attempted to validate the theory, replicate the duo's results, or even vilify anyone who would consider the possibility of EFC theory's righteousness (remember Reinhart and Rogoff?). After taking a closer look at the policies of countries across the EU from 1981 to 1989, as well as in the United States, the now famous article demonstrated how tax policies exhibited the traditional Keynesian response, that increasing taxes to cut deficits had a contractionary effect on private consumption, while FCs that focused on spending had an opposite effect.

The study focused on the early 1980s, a magical moment in history in which high debt flowed from the light-hearted fiscal policies undertaken in the 1970s to combine with high interest rates of the early 1980s, making for an uncomfortable affair. Borrowing suddenly became much more expensive than in the past, providing an incentive for countries to cut back (or be cut by the world's lenders). As explained in chapter 2, there were a lot of ways to do so during this time period as well, and some pretty grandiose disputes about which would do the best. The typical Danish view was that FC would "dampen private consumption" by way of an increase in unemployment and a slow-to-invest response by the business community. The fact that the traditionally tough financiers of Denmark (as of 2017, Denmark has a public debt of close to 36 percent debt-to-GDP ratio, compared to Germany's 64 percent, or France's 97 percent[1]) decided that the benefit of having smaller deficits outweighed this expected result allowed for a study of the effect of a steep spending cut on the country's consumption. The Germans, on the other hand, refuted the conventional wisdom, providing a more nuanced fiscal world view that agreed with the probability that FC will directly reduce aggregate demand, but also added that this response can be countered by the "role of expectations, if the measures taken are believed to be part of a credible medium-run program."[2] Consumers who believe that policymakers are offering up a sincere attempt at a longer term fiscal fix will reward policymakers by going out there and producing some GDP, according to the line of thinking that closely follows the now neoclassical dominated idea that was made popular by Milton Friedman and others (see the term "rational expectations" used at the end of chapter 2). The challenge to date, however, has been to find empirical evidence to support Deutschland's intuition.

To test the theory, the Italian investigators put together some crafty (at least, at the time) statistical studies. Understanding these empirical techniques requires a bit of econometrical knowledge (if you need a little help in this area, feel free to add Jeffrey Wooldridge's *Introductory Econometrics*[3] to your nightstand reading pile), but they basically contrived a standard statistical model that regressed real private consumption (as a share of potential output) on lagged consumption (as a proxy for the international business cycle), cyclically adjusted taxes, government expenditures, and the money supply for ten countries over the period from 1973 to 1989. The hope is that applying a similar *regression analysis* allows a researcher to evaluate the relationship between a dependent variable, in this case real private consumption, and other independent variables (everything else). This particular approach is considered simplistic today, but was meant to test the connection between government expenditures (and taxes) and economic performance, while accounting for effects that can be attributed to changes in the money supply (monetary policy effects) as well as those that may be credited with business cycle shifts, which are not discretionary policy-related (because we want to learn the impact of the policy decisions we've made). In the end, the choice of which policy choices had which impact is really what we want to study, so virtually all related studies attempt to trim the noise to view how these choices relate to a country's economic wherewithal.

The results of their model were certainly interesting, to say the least. Despite finding that there was a traditional Keynesian response in the tax channel (a 1 percent increase in taxes had a significantly negative effect of approximately a tenth of 1 percent to the downside on private consumption, for the countries studied across the time period studied), they also found the contrary possibility that spending reductions have the opposite response, but with a larger magnitudinal response and with even greater statistical significance than the taxation effect. In other words, their general results were even more conclusive that government spending had a negative relationship with private consumption than the more well-known and rarely disputed Keynesian theory that tax increases have the same effect.

To be certain that the statistical results made theoretical sense, Giavazzi and Pagano took a deep dive into two of the most extreme cases within their study. Both Ireland and Denmark brought the thunder when it came to serious FCs. Denmark cut public consumption and increased taxes so vigorously in 1983 that it reduced yearly public debt growth from 10.2 percent between 1979 and 1982 to zero, with a big chunk related to the shift in government spending from 4 percent year-over-year growth down to less than 1 percent (if you have to read this line four or five times, you will have read it fewer than me). Ireland did virtually the same thing at the same time, but then doubled down in 1987. During the first episode of consolidation from 1982 to 1984, they reduced public consumption to almost the same degree as Denmark, but raised taxes even more intensely. In the plan covering 1987–1989, however, public consumption decreased at a rate of nearly 4 percent per year, public investment fell by more than 13 percent, and taxes were relied on to a lesser extent. The more dramatic maneuvers in Ireland's deficit shrinking regime part II finally started chipping away at total public debt.[4]

But there are so many macroeconomic factors that can influence economic output; one has to closely scrutinize such a policy shift and all of the surrounding circumstances to really understand what caused what. Both countries, for example, shifted monetary and exchange rate policies at the same time they consolidated national budgets. Denmark fixed its kroner to the German mark, removing the usual suspect of monetary devaluations from the list of potential side contributors to GDP improvements. Per the study's authors, the total package resulted in a Danish reward of 3.6 percent growth for several years. Ireland's monetary authorities also pegged to the mark, but without the same positive results (despite a boon to exports). During its second attempt in 1987, Ireland decided to go hardcore and cut the deficit by 7 percent of GDP, mostly from reduced government spending and investments.[5] Growth ensued, but some debate how much influence monetary policies really had on the country's stabilization.

While the impact of EFC theory on the study of policies to cut fiscal deficits is irrefutable, unfortunately for the Italian duo, their results didn't go without a ton of debate and an eventual refutation of their methodologies. Some did confirm their conclusions, yet most today (including the original authors themselves) submit that the methodologies used at the time led to biased results.

IF NOT EFC, THEN WHAT?

In the decades since Giavazzi and Pagano's paper, numerous studies supporting and negating EFC theory have been published; some lean theoretical, but most are empirical examinations. Some question why and how such a phenomenon could happen with the ardent protestation of well-established economic theory and its historical support, combined with the hardheaded response of a grandparent from the old world: this is how I did it, so this is how you should do it. The rest rely heavily on their own econometric approaches, responding with vigorous criticisms and new insights that linger into the world of mathematics and statistics. In general, this type of academic debate is a professional and cordial process (though, for fun, I imagine a few rounds of fisticuffs at the annual American Economic Association's meetings) of writing, getting peer input, rewriting, getting unsolicited rebuttals, and responding—an exercise that is useful to improving and adding to the existing body of work. For nascent investigators it's useful to see the trail of history that any good paper's literature review will guide one down, but is especially helpful to better understand the reality behind it all so we can improve on past work and create better, evidence-backed frameworks for the next generation of policy leaders.

Whether related to the claims of an expansionary effect, or alternative debates about the implications of various FC policies, a few major barriers have contributed to the wide-ranging results in FC studies. The first is the method by which a period of FC is defined or identified, which has comprised a major chunk of today's infighting. The second is the specific country or countries' data that are used, along with the incorporation (or lack thereof) of tests that integrate a slew of policy variables also known to affect output. Lastly, and more broadly speaking, is the debate about how austerity policies are approached in the first place, whether we need them at all, and if they end up doing more harm than good based on other correlated implications that are harder to measure, but still concerning to a society at large. Some of these issues will be discussed in the following sections as they have been presented in academic journals over the decades before the 2008 global crisis, along with the potential for further analysis using alternative methods, or different sources and updated data.

Hide-and-Seek with FCs

One of the biggest problems with studying FCs is how to find them. I know, this seems like a silly problem to have. With all our technological advances and fancy software why can't we just Google "when did Aldovia consolidate their fiscals?" and get every answer we could imagine. (Don't try to search for Aldovia. It's a made-up country from a Hallmark movie that I may or may not have been forced to watch.) Doesn't the World Bank have a consolidated list of all known FCs? If not, can't we just send an email to the financial department administrator of any country and get a quick answer? These questions befuddle even the most accomplished of researchers with prize-winning economic skills who are used to going to their friendly website of choice to slap together almost any chart they can imagine—with grayed-out bars showing precisely when we officially entered and exited a recession. The answers are a pretty wishy-washy, yes and no.

While simple econometric techniques can be deployed to identify periods in which fiscal balances have merely changed (the closest thing to a Google search in the economist's world), the researcher's task is not simply to find movements in fiscal balances, but to identify periods in which policymakers *intended* to enact an FC, as well as changes in economic indicators that directly result from those intentional policy shifts. What's the difference? Well, if you pull up all of the data on the national income statements of a country—let's use Aldovia as an example—and simply look for moments in time in which the deficit was shrinking, it would be easy to assume that anytime you find one, the country of Aldovia must have had some stingy financial leaders who enacted an austere fiscal policy to make it happen. But, that's an assumption that ignores all the other possibilities. For example, the natural course of a business cycle upturn may cause automatic stabilizers to tighten up (when more people have jobs, for example, fewer receive unemployment insurance or social welfare benefits), leading to less spending and a likely improvement to tax revenues, without the guided hand of a policymaker. As much as the Honorable Aldovian Chancellor may like to take credit for these fiscal improvements, he wasn't responsible for any policies that can (directly) take credit for the fiscal turnaround. It would be erroneous to assume that because Aldovia's deficit shrunk, policymakers must have done something brilliant that the rest of the world needs to copy.

In a slight variation of this example, what if the Aldovian Chancellor did enact a policy to fiscally consolidate, but it happened to be at the exact same time that the economy began booming. In this particular case, FC policy creation, a shrinking deficit, and a business cycle going into full peak mode may all be correlated, which leads the untrained eye to assume that one necessarily caused the other. What if the fiscal policies had zero impact on the new shifts in the nation's finances? How would you know?

Without eliminating the background noise that works alongside, or in lieu of, policymakers' handywork, a policy practitioner may mistakenly assume that Aldovia created policies to shrink the deficit which also caused the economy to expand. *See, Aldovia implemented a massive austerity plan and they came out great!* But, you the intelligent reader and diligent economics student now know the truth. Even when you do think you've found a time when policymakers have managed to somehow shrink a deficit, there will be more questions than immediate answers.

The task, therefore, is to find an episode of FC that was preceded by a policy that meant to make it happen, study the economic ramifications that occurred directly after—while filtering out the junk that may have also had a marginal contribution—and apply some good common sense to be sure it's all compatible. If we found that Aldovia cut its deficit growth in 2009 from 10 percent of GDP to zero the following year and discover that the Chancellor Doe issued a decree halting all government spending just before this, we might be on to something. In this case, we can take a close look and see how cutting all government spending to zero affected Aldovia's growth into the future. If the economy survived, its government likely didn't fare too well. If the economy boomed, then the chancellor will be asked to apply his magical powers to the fiscal plans of other countries with similar deficit and debt concerns.

Intentionality is also a difficult thing to parse out. Gaining a thorough understanding of policymaker intentions is an arduous task requiring a researcher to scour a large breadth of documents, to interview multitude policymakers, and/or to scan the historical record across multiple countries. No one wants to do that much work, few have the time, and even fewer have the resources and patience required for such a serious investigation.

Given the enormous amount of data present in macroeconomic studies of this nature, most have, therefore, resorted to various statistical techniques to resolve the issue of identification related to FC policies. When constructing an empirical analysis of the various data in this field, the most common and conventional approach is to apply a statistical tool known as *regression analysis* using a variation of a basic specification on an econometric model that intends to explain the relationship between a dependent variable (such as aggregate demand or private consumption) and a number of independent variables that may contribute to the movement in the dependent variable over time. Though there are some interesting ways in which one can do all of this via the old pen and paper (a whole other level of insanity), most go the old route of throwing some numbers into an Excel-type file, then feeding them into a sophisticated software tool (see SPSS or Stata as some recent favorites).

Outside of the attempt to validate a relationship between theorized variables, those who employ these types of techniques really want to mitigate the biases related to endogenous variables common in macroeconomic studies—known or unforeseen—by using the various econometric techniques discussed in subsequent sections. Translation: it's tough to see whether the GDP of countries similar to Aldovia's has improved because of a policy introduced by its policymakers, or if the policy was effective at shrinking its stubborn Aldovian deficit because of the improving economy that just so happened to be moving as part of its normal business cycle fluctuations. Which part of the dog is really doing the wagging?

To try to figure this out, the basic model generally consists of a regression of real GDP (or real private consumption) on a variable that accounts for changes in a fiscal balance (to identify FCs), along with an array of other variables that are theorized to affect output. This truncated version (if this looks complicated, keep in mind that you'll never see it written so simplistically in any recent study) looks like this (see figure 3.1):

$$\Delta Y_t = \alpha + \beta_1 \Delta \text{FB} + \mu,$$

Figure 3.1   Author Generated.

where Y= the log of real GDP, FB is the fiscal balance variable of interest, and you'll have to know a bit about regression analysis to understand the rest, but μ just stands for "everything else."

Since the first major problem for researchers has been related to the techniques used to measure changes in a country's fiscal balance that reflect intentional decisions, and not simply the automatic effects of business cycle fluctuations, a lot of studies have been dedicated to finding statistically significant independent variables that are exogenous in nature. That is, we are looking for variables that affect GDP or some other measure of macroeconomic performance, that are not also impacted by shifts in GDP or other measure of macroeconomic performance, which would lead to a problem known in econometrics as *endogeneity*. Searching for realistically exogenous variables and implementing them into a model to replace those that are known to be endogenous should control for potential biases that lead to inconclusive or incorrect conclusions. And no one wants inconclusive, incorrect, or generally biased conclusions (it's not easy, though still possible, to get stuff published that is just plain wrong).

The methodologies used to find and properly determine such variables related to periods of FC vary widely, may exclude or reduce the above discussed problems of endogeneity, and have led to a significant body of research and wide debate on the usefulness of previous studies' outcomes.

No Cycling Zone

Previous research has tried to find a variable that isn't itself impacted by our measure of economic performance by taking into account fluctuations that persist in the business cycle. As a reminder, the normal ups and downs around a long-term trend in a nation's GDP are known as the *business cycle*. When we're in an upward growth short-term trend, we are in a period of *economic expansion* (or growing GDP), recovery, or upturn, until we hit our peak, then enter a *recession* (period of economic contraction, or shrinking GDP) and eventual trough when we're bottoming out. The phases of a business cycle are expanded to more than the several presented here by some, but explain the same up and down movement within any normal economy over a period of time. Given that we are always in one part of the business cycle, and are always moving to another (n.b., it is impossible to know within which part of the cycle we currently reside as only in hindsight is this discernable), the so-called "natural" flow of the cycle also has an impact on the variable that we would like to measure as our outcome variable of interest when studying policies that consolidate a nation's finances. If GDP is already expanding, or contracting, when a particular policy is put into place, we want to know how much of that movement is due to these normal movements and how much credit we can really give to the policymaker and his respective genius, for coming up with said policy suggestion. If you only see the talking points coming out of your nation's capital, the following is an accurate description: if economic times are good, it's because of the policymaker, who may be an elected official in need of some new fundraising bullet points. If times are tough, XYZ policy is a hot potato that was "forced upon" the country by the circumstances of the time. After all, *it would have been worse if I didn't act!* We want to know if either is really true.

By theoretically removing some of the issues caused by "normal" movements in the business cycle, we should be able to get down to the nuts and bolts of what we really want to know. The *cyclically adjusted primary balance method* (CAPB) was created to do just that. It's less complicated than it sounds. The CAPB approach basically identifies FCs using data on a country's primary budget balance, adjusted for fluctuations in the business cycle. The *primary balance* can be found by finding the regular government balance, then subtracting interest payments. The idea is that we want to be left with components of a nation's revenues and spending that are controlled by a policy choice; in other words, we want to see only those that are discretionary. Since interest payments on existing debt are compulsory, unless your country is trying to default (see Puerto Rico in later chapters), they shouldn't be included in a study of policy decisions that impact a nation's deficit and economic performance. Once we have only these discretionary components left, the CAPB method was then developed to try to remove the effects of the business cycle.

The CAPB has been used since the early 1990s to distinguish between policy and adjustments to economic performance and the fiscal balance that are related to normal economic movements. To get rid of these cyclical and automatic effects, estimators find the very mysterious point of *potential GDP* and compare it to where it currently stands, then eliminate the effects of shifts in spending and taxes that have occurred due to this deviation from economic potential. Potential GDP isn't really as much of a mysterious guess as you might think. In reality, it's essentially a guess of what GDP should have been (or should be) based on a known trend in GDP over a certain time period. If economic performance deviates from this trendline, it is moving according to the normal business cycle ebbs and flows. As you may guess, there is a lot of disagreement over whether potential GDP is truly measurable in the first place. Certainly it is difficult to know what our potential GDP is for this year or next, since we are always in the middle of a developing trend. If the economy begins a slow, steady contraction that lasts over the next three years, the trendline that crosses through today's period will be lower than we might anticipate contemporaneously. It is one thing, therefore, to say "France was operating below potential GDP from 1982 to 1983," which may have some wide agreement as to its true deviation; however, it is another thing altogether for an economist to suggest that we are currently operating at, below, or above potential GDP. No one really knows that answer for sure, which, to be fair, makes it difficult for policymakers to make decisions based on this best-guess type of information.

However, if we're using a transparent methodology that corrects the GDP using a CAPB based on a similar concept, it's fair to make certain assumptions that can be used as points of comparison across others who have deployed similar methodologies. An abundance of researchers have used it across a wide range of studies over the years. Related to fiscal adjustment policies, Oliver Blanchard, former chief economist of the IMF, created what he deemed an "index of discretionary change" in a 1990 paper (before he was the chief economist at the IMF) that found the value of the primary budget which "would have prevailed, were unemployment at the same value in the previous year, minus the value of the primary surplus in the previous year."[6] If other economic factors (that are all construed to be captured in employment) haven't really changed much from last year to now, what would the primary balance be and what is the difference from what it is? The difference is what Blanchard would have defined as the discretionary changes due to policy intervention.

Others built upon Blanchard's idea, or created their own similar indices or corrections to control for business cycles effects.[7] The previously noted Messrs. Giavazzi and Pagano used cyclically adjusted fiscal data to get rid of those pesky business cycle concerns and found their famous EFC theory, proclaiming some forms of austerity to be expansionary. Others supported their findings using variations of the CAPB method, but as interest in the idea grew, new discoveries led to the final admission that the CAPB adjustment just doesn't cut it because it generally leaves researchers with a bit too much positivity. That is, results tended to be inappropriately skewed in the direction of economic growth. Most today submit that such methodologies, therefore, lead to biased results. FCs may not have been as favorable to economic performance as CAPB supporters once proclaimed.

There are a number of reasons why reliance on CAPB data may lead to erroneous conclusions and misspecification in econometric approaches. Remember that final variable in the basic CAPB model specification that stands for "everything else?" The problem is that there are a lot of important little nuggets within that everything variable that the CAPB model doesn't account for well. If those that are left out of consideration are also correlated with other non-policy variables contained within this all-encompassing *error term*, which also affect economic output, then we have a bias that will lead to problems within our statistical results and incorrect conclusions.

For example, suppose the economy is killin' it and we enter a stock market boom. As portfolio values rise, institutional investors, fund managers, and even you and I at home will see an opportunity to start taking some gains. Those capital gains, or the profits we receive from the sale of stocks, add up across the country. As we pay taxes on those gains, aptly called capital gains taxes, we inadvertently improve the CAPB by increasing cyclically adjusted tax revenues. Because we're all doing much better, financially speaking, we're also more likely to have a bit more confidence in the way the world is spinning. Investors are likely to add to the nation's aggregate investment and we'll all consume a bit more, both of which mean there is a probable increase in the correlation between the CAPB figure we use to identify FCs and those factors that are not represented in the remaining parts of the model (that "everything else" error term).[8] If we don't take these factors into consideration, these non-policy attributes make it seem as though the policies we did implement were the real reason for all the gains, which makes policymakers feel better about themselves than they rightfully deserve.

The IMF gave an example in a 2014 paper of when the opposite might be true—a *fall* in asset prices can also obscure the case of an FC policy. In 2009, Ireland experienced a stock price gut punch (like the rest of us), as well as a housing bubble bust (like the United States). The resulting slide in stock and housing prices decreased the CAPB substantially. However, at the same time, Ireland unleashed a barrage of FC policies that amounted to more than 4.7 percent of GDP. Since the standard CAPB approach looks for an increase in the CAPB (cutting the deficit should increase the primary balance, not decrease it), it would not identify this particular case as the fiscal shrinkage that it was. This may be just one example, but how many cases across time may have led to the same misidentification scenario? Ostensibly, removing enough similar cases that have led to, or ran parallel to, a dive in the GDP and you've helped provide evidence that an FC has a more positive effect than otherwise might be found.[9]

Others have gone so far as to make the point that stronger-than-normal economic contractions have an even greater automatic effect on fiscal adjustment variables. This means that we are likely to completely overlook important periods when FCs coincide with the most dramatic downturns.[10] It's easy to overstate the positive benefits of FC when you remove data that says the opposite, whether intentional or not.

The misidentification of FCs doesn't end with overlooking or overstating the effects of consolidation policies. What if a policymaker pushing for an FC was motivated by an interest in restricting growth? The lack of independent monetary policy for those in the EU has allowed for examples of this. In 2000, for example, Finland decided that a boom in asset prices and a fast-growing economy needed to be controlled or face the consequences of inflation.[11] But, in 2000 Finland also gave up its ability to implement traditional monetary policy tools that are generally used to counter concerns related to an overheating economy when it joined the EU (for example, a central bank can increase interest rates, or tighten the money supply, if a country has an independent bank; Finland handed over its monetary policy reins to the ECB). The only power they had left outside and independent of the EU's authority resided within its localized fiscal policies, so Finland implemented austerity in the hopes that it would do the trick.

Given that Finland's motivation was to cut back on its growth by cutting spending and raising taxes (which would improve the CAPB), it doesn't make much sense to consider what effect their policies had on short-term growth. The researcher wants to find a period in which policies were implemented to improve an economy, which then did what they wanted it to do. Finland's policies in 2000 did the opposite of what they intended, yet the traditional CAPB method would have picked this up as an example of an FC policy that intended to improve the fiscal bottom line, which also led to a positive growth outcome.

The criticisms of the CAPB method hasn't stopped with the above examples, and continued to build over time, with new additions, twists, and updated ideas from various investigators. Some merely updated Giavazzi and Pagano's original methods to resolve what they saw as the most important issues, others threw in the adverse effects of employment as counters to any benefit attributed to GDP or private consumption growth, others weighed the very important distinction between temporary and permanent consolidations (we give less serious consideration as consumers to those that are temporary, goes the theory), some results concurred with the Keynesian-dominated principle that the multiplier effect will lead spending cuts to have a worse impact on economic performance than tax increases, while others found opposing results. The one result that did become clear, however, is that the CAPB method may not have been the best econometric idea leading to the most trustworthy of results. New methodologies were creatively deployed.

Getting Tricky

If you think the mathematical and statistical tricks were complicated before, they only got trickier over time. A wide variety of empirical methods have been created and applied since the 1990s to overcome the shortfalls of the CAPB method and provide more conclusive direction to policymakers. Before you get too scared of what I'm going to talk about in this section, I promise to keep the discussion on the lighter side, leaving room for further investigation on the various methods that others have used.

There are substantial variations within each of the following, yet two of the more prominent models for classifying periods of FCs are vector auto-regression (VAR) and dynamic stochastic general equilibrium (DSGE) econometric model techniques. Econometric modeling innovations of the early 1980s combined with recent theoretical inquiries into the identification of fiscal and monetary policy shocks to form research that applied VARs, which are fancy matrix-embedded modeling techniques that are useful for describing the more dynamic behavior within macroeconomics, especially related to the types of data that econometricians use in this field: multivariate times series (multiple variables and their values over time). Ramey's 2016 summary of the various techniques for recognizing fiscal policy shocks provides a solid review of how the technique came about.[12] Rotemberg and Woodford's work helped advance the VAR technique by analyzing military spending adjustments and the impact on the macroeconomy,[13] while Cochrane leveraged established VAR practices to search for a variety of shocks, including consumption shocks.[14] Despite these unique advancements, the developers themselves were often unsatisfied with their models' abilities to figure out the causes of economic fluctuations, while Ramey's high-level overview of the various techniques that employed similar methods found a common thread of inherent weaknesses, such as invalid restrictions based on a lack of acknowledgment and ability to account for information on forward-looking behavior that may be imbedded in policymakers' decision.[15]

DSGE models are pitched as a means for providing "a more structural way to identify" fiscal policy shifts in government spending and taxes, by looking at how the entire economy is impacted by random shocks and evolves over time, applying microeconomic principles to the theory of general equilibrium. The real means for implementing these types of models is outside the scope of this book, but it's important to note the methodology as a step in the evolution of fiscal policy analysis as it relates to macroeconomic analyses. Those who have relied upon DSGE models have found Keynesian responses to FCs as well as non-Keynesian, from less dynamic DSGE's that found different responses to FC based on the type of plan to a "new Keynesian DSGE,"[16] which found that all forms of FCs are harmful to economic performance in the short run, while spending cuts provide the optimal short-run path.

During a congressional inquiry into the validity of some of these models, Nobel Prize winner Robert Solow had one of the most humorous responses when asked what he thought about DSGEs:

> I do not think that the currently popular DSGE models pass the smell test. They take it for granted that the whole economy can be thought about as if it were a single, consistent person or dynasty carrying out a rationally designed, long-term plan, occasionally disturbed by unexpected shocks, but adapting to them in a rational, consistent way. I do not think that this picture passes the smell test. The protagonists of this idea make a claim to respectability by asserting that it is founded on what we know about microeconomic behavior, but I think that this claim is generally phony. The advocates no doubt believe what they say, but they seem to have stopped sniffing or to have lost their sense of smell altogether.[17]

Dr. Solow's love for idiomatic expressions related to the senses aside, he isn't alone in his sentiment that some methods allude common sense (though most are less dramatic, especially when entertaining an audience of members of Congress). For the same reasons that eliminated the usefulness of their antecedents, DSGE models still have their own weaknesses that lead to biases, as well as issues with various omitted variable and identification concerns.

Despite the bragging rights that came along with the creation of these unique approaches, and the "cool" factor associated with putting into practice what most of us can't possibly understand, they still aren't quite good enough for figuring out exactly what is causing what and when in the fiscal policy world. Without really knowing what policymakers are thinking, figuring out real intentions over time, and knowing that the reactions in economic performance are actually related to the referred-to policies, we still have unaccounted for flaws, regardless of the statistical tricks and excessively complicated math models that may be thrown into the analysts' economic blender.

There had to be something better.

Storytime

Everyone likes a good story. Economic theorists are no different. After all, a good economic theory is not much more than a reasonable-sounding story, based on enough fact and supported evidence to make it intriguing, with the rest filled in by the imaginations of our logical minds to make it complete. Since the social science that is economics is marked by its unique inability to be tested in a controlled experiment, unlike the natural and physical sciences, we are left with but a set of economic theories (some strengthened by far more evidence than others) and the real-life stories and examples that help to support them.

If statistical techniques and quantitative methods lack the sufficiency to provide suitably unbiased results, should we just throw our hands in the air and proclaim it to all be in vanity? Other departments across the world's universities have long awaited a time when they can officially denounce the "dismal science," but economists have refused to give up: instead they dug in deeper, developing the arduous and labyrinthine procedures that try to connect policymakers' direct intentional act of attacking deficits and debt with subsequent movements in economic performance. The only way to ensure that intention led to an action that produced a consequence is to get inside the heads of policymakers. Without an ability to read policymakers' minds, it's really difficult to know the reality of their thought processes; therefore, most just assumed it was impossible to do. Most, but, not all.

A more recent development, therefore, attempts to account for many of the issues in prior FC identification research by examining the historical record to determine policymakers' intentions for implementing consolidation policies. While you may wonder why everyone else didn't just think of that, consider what that really means. The "historical record" isn't just something you can find in a Wikipedia entry, or even look up in your local library's card catalog, it basically means every written account related to a particular topic. As you can imagine, reading *everything* is a bit time-consuming. To pare that "everything" down to something more manageable, researchers generally omit obscure blogs, tweets, and opinions from your local news anchor, but that still leaves one with quite a bit of reading to do. But first, a reminder about why the last resort method became so necessary.

In many of the previous models, the identification variable is found to be endogenous as it is affected by the dependent variable (a measure of economic output), which reduced the statistical validity of results. To ameliorate these concerns and the associated biases, researchers had to find unique instruments uncorrelated with omitted variables, as well as business cycle effects, which also capture policymaker intentions. In theory, if it is possible to identify discretionary changes in fiscal policies that are not implemented due to concerns of current or expected economic conditions— therefore motivated purely by a desire to improve a fiscal balance and reduce deficits for long-term growth—one can test the resulting economic output properly. But, as we've established, it's just not that easy to pick out FCs without making some grave errors. More time-consuming methods that rely on an intense reading of history, therefore, have remained one of the last untackled means for circumventing previous criticisms. Though not an entirely new concept, the most thorough and accepted practices for similar processes as applied to the study of fiscal adjustment policies go by a number of names, such as the narrative approach, narratively defined, the historical approach, or storytime for the bored and/or highly motivated economist.

Though more prominent in contemporary research, narratively defined methodologies can be found in the literature at least as far back as the 1960s. Nobel laureate Milton Friedman, along with good buddy Anna Schwartz, applied narrative identifications to monetary policy shocks in their 1963 *A Monetary History of the United States*.[18] It takes a special person to want to spend your days reading historical documents on monetary policy that date back to the 1860s, but these two raised the bar for understanding the context of the data before every other researcher of their day.

However, most stayed away from narrative approaches until the 1980s and 1990s (because it's hard). When competitive forces compelled some to finally reenter this frontier, early approaches used narrative methods to identify the oil shocks that were prominent in the 1970s,[19] or tax policy shocks of the 1980s.[20] The most influential contributors to today's innovations in contemporary practices, however, developed much more recently.

David and Christina Romer are about as prominent and powerful as a power couple can be in economics. After agreeing on a plan to join forces and dominate the world of economics, the two quickly solidified their partnership through marriage and began creating one of the most rigorously applied narrative approach techniques. Beginning in the late 1980s, the king and queen of macro developed their own story-based approach after reading Friedman and Schwartz's famous try. In 1989, they did so by reviewing the U.S. Federal Reserve Bank's *Federal Open Market Committee*'s (FOMC) recorded minutes for every meeting since World War II to seek out "episodes in which the Federal Reserve in effect decided to attempt to create a recession to reduce inflation"[21] that were not brought about by business cycle shifts in economic output. Ramey and Shapiro chose to instead have a bit more fun and put their living room hobby to practice in 1998 when they scanned magazine articles to find political events exogenous to current economic conditions as well as shocks that were "unanticipated."[22] As hard as they and many others tried to dethrone the dynamic Romers, the royals of macroeconomics were destined to dominate.

In 2010, Romer and Romer came back with a vengeance and earned the coveted "seminal work" designation reserved for only the most warranted of peer-approved academic work. To counter that irritating "omitted variable bias in any regression of output on an aggregate measure of tax changes,"[23] the authors examined a comprehensive primary record of contemporaneous federal reports and speeches between 1945 and 2007, including the *Economic Report of the President*, the *Annual Report of the Secretary of the Treasury*, and presidential speeches such as the *State of the Union Address* from the executive branch; reports by the House Ways and Means and Senate Finance committees to include legislative discussions, as well as the *Congressional Record*; and additional reports that provide insight into Social Security, such as the *Annual Report of the Board of Trustees of the Federal Old Age and Survivors Insurance Trust Fund*. If that sounds like a lot, it's just a small sample of the total documents they reviewed, and they did so for *every* year it was available.

By examining these records, the Romers hoped to find tax changes that were implemented as an exogenous response to counter the budget deficit or improve the national debt and long-term growth, as opposed to changing fiscal policies in order to offset another variable that may additionally impact economic output. To do so, they sought to identify tax-focused consolidations that were "motivated by past decisions, philosophy, and beliefs about fairness"[24] that would not be correlated with other variables captured in the econometric model's error term, which would otherwise lead to a statistical bias and a demotion to the macro kingdom's court jesters.

Over the period surveyed, they found fifty-four "relatively" exogenous tax changes. Does that seem like a lot of work to find fifty-four datapoints? Compared to your typical microeconomic studies, it is a low number, but in the world of macroeconomics, this is the type of data you are often left to work with, which does lead to critiques of macroeconomic studies in general. (With few, or relatively few, observations, results can be less precise and more sensitive to errors.) However, this particular study was the most robust of the time and has arguably overcome many of the issues related to its small dataset.

Their detailed descriptions of how "motivation, revenue effects, and other characteristics of each legislated tax change" were classified might lead one to concede to their methodological righteousness, if nothing else for the mere sake of not having to dig deep enough to dispute them. As a sample of their methods, they offered a comparison between the decision to classify an FC as endogenous—and thereby excluded from the dataset—and an exogenous finding that is more useful to their study. The summary of this example alone spanned thousands of words, providing a comparison between the United States' *Tax Reduction Act of 1975*, which was classified as an endogenous tax adjustment because it intended to counter the effects of a recession, and the *Revenue Act of 1964*, which was motivated by a long-run growth strategy and therefore considered to be an exogenously defined tax policy.[25] It's hard to imagine the amount of work that went into identifying all fifty-four periods they used in the final dataset (nor the heartbreak of someone who spent an inordinate, and likely unhealthy, amount of time studying a particular tax policy, only to find that it was not useful in the final research project).

Perhaps equally important, Romer and Romer knew that they had to compare the new methods to the way of the old guard. To do so, they looked at the new narrative approach alongside the CAPB method of yesteryear by rebuilding estimates of the CAPB over the examined time period using current best practices, then put them into regression models to demonstrate a relationship between the new series and the CAPB method. Movements in the two series were similar, but with a slight variation in timing. However, they found a substantial difference between changes in the CAPB and the narrative series, demonstrating an important difference from the onset. The results of the new model were consistent with the theory that tax-based fiscal adjustments had negative effects on GDP growth. A 1 percent tax increase (as a percentage of GDP) slightly negatively affected output over the first three quarters subsequent to an increase in taxes, and increased in magnitude over the following two years, lowering real GDP by up to 3 percent. The measured effects using the narrative approach were also substantially larger in magnitude than with other CAPB approaches. Given the narrative method's adherence to more sound econometric philosophy, the results were given that much more credibility.

Despite the Romer Monarchy's dominance, criticisms still arose, with many focused on contradicting the appropriateness of their narrative model. One issue that IMF researchers couldn't forget about was that of the timing of the implementation of FC plans. While an FC may be properly identified based on legislators' intentions, what if the policy adjustment was not officially put into practice until an economic recovery commenced? Such timing nearly guarantees that results will be correlated with a positive shift in economic output. Contrarily, if a country doubles downs on its initial consolidation plans to try to control for the onset of a contraction, results may also be inappropriately associated with *shrinking* output.[26] Both are flaws that, again, can misalign policies with either growth or contraction.

Additionally, economic actors, who *generally* act rationally and according to their incentives, may respond differently based on whether they anticipate a particular policy to be enacted in the future, are shocked by its inception today, or just plain don't believe that it will ever come to fruition. In the United States, for example, months—or even years—sometimes separate the date a bill is signed into law by the president and its implementation by regulators. The *CROWDFUND Act* was made official by President Barack Obama in 2012, but wasn't fully written by regulators and put into practice until . . . *four years* later. Such delays, and the associated reactions by economic actors, may have been ignored in others' identification methods. Valerie Ramey wrote substantially about the distinction between anticipated and unanticipated consolidations and the way they impact behavior and output, for example.[27]

Despite some of the perceived flaws, many in their field thought that the Romer couple was on to something. Few other econometric methods were able to build data and observations that had the level of exogeneity, and therefore statistical validity, that could be found within their narrative-based dataset. However, improving upon an already immense undertaking to build a larger dataset would require the efforts of those with resources, manpower, and lots of time on their hands.

The IMF decided they were up to the task and worked on an expanded set that catalogued exogenous FCs across OECD countries up to and partially through the most recent global shock.[28] Its researchers were among the next to enlist the insane level of dedication needed to get a lot more datapoints based on the narrative methods. While Romer and Romer's work read legislative, regulatory, executive, and other reports that better captured policymaker intentions related to taxation policies in the postwar United States, the IMF, however, upped the ante when it examined similar sources (speeches, legislative records, central bank reports, etc.) for seventeen OECD countries (including the United States) from 1978 to 2009, but also expanded the search to include FCs that were based on government spending adjustments as well as taxation policies. The new set's objective was to also break down the episodes of FCs into those that were based on an interest in controlling out-of-control domestic demand (to ostensibly counter that problematic economic "overheating" issue) and, therefore, not considered exogenous in nature, and those adjustments that were motivated to get things fiscally right and hopefully create an enduring fiscal atmosphere that was conducive to long-term sustainability.

Two notable episodes in which countries wanted to reduce a deficit and get their fiscals back on track were Austria in 1996 and the United States in 1993. According to the IMF, Austrian policymakers wanted to shrink the deficit to conform to the new EMU standards that they had to comply with as part of the *Maastricht Treaty* of 1992; the powers that be also wanted to ensure a long-term fiscally stable path when they passed the *Omnibus Budget Reconciliation Act* of 1993 in the United States. On the other hand, Finland's consolidation plan in the mid-1980s was designated as one that planned to restrain a potentially overheating economy, specifically noting that net exports were expected to rise (and subsequently did), which would have helped instigate a period of economic growth that might lead to uncontrolled (or unprepared for) inflation.[29] And this analysis went on for hundreds of different periods of potentially exogenous FCs, all for the sake of being just a little bit more right than others.

All in all, they found 173 exogenous fiscal policy shifts, or more than three times that of Romer and Romer. By applying Romer and Romer's 2010 approach to a larger dataset, they were able to improve the validity of results, further distinguishing the narrative approach from the more conventional CAPB method. Their statistical model analyzed short-term effects (three years post policy implementation), similar to Romer and Romer, but their results differed. Romer and Romer's famous 2010 findings that FC is indeed necessarily contractionary seems to have stood up to a test that included more countries and a wider variety of the types of FC policies that Romer relied upon, but to a lesser degree. For a 1 percent consolidation (relative to GDP), the major conclusion from the more robust dataset was that real private consumption contracted by as much as 0.75 percent and GDP declined by 0.62 percent.

The conventional CAPB model was much more supportive of austere fiscal policies. Applying an updated version of the old model to this dataset, the IMF found a positive benefit to economic growth, even in the short run. The paradox again reared its head in the CAPB model: *Implementing austerity could actually be good for the economy . . . and almost immediately!*

Austerity-supporting policymakers haven't been so accepting of the day's narrative approach, deriding it for its subjectivity and other defects that led to the contractionary findings. But the CAPB's adherence to antiquated thinking may finally have been proven and the new story-based narrative method amplified by the IMF quickly proliferated as one of the more famous and accepted approaches to FC analyses.

Given its flexibility, inherent ability to pick apart and deeply delve into every detail related to a fiscal policy, simple-to-understand (though not easy to develop) methods for identifying FCs, and adherence to econometric foundations for valid and efficient statistical results, the narrative approach became (and remains today) one of the favorites of analysts across disciplines. But, given its methodological simplicity, the demand for and debate of austerity measures since the global shock in 2008, and ability to manipulate its findings to support one's own political persuasions, the debate about its correctness has flourished.

Parallel policies such as those traditionally left to the realm of the monetary world, as well as influences related to exchange rates and its subsequent adjustments (or inability to adjust), combined with the financial and fiscal tragedies of the global shock surrounding 2008, too often bring about even more questions: Do monetary policies have a greater impact on the effectiveness of fiscal policy than we knew? How have previously decided exchange rate regimes impacted the efficacy of either? Should FCs of yesteryear still be applied to countries with far worse economic conditions of the post-global recession world? What led to the development of FC studies prior to 2008 was flipped upside down as massive new debt loads, combined with greater worldwide interest, more methodological transparency, and better methods, to lead to one of the most complicated thrillers that story-time advocates could have ever hoped for.

The next chapter will discuss how some of these studies and methods developed, some of the debate about it all, and will look into the updated research that has developed since that has many of the old guard Keynesian policymakers discouraged by updated narrative-based methodological treatments and outcomes.

NOTES

1. "General Government Debt," *European Commission*, accessed February 18, 2019, https://ec.europa.eu/eurostat/web/products-datasets/-/sdg_17_40.

2. Francesco Giavazzi and Marco Pagano, "Can Severe Fiscal Contractions Be Expansionary? Tales of Two Small European Countries," *NBER Macroeconomics Annual* 76 (1990): 76.

3. Jeffrey M. Wooldridge, *Introductory Econometrics: A Modern Approach*, 6th ed. (Mason, OH: South-Western Cengage Learning, 2016).

4. "Government Expenditure," *OECD National Accounts Statistics*, accessed January 15, 2019, https://www.oecd-ilibrary.org/economics/data/oecd-national-accounts-statistics_na-data-en.

5. Giavazzi and Pagano, "Can Severe Fiscal Contractions Be Expansionary?" 90.

6. Olivier Blanchard, "Suggestions for a New Set of Fiscal Indicators," *OECD Economics Department Working Paper no. 79* (1990).

7. See, for example, Alberto Alesina and Roberto Perotti, "Fiscal Expansions and Fiscal Adjustments in OECD Countries," *Economic Policy* 10, no. 21 (1995): 205–248.

8. Jaime Guajardo, Daniel Leigh, and Andrea Pescatori, "Expansionary Austerity? International Evidence," *Journal of the European Economic Association* 12, no. 4 (2014): 955.

9. Guajardo, Leigh, and Pescatori, "Expansionary Austerity?" 956.

10. Guido Wolswijk, "Short- and Long-Run Tax Elasticities: The Case of the Netherlands," *European Central Bank Working Paper Series No. 763* (Frankfurt: European Central Bank, 2007).

11. Mika Kuismanen and Ville Kämppi, "The Effects of Fiscal Policy on Economic Activity in Finland," *Economic Modelling* 27, no. 5 (2010): 1315–1323.

12. Valerie Ramey, "Macroeconomic Shocks and Their Propagation," in *Handbook of Macroeconomics, Volume 2*, eds. John B. Taylor and Michael Woodford (Amsterdam: Elsevier, 2016), 71–162.

13. Julio Rotemberg and Michael Woodford, "Oligopolistic Pricing and the Effects of Aggregate Demand on Economic Activity," *Journal of Political Economy* 100, no. 6, (1992): 1153–1207.

14. John Cochrane, "Shocks," *Carnegie-Rochester Conference Series on Public Policy* 41 (1994): 295–364.

15. Ramey, "Macroeconomic Shocks," 81.

16. Apostolis Philippopoulos, Petros Varthalitis, and Vanghelis Vassilatos, "Fiscal Consolidation and Its Cross-Country Effects," *Journal of Economic Dynamics and Control* 8355 (2017): 106.

17. Robert Solow, "Building a Science of Economics for the Real World," *Prepared Statement*, presented to the House Committee on Science and Technology Subcommittee on Investigations and Oversight (July 20, 2010).

18. Milton Friedman and Anna J. Schwartz, *A Monetary History of the United States, 1867–1960* (Princeton: Princeton University Press, 1963).

19. See, for example, James D. Hamilton, "Historical Causes of Postwar Oil Shocks and Recessions," *Energy Journal* 6, no. 1 (January 1985): 97–116.

20. See, for example, James M. Poterba, "Explaining the Yield," in *Studies in State and Local Public Finance*, ed. Harvey S. Rosen (National Bureau of Economic Research Project Report series, 1986), 5–49.

21. Christina D. Romer and David H. Romer, "Does Monetary Policy Matter? A New Test in the Spirit of Friedman and Schwartz," *NBER Macroeconomic Annual* 4 (1989).

22. Valerie A. Ramey and Matthew D. Shapiro, "Costly Capital Reallocation and the Effects of Government Spending," *Carnegie-Rochester Conference Series on Public Policy*, 48 (June 1998): 175.

23. Christina D. Romer and David H. Romer, "The Macroeconomic Effects of Tax Changes: Estimates Based on a New Measure of Fiscal Shocks," *American Economic Review* (June 2010): 763.

24. Romer and Romer, "The Macroeconomic Effects of Tax Changes," 764.

25. Romer and Romer, "The Macroeconomic Effects of Tax Changes," 771–774.

26. Jaime Guajardo, Daniel Leigh, and Andrea Pescatori, "Expansionary Austerity? International Evidence," *Journal of the European Economic Association* 12, no. 4 (2014): 956.

27. Valerie Ramey, "Identifying Government Spending Shocks: It's All in the Timing," *Quarterly Journal of Economics* 126, no. 1 (2011): 1–50.

28. Pete Devries, Jaime Guajardo, Daniel Leigh, and Andrea Pescatori, "A New Action-Based Dataset of Fiscal Consolidation," *IMF Working Paper No. 11/128*. Washington: International Monetary Fund (2011).

29. Devries, Guajardo, Leigh, and Pescatori. "A New Action-Based Dataset," 4.

Chapter 4

How'd It All Work Out?

Remember that time when you just knew you were right, told everyone so, then found out later you were completely wrong? (I know I'm not the only one.) Some people, and *most* researchers, have character and are willing to admit when (a) they write papers with significant results that are based on imperfect information or tests or (b) they come across new economic data (which inevitably happens as time keeps on ticking) that proves their old results wrong. On the other hand, given the proliferation of social media and professional echo chambers, it's increasingly easy and too often desirable to defend one's wrongness.

Well, economists are no different as there are many examples of economic researchers who have published results on the impact of FCs on economic growth, only to then find out they were wrong. It turns out, we are all going to be "wrong" at some point as new data comes to light, new methods are invented and implemented, and new research is built upon the old. This is especially true since the onslaught of the 2007 to 2009 Great Recession in the United States, which spread to the rest of the world and provided a new chance for nearly all advanced countries to pull out all the FC tricks to try on their respective economies. Some turned out okay, others not so much. Regardless, there is a new body of data continuously building upon itself, each and every day and a substantial number of researchers who have been groomed to update old methodologies and construct new datasets that have led and will lead to new results, which should change the minds of even the most stubborn of policymakers. Considering the quickly accumulating debt loads around the world, today's research advances may be arriving just in time (buyer beware: like with any new technological advancement, new policy solutions are better served and understood with a dash of hindsight).

LOADS AND LOADS OF DEBT

The most recent worldwide recession didn't bode well for the globe's government debt hawks. I discussed some of the reasons for the access to, availability of, and increased love affair with public debt after the latest worldwide economic downturn in chapter 1 (see, for instance, Figure 1.3, *GIIPS Public Debt*). Whatever the cause of record levels of debt, it's easy to visualize the results. Figure 4.1 gives a brief glimpse into the average amount of government debt across the OECD's relatively developed world. Notice the greater than 10 percentage points increase in average public debt over the two years spanning 2007 to 2009. Figure 4.2 includes emerging markets (in addition to developed countries) and shows how the trend of average public debt growth has accelerated over recent years.

The traditional response has been what many may call the "textbook" answer to increased debts and deficits: governments need to get things under control before we end up in a full-blown debt crisis. If they don't, the increasing deficits will lead to higher interest rates via central banks' increasing rate targets in their respective countries. Central banks increase their rates to counter potential economic overheating that may occur after all the government spending increases; retail rates increase as investors demand a higher premium to cover what they perceive as greater risks associated with more

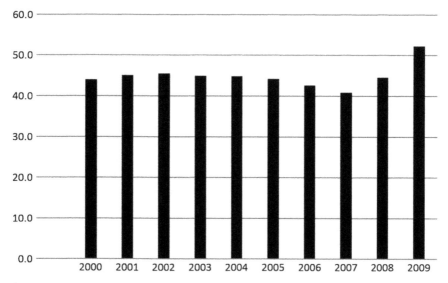

Figure 4.1 OECD Average Public Debt. Author Generated from "General Government Debt," OECD, Accessed July 22, 2019, https://data.oecd.org/gga/general-government-debt.htm.

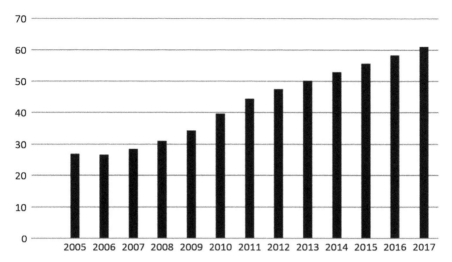

Figure 4.2 Global Public Debt. Author Generated from "Global Debt Monitor," Institute of International Finance, Accessed July 22, 2019, https://www.iif.com/Research/Data.

government borrowing. An increase in deficits which leads to higher interest rates may then "crowd out" private borrowing, since it's harder to justify an investment when more of your top-line revenue has to be spent on borrowing costs. The cost of borrowing money is a significant line item in every investor's or entrepreneur's pro forma; if that cost increases, the expectation of profit decreases and the motivation to invest falls. Traditionally, this has more or less been the prevailing case, especially across those countries that are less developed than, say, the United States. However, even in the United States, this crowding out effect has been especially dominant when deficits were high. Many consider fiscal reduction measures of the early to mid-1990s (see figure 4.3, *U.S. Deficit/Surplus*) to be the reason why salivating investors unleashed everything they had (figure 4.4, *U.S. Gross Private Investment*), increasing aggregate private investment so much that it led to the ensuing economic boom of the 1990s.

Government debt as a share of total GDP is far higher today, so shouldn't identical deficit reduction strategies create the same, or even more pronounced investor-led, success stories than it has throughout history? Well, like everything else in the wonderful world of policy, the answer to this question is almost always *maybe yes and maybe no*. While a lot of the early research into FCs focused on the potentially positive outcomes and benefit to GDP growth (see Giavazzi and Pagano, for instance), later research focused on the new data that began to question the supposition that FC policies can lead to anything good at all, while some even questioned the necessity of austerity in the first place.

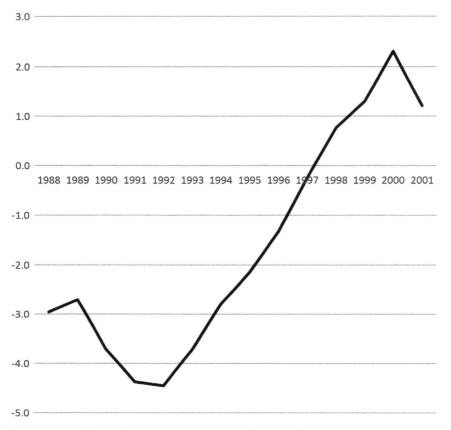

3.0

2.0

1.0

0.0

1988 1989 1990 1991 1992 1993 1994 1995 1996 1997 1998 1999 2000 2001

-1.0

-2.0

-3.0

-4.0

-5.0

Figure 4.3   US Surplus/Deficit. Author Generated from "Federal Surplus or Deficit," U.S. Office of Management and Budget, Accessed July 22, 2019, https://fred.stlouisfed.org/se ries/FYFSD.

If there is a consistently high correlation between cuts in spending—and/ or tax increases—and contractionary effects (shrinking GDP), then the case for FC plans may have been wrongheaded all along. A recent research article published by the National Bureau of Economic Research (NBER)—the organization responsible for deciding when the U.S. has officially entered or exited a recession, along with producing an inordinate number of Nobel laureates—seems to support this possibility with its finding that FCs "negatively affect economic performance by reducing GDP, inflation, consumption, and investment."[1] This particular study focused on mostly European countries (plus the United States) and made the point that such policies are especially counterproductive when implemented during a recession (more on the potential thriller that combines recessions and austerity soon). However,

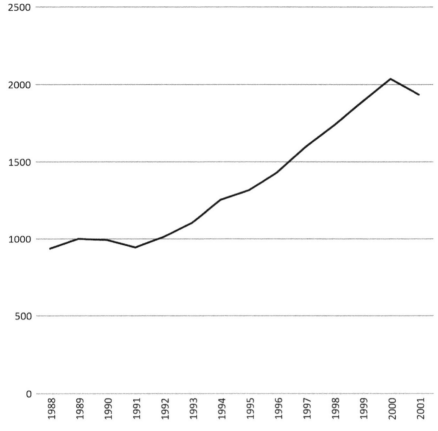

Figure 4.4 US Gross Private Investment. Author Generated from "Gross Private Domestic Investment," U.S. Bureau of Economic Analysis, Accessed July 22, 2019, https://fred.stlouisfed.org/series/GPDI.

the authors found, not that FCs necessarily begat shrinking economies, but that the economies that experienced fiscal austerity grew less quickly than they would have otherwise.

Given the high and rapidly growing debt-to-GDP ratios that transpired in the years after the recession, it might seem obvious to those with textbook knowledge of government debts and fiscal deficits that the central government needed to find a way to pull back on the spending, increase revenues, or adjust fiscal policies in some manner to counter the potential for total fiscal calamity. Having loads and loads of debt isn't a sufficient metric for imposing a round of FCs, according to some. Paul Krugman was well known for his high-profile *New York Times* diatribes against austerity, especially in the face of economic crises, and often (okay, always) criticized policymakers that advocated for austere fiscal policies in the wake of the recent worldwide recession:

> Somehow it has become conventional wisdom that now is the time to slash spending, despite the fact that the world's major economies remain deeply depressed. This conventional wisdom isn't based on either evidence or careful analysis. Instead, it rests on what we might charitably call sheer speculation, and less charitably call figments of the policy elite's imagination—specifically, on belief in what I've come to think of as the invisible bond vigilante and the confidence fairy.[2]

Krugman doesn't pull punches. His reference to the "invisible bond vigilante" refers to the theory that lenders—a.k.a. purchasers of government debt, whether private citizens, major investment banks, other central governments, or a country's own government or regulatory authority—will lose faith in a government's ability to make good on its debt obligations and quit buying bonds cold turkey, leaving a government without cash to continue operations. For places like the United States, Germany, and even outrageously indebted Japan, that hasn't happened to the scale that some have forecast, yet. In other places like Greece, Puerto Rico, and Argentina, it has.

In light of the recent crisis and fashionable upswings in debt, long-term rates on government debt should increase (as debt increases, lenders perceive an increased risk of default and compensate that risk by demanding higher premiums in return, known as the *risk premium*, before they will purchase more bonds). Yet, the United States experienced multiple periods of falling long-term interest rates just after the deepest depths of its recession, exhibiting the opposite effect (see figure 4.5, *10-Yr U.S. Treasuries*). What economic theory couldn't predict is that a country backed by the credibility of the U.S. government and its healthy long-term record of making its obligatory payments may actually attract investors when the rest of the world is experiencing similar or worse economic conditions. An it's-all-relative philosophy often prevails, even in the global financial sector. In a world of economic chaos, investors who had to do something with their money simply chose the least-bad alternative, so they chose U.S. Treasuries, which is generally considered the safest investment on Earth. Market forces didn't compel that nasty risk premium to increase as it might have if the U.S. economy was faltering or if its government was the lone wolf, increasing deficits and outstanding debt all by its lonesome.

If countries are able to keep their interest rates low, maybe they shouldn't be so concerned about debts and deficits, especially during an economic crisis. That's the conclusion that many have drawn from recent data. An

Figure 4.5 Ten-year Treasuries. Author Generated from "10-Year Treasury Constant Maturity Rate," Board of Governors of the U.S. Federal Reserve System, Accessed July 22, 2019, https://fred.stlouisfed.org/series/GS10.

IMF researcher, for example, recently compared nominal interest rates of government debt products with long-term growth rates to analyze whether having high levels of debt is really problematic. Many countries with long-run growth rates that are expected to be larger than long-term interest rates on new loans can essentially borrow to infinity and beyond (and some are trying it!).[3] Does this seem irrational, unreasonable, and contrary to everything you ever learned in life? Well, debt growth "without bound" assumes that one keeps that ratio inverted. In other words, growth rates have to outperform, and be expected to continue outperforming, long-term interest rates forever. For a country like the United States, some contend that this is a fact we have to get used to. Today the aggregate national debt held by the U.S. government is much higher (as a percentage of its GDP) than it has been in the past, but its average interest payments on this debt (adjusted for inflation) have been about the same since the late 1940s, according to Jason Furman, former chair of the *Council on Economic Advisers* under U.S. President Barrack Obama, and Larry Summers, former director of the *National Economic Council* under the same president.[4] Higher debt has not automatically increased the portion of spending the United States has allotted to interest payments, giving credence to the argument that debt may have no bound, according to these two. Given that additional debt added to the U.S. total public debt grew anywhere from 6 trillion dollars to more than 10 trillion (depending on how you measure the portion of new debt that can be attributed to a sitting president—for example, the total deficits from every budget signed by a president may be a different amount than all of the deficits directly created by his policies, since members of Congress get a bit of say into what gets spent), ending by nearly doubling the total tally of aggregate public debt, and it seems that this particular administration heeded Summers and Furman's advice. (To be fair, the deficit did shrink across subsequent budgets under President Obama, with some sleight-of-hand borrowing from other government funds intended to support elderly and retired individuals, i.e., the *Social Security Trust Fund*, which does not count as an addition to the national debt.)

Lower rates of borrowing in developed and credit-worthy countries like the United States can also counter the traditional theory that high debt necessarily increases rates and hurts investment. If higher levels of aggregate debt lead to increasing interest rates for borrowers in the private sector, then the cost of investing in economic capital can rise, stymying total investment. But interest rates have continued to remain low in the United States, as noted previously, which have justified new investments and increased company values (as reflected in stock market indices).

It's easy to find examples of countries that have experienced fiscal crises due to huge debts and unmitigated deficit growth (see case studies in Part Two of this book). This simple fact leads news media gurus to make an incorrect generalization to other countries, no matter the size of an economy, level of development, location, resource advantages, monetary system, rule of law, history, military dominance, and so on. But it's an erroneous and illogical mistake to compare debt crises in a place like Chile in the early 1980s—or almost any Latin American country of that time that were heavily reliant upon the lending and subsequent bailing out powers of the IMF's combined economic and financial authority—to that of a developed and advanced country such as the United States or many of those in Europe. Nonetheless, too many draw the conclusion that circumstances in one place must also apply everywhere; high levels of growing debt in the United States will inevitably lead to lost access to the credit markets and an eventual economic catastrophe, debt crisis, and general looting and pillaging from sea to shining sea.

One of the major distinctions between most lesser developed countries and a U.S.-type behemoth is that the United States can print its own currency, and then borrow from itself. This gives the United States a lot of control over the variables that generally contribute to interest rates, debt-to-GDP ratios, and the money it has to pay back those debts. In fact, many advance the idea behind a newly popular theory known as *Modern Monetary Theory* (MMT). Under this theory, a country with a sovereign currency won't really have any debt "problems" per se, and needs to worry little about restraining spending, since it has the keys to the printing offices. If you can finance your debt by keeping the print shop doors open just a little longer each day, then you may also be able to push rates low, increase investment, improve private savings rates, feed the hungry, build out unlimited infrastructure, give everyone a free university education, and supply every graduate with their own Subway franchise. The *only* constraint to this type of self-financing is the potential for inflation. Given the low levels of inflation in many countries (especially in the United States) since the massive increases in debts and deficits after the Great Global Recession, MMTers have a bit of evidence on their side that inflation fears are a bunch of cockamamie nonsense.[5] But what happens as Central Banking policies normalize (rate targets increase) and economies recover and/or boom, reaching and growing beyond full employment, which increases inflationary pressures (as can be seen in the United States as of the writing of this book)? Furthermore, MMT seems to have some credence in good times, but what happens when the next, inevitable economic downturn causes credit ratings to waiver, borrowing rates to go up, increases limitations on spending programs dependent on more borrowing, or substantially increases the proportion of a government's spending on interest relative to GDP or tax revenue? As many less successful countries can tell you (and many successful ones), a country's fiscal status can get out of hand very quickly during an unpredictable economic wobble, leaving unprepared countries far behind in the aftermath.

Very few deny that we can just print money in perpetuity without consequence (here's looking at you Venezuela[6]), nor that there aren't other problems with spending taxpayer money faster than the government can take it in (see upcoming interest expense discussion, for example). But having your own sovereign currency does provide for a set of tools that others aren't afforded. Look at the relatively small, isolated country of Japan, which issues and prints its own currency, and borrows in the Yen. Its debt-to-GDP is the highest in the world, by a long shot, with a ratio of well over 250 percent. Why haven't they imploded and sunken to the ocean floor? Not only have they not submerged, remarkably, real interest rates on their long-term debt are negative, due to the existing state of *deflation*, or an overall falling level of market prices. This means that some banks are crazy and/or desperate enough to be willing to pay the Bank of Japan (the central bank of Japan, aka BoJ) a rate of interest to hold their money.

I will discuss the unusual case of Japan more in the case studies section, but the theory behind the seemingly odd choice of Japan's central bank to impose negative rates is that it wants to reverse deflation, and even try to get some inflation and economic growth going. To do so, the BoJ has tried to reverse the dominating incentive to take money out of more productive resources and simply let it sit and earn interest in the central bank's vaults. Having to pay another bank to hold your bank's money is pretty strong motivation to seek other opportunities. If there are any viable investment alternatives in the private sector (hopefully more productive households and businesses), the theory is that private sector banks will start to seek those, and the economy may again have a chance at life. Despite such an unusual monetary and fiscal policy, Japan has been able to maintain high levels of debt and deficits without causing an uncontrollable acceleration to the rates of interest that may otherwise have been brought about by a lack of lender confidence. Are such monetary tools a benefit to the grandiose economies of the world, or a detrimental moral hazard that will lead to even greater debt that will deter economic growth and a well-oiled overall economy?

CONFIDENCE IS KING

Whether asking the one you admire out on a first date, giving a speech in front of a crowded auditorium, or taking the necessary steps to invest your life savings in a business concept that you just know is going to work, your success will likely depend on your level of confidence. Confidence can also be king when it comes to economic improvement. Related to the average citizen who consumes goods for his or her family, as well as businesses that need to feel good about their investments, it's important for economic actors to feel as though the economy is on the right track before being comfortable enough to make the decision to consume and invest.

How does consumer and business confidence relate to fiscal policy? When country debt is high, investors may grow concerned that a central government lacks the competency to improve or maintain economic prosperity, leading to a reduction in confidence in the economy and an accompanying reduction in investment. Without confidence in our policymakers' ability to control the debt, we as a society cut back on our spending and investing concerned that either harsh austerity measures will have to be implemented soon or an economic battle to the bottom may take place. Therefore, one of the arguments by some fiscal adjustment supporters is that policymakers need to do something now to restore confidence, which will then translate to an economic contribution by economic actors, which will propel an economy in the general direction toward Nirvana.

Referring to what he called the "confidence fairy," Paul Krugman wasn't a fan of this philosophy, especially in a tough economic climate. Being an anti-austerity, spend-and-invest-taxes-back-into-the-public kind of economist, Krugman frequently dismissed such ideas as "fantasy," noting that few cases substantiated this idea, and more often than not other factors were the real culprit behind economic restoration, not confidence.[7] Yet many other researchers focused on FC policies have found the exact opposite results: consumer and investor confidence play a major role in our economic well-being.

Having worked with countless investors over the last couple of decades, from institutional sized hedge funds to college savings–funded start-ups, this idea strikes a practical chord with me. Though there are a lot of factors that eventually culminate in the decision to make an investment, every (good) investor takes a top-down analytical approach to the future direction of their efforts that begins with consideration of the current macroeconomic climate. Clearly if we're entering or in the middle of a deep recession, it's a more difficult decision to pull the trigger and release your funds and efforts into the wild (unless you have the marketing skills of Looney Larry and his mobile surgery truck). Within this macroeconomic analysis, investors have to consider how accurate their assessments of future revenues and costs are. Ascribing to the theory that *a rising tide lifts all boats* one will consider an economic expansion as a probable positive contributor to future revenues, and conversely, a recession will inhibit revenue growth (though you rarely hear someone say *an ebbing tide leaves boats stranded*).

Revenues aren't the only factor in the business assessment mix. Costs, in this case costs controlled by policymakers, have to always be considered. If your investment is headed toward an industry that you know is about to be slapped with new red tape, you have to ponder whether these new costs of doing business will be a limitation on profitability (in general, they are). By the same token, if an investor foresees that an industry will incur higher tax rates, business confidence can wane, investments may be withheld, employment growth will fall or stall, and so on. So, what if an astute investment analyst in a country with a booming debt and deficit sees—what he or she considers to be—the writing on the wall, knowing that at some point in the future FC policies will need to be enacted? If this consolidation is expected to be composed of a large cut to government spending, aggregate spending may hit a business in the wallet (depending on where the spending is cut and how closely related that segment of government spending is to your business). If the consolidation is expected to be driven by a set of significant tax increases, chances are high that the profit machine that you invested in will not be quite as profitable in the future. Add up all of the consumers and investors in the economy who think along these lines and confidence indicators will begin to shilly-shally. Dr. Krugman might think of "confidence" as a mythical variable with little influence, but in the practicing world of business and investment, that gut feeling about future costs has a real effect on investment.

If today's FC, therefore, takes away this uncertainty (for the moment), then it can be assumed that confidence in the future will improve and consumption today will be stimulated. Alesina and Drazen discussed this possibility as it relates to fiscal policy back in the early 1990s, when they found that out-of-control debt—debt that was universally thought to eventually require a fiscal adjustment—hampered confidence until an adjustment actually occurred.[8] While policymakers are motivated to avoid taxation for political reasons, delaying what is perceived as an inevitable FC can lead to waning confidence.

Investors aren't thoughtless oafs in the art of economics. They tend to realize that the longer policymakers wait, the more dramatic government spending will need to be cut or that taxes will need to be raised in order to return the nation's finances back to the stable fiscal path that policymakers knew it needed to be on. The business owner and investor class seems to strongly prefer stabilization and certainty—even if it means the implementation of a policy that lowers profitability today—rewarding required austerity with their confidence, purchases, and investments.[9]

Within these confidence-infused models, it's important to note that the distinction between the various compositions of FCs is especially important. If you run a business, or are an investor, would your outlook be more unenthusiastic toward a FC that was built on an adjustment to spending policies or tax policies? The answer is, of course and as always, *that depends*. Firms that are direct contractors to the defense sector, for example, might not be too happy if legislators come up with a plan to curtail the deficit with massive cuts to national defense. Northrop Grumman, one of the largest defense contractors in the world, develops "precision weapons, tactical rocket motors . . . ammunition and gun systems, advanced fuses and warheads, weaponized special-mission aircraft, and propulsion control systems."[10] Needless to say, Northrop doesn't take these types of policies kindly. A fiscal adjustment that includes a shock to government spending, especially focused on defense spending, would get you on their bad side (given Northrop's line of work, there may be a reason why not many legislators advocate for spending cuts that will harm Northrop's revenues).

However, more businesses (all of them, to be precise) are impacted by general increases in corporate taxes than they are by negative government spending shocks. While policymakers probably aren't too keen on getting into a fight with Northrop Grumman and its raucous band of defense sector buddies, they are also not fans of having long lines of business lobbyists knocking on their door to offer statements such as "If our business clients have less money, you will have less money—get our point?" Aside from my politically skeptical arguments for why policymakers may not always depend on tax adjustments as their preferred tool in the FC kit, researchers also present loads of data concurring with the notion that government spending needs to be addressed in order to appease businesses and corporate investors; otherwise these investors realize that there is nowhere to turn but to taxes in order to cover the endless increases in government spending.[11] Since it is generally easier (and more appealing to lovers of instant gratification) to increase taxes today as a means to improve revenues and trim deficits, it is important for policymakers to have an understanding that investor confidence does impact investor action and tends to be more negatively correlated with tax-focused FC policies than with alternative versions that focus on spending. How much that real-world "confidence" translates to economic data variables that impact economic performance is a grander question that the Krugmans of the world are ready to fight (unless Northrop Grumman is involved, in which case they win).

KILL THE DEBT OR LET IT RIDE

Given what some see as more contemporary evidence dismissing the need to fear bondholders' henchmen or mythical confidence genies, when our economic winds turn unfortunate, should central governments simply invest in our economy and help those in need, to heck with the debt and deficit? Plenty of developmental economists make the ardent point that investments in human capital that help provide jobs for citizens, healthcare for those without, pension security programs that offer basic incomes to the elderly, and enhanced educational opportunities for the next generation of economic contributors are well worth any potential curse placed upon society by high debt. But, maintaining existing public transfer and welfare programs in most countries demands consistent increases in spending. Add an allotment for new needs, plus the general trend toward aging societies across the developed and developing world, and it's difficult to find the justification for what looks like a guaranteed deficit hole that can only get bigger.

Others wonder why central governments can't just maintain a middle-of-the-road philosophy that ensures that FCs are paid for by improved revenues. The idea of a balanced budget amendment added to the constitution of a government is nothing new: Germany, Hong Kong, Italy, Switzerland, and Spain have versions, while the United States has debated the idea for some

time (almost all of the states have their own separate balanced budget requirement). The effectiveness of such legal mandates is debatable, however.
While Germany and Switzerland are known for their fiscal dominance and
budget forethought (Germany had such a high, record surplus in 2018 that
it had to call for immediate tax cuts to quit taking so much money from its
citizens unnecessarily;[12] Switzerland had its own surplus at the same time.
which drew anger from citizens who called its budgeteers "tightfisted"[13]),
it's doubtful that anyone will say the same for Italy or Spain anytime soon.
At the time of writing this book, Italy was strong-armed by the EU to keep
their deficit from growing more than 2 percent of GDP in 2019.[14] Spain, on
the other hand, is just trying to keep it below 3 percent,[15] a vast improvement
from recent years.

Maybe reducing deficits shouldn't be the prerogative of a prudent policymaker, but we should instead focus more on societal benefit spending that
anticipates future returns, paid for by tax increases for the wealthy among us.
Unless of course, we're in an economic downturn, then it's a debt free-for-
all. Most of these types of arguments, however, are generally made on behalf
of countries that are perceived to have the financial ability to sustain such
spending and investment levels, even in contractions, have the ability to print
and spend with few repercussions (relative to the rest of the world), and have
a class of wealthy individuals who may be willing to give up a bit more of
what they own without packing up, firing up the GV, and moving to (add the
name of your favorite tax haven here).

Even if big debts and deficits are sustainable for some, and those developed
economies have the ability to spend more on supporting transfer, welfare,
educational, or other investments in society, one can't help but imagine if
there were no debt payments at all. The United States, for example, currently
has a monthly payment for interest on its existing debt of nearly 44 billion
dollars[16] (keep in mind that these are just expenses for the interest on total
debt, not including principal). If the United States miraculously eliminated
all of its debt and was able to spend 523,000,000,000 dollars a year on something else, it could provide every impoverished person in the country with a
monthly income of $927. With an average household size of 2.56 people[17] (I
will round up to three so you don't have to imagine what 0.56 of a person
looks like), an impoverished family could gain 2,781 dollars per month,
entirely eliminating poverty within the United States (the Federal Poverty
Line for a family of four stands at an income of approximately 2,100 dollars per month). If Germany were to do the same, it could give more than
300 dollars (USD) to each of its impoverished citizens monthly. Add up the
number of impoverished persons in a single family, and the amount of basic
minimum income could easily reach into the thousands. Fan of a *Universal
Basic Income*? Find a way to eliminate the debt, and you just might be able to

convince a few people to support you. Though, with freed up funds, comes a lot of new, outstretched hands looking for innovative ways to spend it.

Of course, the idea of total debt elimination is a mere fantasy; no serious person thinks we can ever eliminate any country's public debt and interest payments. But the illustrations are demonstrative of the power of government debt and the opportunity costs of its existence. Consideration of both extremes of the debt spectrum—spend like there's no tomorrow versus eliminating the debt—leads us to a debate common in political discussions around the world: Who is better suited to efficiently use and invest the public's money, the government or individual, private citizens?

NEW DEBT DATA

If you haven't asked already, you should be wondering: What policies have been enacted since the latest worldwide recession and how have they all panned out? If you are the type that likes to save time and just get to the heart of the matter, you might be disappointed to learn that no one really knows. At least, that's my highly skeptical view of the existing academic, policy, and political debate. Though it has been a decade since the Great Recession ended in the United States, it is still relatively early to understand the data related to FCs. We're also too fresh out of the recent global recession to know, with certainty, the full economic impact of policies enacted during the recession and how they will fare in the long run, especially for countries that experienced recessions that ended far beyond 2009. The literature investigating the short-run macroeconomic impact of FCs is also still in its nascency, attempting to wrap its head around the distinct and separate effects of FCs, outside of the noise of accompanying policies and other macroeconomic variables. In the second half of this book, I'll investigate a few cases that extend to times before the recent big recession to provide some context to periods studied since the Recession.

Perhaps the facts are more accurately captured by stating that no one really knows of a particular policy solution that has worked one way or another for more than a small homogenous group of countries. In other words, there is no austerity solution that can be generalized to any given country at any given moment in time. To that end, no one can be perfectly certain of how austerity has impacted the world, whether FC policies have been overwhelmingly ineffectual (as related to their impact on economic output and overall performance), whether policies that have been incorporated tangential to FCs have had a greater impact on output than the fiscal adjustment policies themselves, or whether economies have improved or fallen to the wayside all on their own.

Putting my bleak opinion of our mutual knowledge of the world aside, there have been some notable updates that have built upon our current understanding that provide greater insight into how contemporary fiscal policies have been enacted and how (or if) they have benefited their respective countries. Since the conclusion of the Great Recession, interest in the impact of FC plans on output has proliferated. Recent trends in the literature have a wide variety of extensions, having evolved econometrically and theoretically and are far from being concluded, however, are still often based on the same identification and theoretical findings advanced in Romer and Romer's 2010 paper and others throughout the academic world's literary past.

Alberto Alesina and Sylvia Ardagna—both of Harvard University and the NBER at the time—helped kick off the latest collection of studies that empirically analyze the short-run macroeconomic effects of fiscal adjustment policies with one of the first such studies post-Great Recession (2010).[18] Just a few steps outside of the latest global crisis, the researchers took a stab at analyzing fiscal policies presently enacted, knowing that policymakers were seeking solutions to return to normalcy in their budgeting decisions and stop (or at least slow) growing national debts before they become unsustainable. Given the fiscal jolt administered to national finances during economic contractions (due to output slowing, as well as stimuli in the form of tax cuts and spending increases), deficits and debt grew enough to precipitate a discussion on how to create a long-run prudent fiscal path. As policymakers considered how to correct the imbalances, the debate about cutting debt-to-GDP growth wasn't too different from the debate that incurred about which fiscal stimulus created the best economic by-product. Whereas those considering stimulative policies sought answers to whether tax cuts or spending increases were the most beneficial to an economy, when it came time to dispute debt and deficit reductions, the flip side to these policies became the discussion *du jour* right after the crises. Though seemingly simplistic (we'll discuss some of the nuances here as well), the question of *tax vs. spend* is forever at the heart of the debate: Will tax increases or spending cuts lead to the best economic results?

As I've noted in other parts of this book, debates that pit politically charged ideologies against one another are not for the thin-skinned. Nearly everyone has an opinion on where and how they think their government should levy taxes and divvy up dollars—right-of-center idealists try to persuade us that, of course, spending cuts are the only way to bring deficits to their knees, while more liberal-leaning policy analysts passionately defend the need for tax hikes. Surely economic policy experts from academia and beyond too have similar political biases, but they are more adept at supporting them with a bit of data, empirical support, historical examples, and established economic theory. Since many of these "experts" reside as technocratic advisers to the hands that mold future policies, we hope to control for biases with fair assessments based on transparent methodological approaches.

The next-gen Italian Duo of Alesina & Ardagna took it as their calling to investigate episodes of consolidation that include both tax adjustments and spending policy shifts, developing methods for distinguishing between the two types of policies, while also considering which led to the most favorable outcomes. Having a better understanding of how one's beliefs about the difference between taxation and spending-focused fiscal adjustment policies align with the reality that real-world data presents should lead to better answers for the world's authorities. Being well aware of the need for better information, they also understood that many stubborn ideologues merely look for support to help them sell their own unwavering policy prescriptions. Regardless, they tarried on, hoping for the best. Using OECD data from 1970 to 2007 (up to the start of the 2008 global crisis), their 2010 paper studied twenty-one countries, including a number of strong economies in Europe (Austria, France, Germany, etc.) plus some not so well-known for being economic powerhouses (Greece, Italy, Ireland, Portugal), Australia, Japan, and the United States, among others. Their intention was to figure out the exact point at which fiscal policies shifted, then look at how those policies were linked with other macroeconomic variables, specifically considering "the size of the fiscal packages" (i.e., the magnitude of the change of the government deficit) and their composition (such as the percentage change of the main government budget items relative to the total change),"[19] while considering how closely those policies were correlated with changes in economic output. Figuring out when fiscal policies shifted, and whether they adjusted to a degree of magnitude that was worth studying, was, as always, a difficult task. The CAPB—that which smoothed the effects of the usual business cycle's ups and downs—seemed to work well *at the time* and served the job of identifying FCs, as well as fiscal stimuli. Theirs was a valiant effort to reduce some endogeneity issues in an attempt to find fiscal shifts that were implemented for the good of the long-term fiscal outlook and future economic well-being of a country, unrelated to the current state of the economy, to help end the debate between the warring ideologies and find which of these types of plans were really the best.

Applying the CAPB method to the dataset, they decided to select and study only those fiscal movements that were greater than 1.5 percent of GDP. Considering all of the available plans, they anticipated dissenting arguments by picking only the cream of the crop, that is, a 1.5 percent adjustment is pretty large. While this extra care may have overlooked smaller FCs that should have been included into their dataset, the authors wanted to be sure there was no disputing the fact that these shifts were intentionally administered by policymakers to cater to the long-term interests of a nation's fiscal health. A list of 107 FCs (most lasted just one year, but some were part of plans that were implemented over multiple years) and 91 stimulative fiscal policies (an even greater number of fiscal stimuli lasted for just a single year) were compiled. To be considered a "successful" consolidation or stimulus, it had to be correlated with an expansionary period (only around 3 percent of total observations achieved the author's strict definition) as well as a reduction to the nation's public debt (also around 3 percent of the observations of both stimulative fiscal adjustments and consolidations met this threshold).

Applying a simple regression to these most extreme cases with the available pre-recession data, results were interesting and a bit different than the policymakers who enacted the fiscal adjustments may have wanted. Stimulus plans based on spending turned out to not be as effective as expected: stimuli associated with economic booms were correlated with relatively small spending increases (around 1 percent of GDP), while a shrinking economy was correlated with much larger spending increases (around 3 percent of GDP). Large tax cuts were also associated with economic growth (a bit of a surprise), and contractions were linked with slightly positive tax hikes (less surprising). Though not the final answer to the world's fiscal policy problems, enthusiastic supporters of spending stimulus and tax increases as economic activity boosters weren't too happy with these results.

The outcomes related to FC policies were also pretty interesting, running contrary to the common Keynesian beliefs more prominent before and during the global recession. When FCs are implemented, the implementers (policymakers) are trying to do two things. First, they want to, obviously, cut the deficit and debt. So, a successful fiscal crackdown should do just that. It would be fairly embarrassing if one was not able to create a policy to cut the deficit with an FC that explicitly calls for a decreased budget outlay. Second, the whole point of trying to crack down on debts and deficits is because you stand behind the theory that doing so will get the confidence fairy off the couch, stave off bond bandits calling on their loans, or ignite some other variable that leads us down the road to economic growth. Trim the debt and kindle growth and you have a successful consolidation. Surprisingly, success didn't always align with the expected results of the day.

In the Alesina and Ardagna study, economic contractions followed spending cuts of about 0.7 percent of GDP and revenue increases of 1.2 percent. Small cuts and tax increases correlated with shrinking economies. On the other hand, if spending cuts were large enough, economies tended toward expansion. Spending cuts of more than 2 percent and slight revenue increases were strongly correlated with economic growth. Per the authors, there is a substantial and important difference between FCs that focus on cutting spending in order to reduce the deficit, versus policies that focus on raising taxes. While both spending-focused FCs and tax-focused consolidations have a negative effect on the growth rate of GDP, results strongly favored spending cuts over tax increases as the least harmful to short-run economic performance.

The distinction between FC policies that are based on government spending and those that are tax-focused is important for several reasons. Neoclassical theorists traditionally offer up a tri-channel rationale for why one type of policy may be more beneficial than the other: substitution effects, wealth effects, and distortions, all act and react differently to tax and spending adjustments. For example, as noted before, a precipitous fall in government spending (as long as you aren't a government employee getting fired, a contractor losing a new government gig, or have some other major benefit derived from the government's spending) may increase an individual's perception of wealth, since it can be assumed that taxes won't have to go up (or can even be decreased) in the future to take care of rising deficits. When you feel like someone with new money, you spend like someone with new money. The same distinctions may apply when considering aggregate investment within the private sector as well. If the government spends less and the same expectation of future lower taxes prevails, investors may invest more heavily. If those investments pan out (though you may not feel like a lucky entrepreneur, for the most part, increases in total investment lead to positive returns), the economy tends to produce and consume more. With regard to FCs, increases in taxes have virtually the opposite effect of a decrease in spending, per this line of thinking.

Reverting back to the Keynesian system of economic theory, multipliers within a consumption model view tax increases and spending cuts fairly similarly. Large spending cuts must necessarily beget a downward trending economy (reductions in spending will lead to a reduction in total aggregate output), while tax increases should result in the same effect. Yet, more recently, for both old-school Keynesians and models of new-Keynesianism that incorporate some neoclassical elements, the multiplier on spending is similar, but is generally expected to be grander than that for tax increases.

Irrespective of what effect you expect spending and tax policies to have on economic output, before and during the global recession most anticipated that there should be a distinct difference between the various types of policies. Yet, there continued to be a big debate about what that difference is expected to be (theoretically) and what it is (with empirical results and analysis).

A number of economists began separating and studying the policy distinctions in the late 1990s and directly after the global recession in 2010, however, in subsequent and more recent attempts, Alesina and others more finely parse the types of policies to discover how an assortment of spending-based alternatives impact short-run economic output.

In 2017, a larger gang of Italian economists—which included the now famous Alesina and Giavazzi—started digging into the differences between various policies by estimating multipliers for three components of governmental budgets (government transfers, public spending, and taxation).[20] In most prior studies, analysts combined the various components into one single government spending category. However, being distinct categories of spending that impact separate sectors of the economy, adjustments to transfer, investment, and other types of government spending should have different effects. At least, that's how the theory goes.

We previously distinguished transfers from other forms of government spending in the discussion on how GDP is measured. Since transfers simply move money from the government to a private entity without an exchange of a good or service, they aren't counted in measures of GDP. Along the same line of thinking, once transfers are consumed by the transferee, they have little impact on GDP, if any. On the other hand, because the government is providing funds that support welfare and other social goods and services, private sector individuals that would otherwise have purchased those necessary goods and services on their own, no longer will. Adjustments to the amount of government spending on transfers, therefore, should have an impact on private consumption. While in the past, researchers have been criticized for not disentangling the spending categories, thereby leaving open the opportunity for disputes about the validity of results, an improved approach that better separated spending types has opened the doors to a more thorough and nuanced discussion. In recent years (see prior-noted 2017 paper, for example), Alesina, Giavazzi, and crew developed new techniques that provide an opportunity for policymakers to better understand the effects that variously composed FCs will have on an economy. Again countering prior supposition and tradition, transfer-based spending-focused FCs have had a better return on policymaker efforts to improve a deficit than tax increases. Considering the long view of an economy, economic actors realizing that government transfers and entitlements have become a major component of government spending, see cuts to this category as advantageous to their future. Attempts to control a major, long-term consumption category today provides confidence that the government won't have to make up for it on the backend with major tax hikes.

With new, seemingly contrary results, could poorly constructed identification methods be to blame? If Alesina et al. reverted back to the cruder CAPB modeling techniques, wouldn't it be easy to discount their results as inherently flawed from the beginning? Building on Romer and Romer's original narratively defined approach to identifying FCs, as well as on the IMF's previously pugnacious and undeniably thorough dataset that scoured decades worth of paperwork from seventeen OECD countries to identify fiscal adjustments that happened up until 2009-ish, researchers created a new and heartier set of figures that extended beyond the peaks of the economic crises of the 2008 global shock to and up through 2014. This newest iteration was especially thorough in breaking down the finite details of every policy plan, while also emphasizing the magnitude of fiscal policies. For example, if a tax increase was created, was it a sales tax, an income tax, or some other form? An unavoidable poll tax may have a different effect on private consumption than an increase in the EU's VAT, just like different types of spending may have a different impact on macro behavior. Having access to data at its most disaggregated levels provides an opportunity for an assessment "with higher precision in the magnitude and the exogeneity of every prescription," which should reduce measurement errors and more closely examine the true exogeneity of specific measures.[21] Alesina's new results seem to be supported by sophisticated models that have covered all of the bases, to date.

Perhaps even more impactful is the acknowledgment of how policies are directed and implemented in the real world. Since so many fiscal adjustments are created in a time vacuum, it's helpful to see how or if the interactions between variables shift based on whether fiscal plans are designed to be installed and sunset all within a single year, of if they are enacted in such a way that they phase in over a period of years at increasing or decreasing levels of tax and spending changes. The latter case, defined by years-long comprehensive planning, is the more common and real-life scenario.

In the previously cited example of the UK, parliament proceeded with a plan to cut back on the doomsday scenario predicted by the growing deficit of the early 1990s with a multiyear plan that spanned from 1994 to 1997. In the first couple of years, the crux of the plan was based on tax increases, which flipped in the next two-year budget that emphasized government spending cuts. If the impact of one type of consolidation is distinct from the other, it doesn't make total sense to merely define the entire episode as substantially spending-focused or tax-focused. Additionally, to those expectations advocates who think that announced and anticipated future plans have some say in how consumers consume and investors invest, knowing what type of consolidation is going to be running wild on the economy and when may affect private consumption and investment today, or next year differently. The artful creation of a method for differentiating between these multiyear plans was an invaluable and generally underappreciated contribution to FC research. Whereas most previous studies ignored how "real-world" fiscal plans are stylized, such an omission led to results which were impractically applied to present-day solutions that couldn't capture the variation of consumption responses that phased in (or out) over a period of years.

Additionally, the creation of the EU requires an analysis of how plans are derived and administered. To the annoyance of many in the EU since the global recession, the EU has imparted heavy demands on countries that need to comply with its debt/GDP standards, as well as insists on approving the depth of an FC plan (as well as the time frame over which it will be rolled out) to correct deficit trends. While the body generally allows country-level administrators to decide on how they comply with a broader framework, the EU is seen as having the final say and can even "suggest" changes to such plans over time. Treating fiscal plans as if they don't normally operate in this fashion has led to unfair assessments and incorrect assumptions about which variables are causing which effect. Modeling techniques that fail to account for mid-plan adjustments may incorrectly attribute a particular result with an original, yet contemporaneously obsolete, FC plan.

After including data on plans that are executed over time, the Alesina team's decision to bring a unique model to the empirical mix was the most relevant to the policy world. By breaking down the largest and most robust narrative-based dataset of the day in such a way that distinguished between FCs based on public spending initiatives, governmental investments, taxation increases, and transfer cuts, allowing for the estimation of multipliers on these components, research has been able to study FCs in a detailed manner that no other study has allowed. If one is able to determine exactly how a decrease in a particular type of spending, or an increase in a particular type of taxation, can impact a nation's aggregate demand, we may finally be on the road to discovering which policies are the most righteous ones. Per Alesina, letting the tax man clean up the fiscal house led to an average loss to GDP of at least 1 percent, even four years down the line,[22] while private investment responded to tax increases by falling more than 3 percent. To put it into terms more relevant to the policymaker, according to this model, for every 1 percent increase in taxation, private investment is expected to fall by an average of 3 percent immediately, while aggregate GDP will also take a significant hit in the medium term. Policies with a focus on higher taxes as a means to make up for increasing budget shortfalls cause "much larger output losses" than those reliant on cutting back on public expenditure-based FCs, leading to less effective FC plans.

Today's battle ensues, as others have found the precise composition of an FC to be irrelevant and my own research has both supported and negated the findings of Alesina, the IMF, Ramey, Romer, and others. Being that the narrative approach (though increasing in popularity because, well, who doesn't love a good story) isn't used exclusively and still has to compete with more complex approaches such as specialized VAR techniques, DSGEs, and more as methods for identifying FCs, the various techniques often differ in their choices of which consolidations to study, with wide-ranging results. In one recent study, for example, a group from the Netherlands and Germany—known as two of the more fiscally disciplined countries of the developed world—proposed the elaborate-sounding "Bai-Perron structural break" approach, finding little evidence for a distinction between spending and tax-focused consolidation policies as related to their impact on short-run economic performance.[23]

MONEY POLICY CAVEAT . . . AGAIN

I know, I keep promising that this book isn't going to be about monetary policy. But, monetary policy, as it relates to exchange rate fluctuations and targeted interest rates, has been the bane of many researchers' existence when it comes to the fiscal policy–dominated discussions of austerity and its wider implications. Both central banking policies and exchange rate policies have an underlying influence on macroeconomic performance under periods of FC. (Sometimes I consider exchange rate policy decisions to be separate from central bank policies, as they may be implemented at the bequest of a legislative body, although most decisions related to shifts in exchange rates are directed by the all-powerful hand of central bankers.)

As alluded to previously, most countries seem to experience a consistent rise in net exports during—or immediately after—FCs, while such rises in net exports are highly correlated with falling domestic currency values[24] that can counter a decrease in domestic demand. In the IMF's narrative-based investigation of 2014, they found that a rise in real exports combined with a decline in real imports to create a significant net contribution to GDP.[25] They also concluded that the mechanism for shifts in exports could be attributed to the depreciation of domestic currency (given a 1 percent of GDP FC, currency devalued by 1.57 percent within one year), as opposed to a relative price-level shift. This means that something happened within the country to reduce currency value, not that all other countries somehow increased their relative exchange rates or currency values through their own internal monetary policy decisions. Even more specifically related to the distinction between FCs based on spending versus taxation, some studies have found a resulting appreciation of the home currency following an increase in government spending in the Euro area,[26] but others have found opposite effects for the United States,[27] as well as the UK, Australia, and Canada.[28] In these studies, the real exchange rate depreciated in response to higher government spending, which led to an improvement in GDP growth given the offsetting power of increased exports.[29]

Does a country's chosen exchange rate have an impact? Several additional case studies are regarded as classic examples of how various exchange rate regimes have influenced demand. For the most part, a country can choose to follow one of several categories of exchange rate regimes: a complete and total free float, a float managed by an all-knowing hand, and a fixed exchange rate. Within each category are a number of varieties, but theoretically, the different policies should affect the value of a home currency (the whole point of having them), which can then influence how exports and imports flow, and can then affect the overall economy. Thinking back on Denmark and Ireland's fiscal policy experiments of the 1980s, pegged exchange rates were implemented to force a rapid decline in inflation. Under their self-enacted periods of FC (as opposed to what some consider today the forced benevolence of the EU), both relied upon exchange rate–based stabilization policies to improve short-run economic performance. On the other hand, Sweden and Finland—two countries known for their economic turnarounds in the 1990s—abandoned their own pegs to follow a floating exchange rate policy.[30] Whether a float or an exchange, or everything in between, exchange rate variables are seemingly significant contributors to economic performance, but the magnitude and direction of their influence while combined with FCs have been debated.

Besides exchange rate policies, central banks seem to be pretty active in their attempts to stimulate economies, or slow them down, alongside the decision to fix a country's finances. For example, a quick look at IMF data across various FC types shows that monetary policy is substantially different between spending-focused and tax-focused FCs—during spending-focused consolidations monetary policy appears to be more stimulative and central bank targeted interest rates are lower. One reason for this phenomenon may be that central banks are less concerned about the inflationary effects of taxes during spending-focused consolidations, thereby allowing for an easier monetary policy regime.[31] Perotti (2013) noted how the Federal Funds rate in the United States is shifted per "countercyclical considerations," which can impact GDP, but how and when exactly is something up for grabs.

The results seem to be mixed, so what do you do with this data? Well, if you include more robust info on the multiyear plans and consider the "persistency" of the spending and tax shocks that policymakers have implemented to fiscally consolidate, as well as some tricky tricks to test the differences across the EU between pre- and post-EU data, Alesina's Italian analysts propose that the influence of monetary policy never outweighs the impact of spending and taxation on an economy's output.[32] Taxation-focused policies are still significantly worse for an economy under a policy of austerity, even when countered by the positive influences of exchange rate and other monetary influences.

The debate today still mimics the ever-prevalent battle between more Keynesian leaning economists, political leaders, and media personalities that might prefer the ease of implementing (and ease of understanding) tax-focused deficit cuts that garner immediate revenue generation and a more neoclassically styled belief system that submits to the concerns of a growing national debt and begs to start cutting spending and cutting fast, while also tinkering with the idea that we may be able to just ignore the debt altogether, spend to our heart's content, and worry about it all later. To date, the literature has shifted away from a debate about whether consolidations can be expansionary (per EFC theory)—as most now conclude that they rarely are—to the recent discussion that pits tax-cut favored consolidations against those that are more strongly dependent on spending reductions, and is slowly beginning to open the floor to the MMT crowd who doesn't think we need to worry at all.

My research tends to diverge from the fanciful machinations of enhanced econometric modeling (though econometric analyses do provide important insight), instead having a deeper-dive focus on individual countries that allows for a comparison across regions and continents. The failings of virtually all other macro studies becomes evident when focusing on the individual level. Even in the EU, in regionally defined areas such as the countries of the Iberian Peninsula or the Nordic states, individual nations respond to policies in ways that other countries do not, or can't. Sometimes the reason is especially due to the EU's one-size-fits-all application of policies (for example, attempting to apply expansionary or contractionary fiscal policies) to countries that are in different stages of the business cycle, that have been impacted differently by economic downturns, or that are heterogeneous based on other factors. Argentina and the GIIPS are prime examples of countries that have economic systems, policies, and cultures that necessitate a different response to a particular set of FC policies than the fiscally tightfisted and well-developed economies of Germany and Holland. Sometimes spillovers from these less developed countries impact more successful neighbors, and sometimes culture just impedes all logic (the work ethic and expected response in some countries are different than in others, which may indicate that consumption and investment patterns will also react differently to various policies, for example).

While it is especially useful for policymakers to know the history of FCs, how they have been applied, and how economies have reacted, individual countries are often as exceptional in their responses to FC policies as they are in their culture and history, making each country a unique case that should be studied as such. Yes, choosing an FC plan that focuses on spending *in general* will lead to better economic output outcomes than those that follow a more tax-focused route, but there is no blanket policy answer that will apply equally to country X as it will to country Y when trying to answer the question of how to recover from out-of-control deficits and ever-growing debts.

Further considering the diverging political philosophies of different countries, as well as the political (or potential political) influences on fiscal policy decisions (see next chapter) and one can see why it's so hard for anyone to find solutions to the world's toughest fiscal policy questions.

NOTES

1. Christopher L. House, Christian Proebsting, and Linda L. Tesar, "Austerity in the Aftermath of the Great Recession," *NBER Working Paper* (2017).

2. Paul Krugman, "Myths of Austerity," *The New York Times*, July 1, 2010. https ://www.nytimes.com/2010/07/02/opinion/02krugman.html.

3. Philip Barrett, "Interest-Growth Differentials and Debt Limits in Advanced Economies," *IMF Working Paper No. 18/82*. International Monetary Fund (April 6, 2018).

4. Jason Furman and Lawrence H. Summers, "'Who's Afraid of Budget Deficits?' How Washington Should End Its Obsession," *Foreign Affairs*, January 27, 2019.

5. Stonybrook University Professor Stephanie Kelton (also a senior economics adviser to former presidential candidate and self-avowed socialist Bernie Sanders) is one of the preeminent advocates of *Modern Monetary Theory*. Unfortunately, she has yet to use the term "cockamamie nonsense."

6. Venezuela's proud printers were able to ignite the inflation rate to a cool 1,370,000 percent in 2018, per the IMF. Patricia Laya and Andrew Rosati, "Venezuela's 2018 Inflation to Hit 1.37 Million Percent, IMF Says," *Bloomberg*, October 8, 2018, https://www.bloomberg.com/news/articles/2018-10-09/venezuela-s-2018-in flation-to-hit-1-37-million-percent-imf-says.

7. Paul Krugman, "Myths of Austerity," *The New York Times*, July 1, 2010.

8. Alberto Alesina and Allan Drazen, "Why Are Stabilizations Delayed?" *American Economic Review* 81, no. 5 (1991): 1170–1188.

9. Alberto Alesina, Carlo Faverro, and Francesco Giavazzi, "What Do We Know About the Effects of Austerity?" *NBER Working Paper no. 24246*, Cambridge, MA: NBER (2018): 10.

10. According to Northrop Grumman's website (which also shows some pretty gnarly pictures of what they make). "Defense Systems," Northrop Grumman, accessed December 12, 2018, http://www.northropgrumman.com/Capabilities/D efenseSystems/Pages/default.aspx.

11. Alesina, Faverro, and Giavazzi, "What Do We Know About the Effects of Austerity?" 10.

12. Guy Chazen, "Germany's Record Budget Surplus Triggers Calls for Tax Cuts," *Financial Times*, August 24, 2018, https://www.ft.com/content/ce744c1e-a784 -11e8-8ecf-a7ae1beff35b.

13. The Local Switzerland, "Anger as Switzerland Records 'surprise' 2.8 Billion-franc Budget Surplus," *The Local*, https://www.thelocal.ch/20180214/anger-as-swi tzerland-records-surprise-28-billion-franc-budget-surplus.

14. Giovanni Legorano and Marcus Walker, "Italy Says It Struck a Budget-Deficit Compromise with EU," *The Wall Street Journal*, December 18th, 2018, https://ww w.wsj.com/articles/italy-says-it-struck-a-budget-deficit-compromise-with-eu-1154 5169334.

15. Reuters, "Spain Raises Deficit Targets for 2018, 2019," *Reuters Business News*, July 12, 2018, https://www.reuters.com/article/us-spain-economy-deficit/spa in-raises-deficit-targets-for-2018-2019-idUSKBN1K22VA.

16. Average calculated by dividing 2018 total expense by twelve months. Some months (such as December, for example, have much higher payments than others).

"Interest Expense on Debt Outstanding," Treasury Direct (U.S. Department of the Treasury), accessed February 1, 2019, https://www.treasurydirect.gov/govt/reports/ir/ir_expense.htm.

17. Census Bureau, "Households and Families: 2010," *U.S. Census Bureau*, accessed February 5, 2019, from https://www.census.gov/prod/cen2010/briefs/c2010br-14.pdf.

18. The following section borrows heavily from ideas as presented in the following paper: Alberto Alesina and Silvia Ardagna, "Large Changes in Fiscal Policy: Taxes versus Spending," *Tax Policy and the Economy* 24, no. 1 (2010): 35–68.

19. Alesina and Ardagna, "Large Changes in Fiscal Policy," 41.

20. Alberto Alesina, Omar Barbiero, Carlo Faverro, Francesco Giavazzi, and Matteo Paradisi, "The Effects of Fiscal Consolidations: Theory and Evidence," *NBER Working Paper no. 22385*, Cambridge, MA: NBER (November 2017).

21. Alesina et al., "The Effects of Fiscal Consolidations."

22. Alesina et al., "The Effects of Fiscal Consolidations," 4.

23. Rasmus Wiese, Richard Jong-A-Pin, and Jakob de Haan. "Can Successful Fiscal Adjustments Only Be Achieved by Spending Cuts?" *European Journal of Political Economy* 54 (2018): 145–166.

24. Check out any macroeconomics, or even basic general economics, textbook to learn more about the interaction between currency values and export-imports. But, it's a simple concept. All else the same, if the value of a domestic currency falls, exports will rise. This is due to the fact that those who purchase a country's goods do so in the country's domestic currency and essentially get everything at a discount when a country's currency falls in relation to the purchaser's currency. *Export boom.*

25. Jaime Guajardo, Daniel Leigh, and Andrea Pescatori, "Expansionary Austerity? International Evidence," *Journal of the European Economic Association* 12, no. 4 (2014): 949–968.

26. *See* Roel Beetsma, Franc Klaassen, and Massimo Giuliodori, "The Effects of Public Spending Shocks on Trade Balances and Budget Deficits in the European Union," *Journal of the European Economic Association* 6, no. 2 (2008): 414; Augustin S. Bénétrix and Philip Lane, "The Impact of Fiscal Shocks on the Irish Economy," *Economic and Social Review* 40, no. 4 (2009): 407–434.

27. Morten O. Ravn, Stephanie Schmitt-Grohé, and Martin Uribe, "Consumption, government spending, and the real exchange rate," *Journal of Monetary Economics* 59, no. 3 (2012): 215–234.

28. Tommaso Monacelli and Roberto Perotti, "Fiscal Policy, the Real Exchange Rate and Traded Goods," *The Economic Journal* 120, no. 544 (2010): 437–461.

29. Francisco de Castro and Daniel Garrote, "The Effects of Fiscal Shocks on the Exchange Rate in the EMU and Differences with the USA," *Empirical Economics* 49, no. 4 (2015): 1341–1365.

30. Roberto Perotti, "The 'Austerity Myth': Gain without Pain?" in *Fiscal Policy After the Financial Crisis*, eds. Alberto Alesina and Francesco Giavazzi (Chicago and London: University of Chicago Press, 2013), 308.

31. Guajardo, et al., "Expansionary Austerity?" 958.

32. Alesina et al., "The Effects of Fiscal Consolidations," 6.

Chapter 5

It's All Political

Sir Ernest Benn, a writer and political publisher of early twentieth-century Britain (who can add fortune telling to his list of core competencies), knew exactly how politics would unfold in the late 1900s and early 2000s when he said "Politics is the art of looking for trouble, finding it whether it exists or not, diagnosing it incorrectly, and applying the wrong remedies." Being a skeptic of all things political, I find it easy to agree with Sir Ernest. When our political leaders are elected, they are expected to work on national or local issues and are compelled to find the ones that might get them the most notoriety for doing so, whether the "problem" requires intervention or not. As they are also expected to have a general knowledge of wide-ranging issues, they are less frequently the technocratic specialist needed to tackle any particular issue, and too often apply the most politically expedient solution. The very same can be said regarding policies related to national public debts and budget deficits: whether we have a problem or not, politicians know there is one, generally lack an economic or financial background to understand how the problem was created nor what the problem really is, and therefore inevitably make the mistake of applying solutions that put politics ahead of reality. But I suppose Sir Ernest was wise beyond his years, realizing that politics was and always will be politics, transcending time and unconstrained by location.

Attempting to be fair, I do believe most elected officials have the good of their nation at heart (though the correlation between taint and time in office may be high), and politics is a necessity that has a substantial influence over the implementation and eventual outcomes of FC policies. Sometimes, however, when current research points to a clear "best" path forward, the most advantageous political solution may not be the same. The necessity of relying on a populist agenda to achieve and maintain a publicly held office can even be the culprit behind a particular crisis at hand. For example, perhaps a set of policy solutions has been presented to a legislator with the understanding that one is more likely to lead to economic growth than the other, but the latter is more heavily supported by "likely voters," and election time is right around the corner. Perhaps it's a complicated economic issue that few have studied and even fewer understand. Such is the case for legislators considering FC policies amid growing government debt in today's world. The solutions to long-term debts and contemporary deficits may be policies that do not have a visually large impact today, which may lead to the public's misperception of inaction. Doing nothing is a respectable and sometimes required policy prescription (and one that many of us would suggest more policymakers consider), but patience is not a strong characteristic of many legislators' constituencies.

Sometimes the pressure to please is just too great. Enter the knee-jerk, must-do-something-now type of political leader, who proposes a series of fixes that best combines austerity with politics. While such a political champion will nevertheless defend and profess his or her proposal's veracity to the death, the appropriateness of its application may be lacking. If we can just remove political constraints, it would be a lot easier for researchers to convince legislators of what they believe to be the best policy solutions given specific country circumstances. Since politics will never be removed from the real world of policy, the pressures elicited within, the impact of policies that are popular among successful politicos, and the interaction between the political will and the requirement for broad policy shifts have to be considered and scrutinized when studying fiscal adjustment policies.

There is a lot to be said about the influence of politics on the economy, and probably even more to learn.

WHEN POLITICS AND ECONOMICS MARRY

Looking back at the trajectory of deficits in the 1980s and 1990s, and again considering current trends toward unsustainable deficits after the 2008 global crisis, it's easy to see why some see an explicit deficit bias. Figure 5.1 shows the apparent lean toward a deficit (represented by dots that are below zero) within the OECD since the 1980s. Even removing the prodigal Irish who spent themselves into a deficit hole of 32 percent of GDP in 2010 (yes, you read that correctly) while also keeping data from the natural resource lottery winners of Norway who averaged a 10 percent surplus straight through the recent global crisis, and the trend still remains definitely in the red.

The United States exemplifies these concerns, as deficits in this country have already creeped into the 1 trillion dollar range (see figure 5.2, *U.S. Surplus/Deficit*), expected to double in the next ten years, while the national debt

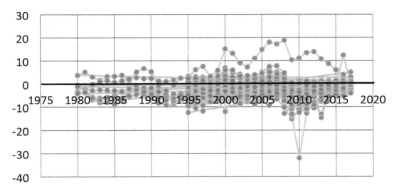

Figure 5.1 OECD Deficits. Author Generated from "General Government Deficits," OECD, Accessed July 22, 2019, https://data.oecd.org/gga/general-government-deficit.htm.

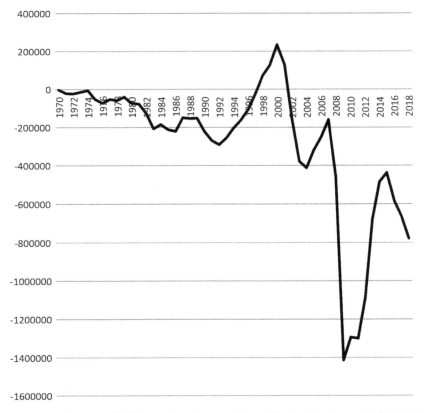

Figure 5.2 US Surplus/Deficit. Author Generated from "Federal Surplus or Deficit," U.S. Office of Management and Budget, Accessed July 22, 2019, https://fred.stlouisfed.org/series/FYFSD.

has more than double since 2008, from 10 trillion to the current 22.5 trillion dollars (by the time you read this you'll be begging for the days of a mere 22 trillion dollar debt). It's pretty clear that we tend toward deficits, at least in recent times, and at least across the developed world of the OECD. What is not entirely clear is why we have such a bias. A ton of research by economists has attempted to combine the incentives of politicians with theories in economics to come up with explanations for our apparent tendencies toward piles of country debt.

In what has become known as the field's seminal work, a political scientist consummated his relationship with an economist to create today's *political economy* research. These new political economy discussions attempt to combine economic theory with political science philosophy to develop a deeper understanding of the inefficient (economically speaking) decision-making of political actors in fiscal policy. Through a more neoclassical lens, analyzing the politics of distribution more often than not leads to a blurry understanding at best. The basic message of political economy thinkers is that there is hope for disillusioned economists—a rational explanation (politically speaking) exists for the "notorious inefficiency" that economists found in the decisions by policymakers.[1]

Per this original line of thinking, there are several basic sources of bias that causes governments to choose to avoid optimal fiscal policy solutions—that is to maintain a surplus in economic booms to counter deficits in recessions. First, political actors don't abide by the economists' definition of "benefits and costs." What benefits the politico doesn't always lead to the maximized benefit to the society or geography in which it serves. Given a politician's propensity to serve his or her constituents, powerful leaders may divert resources to certain geographic locations, locations that may not use the resources to improve conditions in the same manner that others may, but nonetheless are the most beneficial to the elected official. Costs to the taxpayer are also not costs to the politician. While a business manager may attempt to hold or reduce spending on a particular project to the minimum level possible (in order to improve profitability), a politician can be rewarded by the amount of taxpayer funds provided, regardless of how they are used. Unused funds in the latter case (as in many functional bureaucratic departments across large governments) are actually seen as wasteful in the eyes of this governmental actor, therefore creating the incentive for projects financed by larger amounts of taxpayer dollars that maximize the usage of said funds, ensuring that "not a penny goes to waste" (economists will argue that, in fact, a lot of pennies will go to waste). Dividing an economy into disjointed political districts, local projects financed by general taxation, and the incentives provided by election and reelection processes in a democratic society tends to explain the "inefficiency of political choice."[2]

Some describe political economy's basic underlying theories as being comprised of two parts: common pool theory and the time inconsistency of preferences theory.[3] Common pool problems arise, not due to the unsanitary nature of a public swimming hole, but when multiple policymakers come together to set a budget. Both tax revenues and spending deficits are considered shared resources, since taxes are raised through general and broad tax policies and deficits add to the debt that is also shared by all since they will be paid out of future taxes. A policymaker realizes that the burden of an increased deficit is not bore only by himself, but instead is shared among his peers. If all policymakers know that spending which benefits a targeted constituency (and particular voter base) does not translate into an equal cost to that constituency, then the incentive is to spend. In other words, the benefit can more or less be seen as being obtained at a discount, given that the costs are actually subsidized by others outside of one's own geographically restricted constituency base.

For example, say elected member of parliament Bob asks for and is appropriated 1 billion dollars to create a new highway system in his local district in Aldovia. His constituents are super happy and they place a huge value on the benefits associated with better transportation, decreased traffic on local roads, improvements in commerce, and so on. However, Bob's district isn't the only one footing the bill. Poor elected member of parliament James, from another Aldovian district, has to explain why his constituents are also helping to pay for the new highways in Bob's district. "Because Bob promised to help me get reelected" only angers a growing mob. Now, James' district has to cover Bob's district's spending fun, while recouping zero benefit (assuming there are no other spillover benefits associated with being in close proximity to Bob's district). Bob's district gets not only the added benefits of commerce and all that may surpass the total costs associated with the project, but they will receive more tax revenues (including local taxes) and have a burden of future taxes that is but a fraction of the benefit received. The next time, however, James realizes that it is in his best interest to ask his peers to support his plans for a similar project, or the grandest project he can think of. But this time, every member of parliament is now aware of how the game is played and all have the same incentives that Bob did, realizing that their spending pots and their eventual costs to the taxpayer are pooled. When the "benefits" to the politician outweigh the total taxpayer costs in this way, it's easy to see how deficit spending makes sense to every individual voting member of parliament, while it might make a lot less sense to the overall future or current fiscal welfare of Aldovia.

The second underlying theory to political economy discussions relates to time inconsistency problems related to the work of today's legislators.[4] This perhaps is of greatest concern, as sometimes incentives are such that a policymaker has little motivation to be concerned about the fiscal dilemma facing a future policymaker. Since most policymaker power is allotted subject to electability, Bob was motivated to get his for his own, right now. By doing so, he can ensure that he is elected and can then do what he deems best for his constituents. Unfortunately, the cycle is vicious, and Bob still realizes that he needs to win subsequent elections, as do his peers now, and all are vying for opportunities to spend as much as they can (or to increase their own share of a limited pot) at the expense of the future fiscal situation.

In your typical economic environment (at least as economists understand it), when things aren't operating at optimal efficiency standards, market incentives push to get rid of inefficiencies. When Company A produces widgets at a cost of 3 dollars a pop and sells them for 6 and Company B finds out that it can produce them far cheaper and still sell them around 6 bucks or cheaper, Company B will force Company A to find a way to produce them cheaper. Otherwise, as prices fall in a competitive environment, Company A will eventually be undercut in price at the point where it can no longer produce at a profit. The same incentives usually aren't there for the policymaker, leading to inefficient operations in a number of areas. The policymaker doesn't care that price controls in a rental market leads to less housing for low-income individuals (because the incentive for developers to produce housing units falls) and often benefits upper income families as developers spend their time building higher end housing (because they can charge more and recoup higher profits), if his voting base thinks he is doing something good for the population. It would be more efficient in economic terms to impose a higher tax on high-end housing, or to subsidize lower end housing, but that doesn't consider the political benefit and cost. With rent controls a policymaker often gains the perception that he is helping the poor while actually helping the wealthy, winning votes from everyone. With taxes or subsidies, higher income families may lose, leading to a loss in benefit at the polls.

Trade tariffs and subsidies are another example of economically inefficient, but politically prudent policies that many legislators vie for today. Most countries around the world have some sort of tariff and subsidy system in place that attempts to even out what they perceive as unfair trade advantages within other countries or are simply trying to gain an economic advantage for those within their borders. Economists, however, have long known that protectionist trade policies do little to benefit a country's macroeconomy. In fact, the *Theory of Comparative Advantage* states that countries that choose to specialize in the skills in which they are "most good" can more efficiently trade the goods and services produced by these skills to obtain more of the other goods and services that a country needs or wants. The only limitation to the theory is when our policymakers mess it all up. By putting a tariff on a car imported from Japan, for example, (a) causes the car to be more expensive to the end consumer, (b) means that a consumer will purchase an inferior version of what he or she would have in a tariff free world, subsidizing a car manufacturer that produces worse stuff and eliminating its incentive to improve, or (c) means that a consumer will instead decide not to buy a car, leaving behind what may help to improve opportunities and economic advantages for said consumer. On the other hand, politicians are pretty good at pitching a nice tariff as a benefit to the voting base. In the car example, if you want your country's car manufacturers to continue producing inferior cars at uncompetitive prices so that it will continue to employ citizens, a tariff may help to do just that. Jobs retained (though they would have likely shifted to more productive employment otherwise, but that's not how the politician sees it) and votes gained. More often than not, protectionism is simultaneously pitched as a national security issue (we shouldn't outsource the production of military equipment to the Taliban, for example) or a human rights concern (why should we trade with a country that manufactures more cheaply if it allows companies to operate sweatshops full of pre-teen workers?).

Latin American countries applied the same principles in order to bolster economic development at home. If a certain industry was nascent and developing, such as a car manufacturer, one option is to make imports so expensive that domestic producers will proliferate to fill the gap. Eventually, the hope is that these domestic producers become good enough at their jobs that they can create an industry that is globally competitive, creating trade opportunities that improve the contribution to national GDP. A dictator can make himself sound like a pretty nice guy, who only has the good of his countrymen at heart with similar policies. In the long run, however, it never works out. Competitive forces are what compels entrepreneurs to make better goods. When local manufacturers don't have to compete with more successful companies, they just don't have to improve. And now we have a bunch of junk car manufacturers in perpetuity. Initially such policies were politically beneficial; in the end they proved to be impressive economic failures.

The very same inefficiencies apply in the world of fiscal policy. A country that promised an oath to maintain optimal fiscal policy would never need to raise taxes. That sounds like a pretty attractive platform to me. *Vote for me and I will never, ever, ever raise your taxes . . . ever!* Besides the fact that this tactic has been tried before,[5] it also assumes that inaction will be taken in two other areas. First, under an optimal fiscal policy path, it is difficult to cut taxes to the majority of the electorate. This is a popular campaign promise by fiscally conservative candidates across the globe. *Elect me and I will cut your tax rate so hard that the government will never see another dime of your hard-earned money again!* Some try to balance this fiscal policy promise with an equal and opposing hike in taxes to another constituency. These types of pay-as-you-go strategies get the happy juices flowing for deficit hawks, but the politician that proposes it is going to face questions from the unhappy voter base that has to bear the burden of those tax cuts. Why should they pay more so that another class of voter gets to keep more? It's a difficult argument to overcome.

Optimal fiscal policy solutions, or balanced budget proposals, also restrict spendthrift representatives' abilities to support pet projects and major structural reforms, or to create massive social benefit programs that can often be pretty strong vote getters. An increasingly popular trend in the United States is pushing new legislators to propose economic policy reforms that look more like the democratic-socialist agendas of upper European areas, than anything previously advocated for in the United States. In a recent example, a new legislator (also a media darling) has helped to create an environmentally friendly spending proposal that allows the country to reconstruct every building, builds out high-speed rail systems to eliminate air travel, and will provide a job to anyone willing to work. It's one of the more radical proposals the country has ever seen, with an equally radical price tag that surpasses 42 trillion dollars over a ten-year period. The U.S. deficit chart may look a lot more like figure 5.3 in the future. The popularity of this proposal (especially among younger voters) is surprising and is therefore being increasingly advocated by those elected officials that see the political advantage of supporting it; whether or not they believe there is an economic advantage to its implementation.

Of all the political economy theories floating around, one of my favorites is the idea that inefficiencies exist because we all just lack the knowledge to know any better. If we don't know what the best policies are for us, our peers, or our aggregate economies, someone has to tell us, right? We all basically rely upon the best available knowledge we have. In the case of protectionist policies, few understand the nuances of comparative advantage theory (I argue because economics isn't taught well, or at all in some cases, in primary or secondary educational systems), and therefore lean upon an understanding they gain from others. If that "others" category is the media, it's going to be difficult to gain a deep understanding of any policy that isn't tainted by political beliefs. Therefore, many people just listen to who they trust, which is someone they will align with politically or ideologically on other issues. The politician may know this and take advantage of your lack of knowledge, but more likely he or she also lacks specialized training in economics in general, or trade policy specifically. Since both voters and policymakers have incomplete knowledge, new, articulately relayed ideas have a "first mover" advantage that can win over supporters.[6]

Ignorance also pervades the world of fiscal policy, which adds to the proliferation of inefficient solutions. Does this surprise anyone? Yes, your

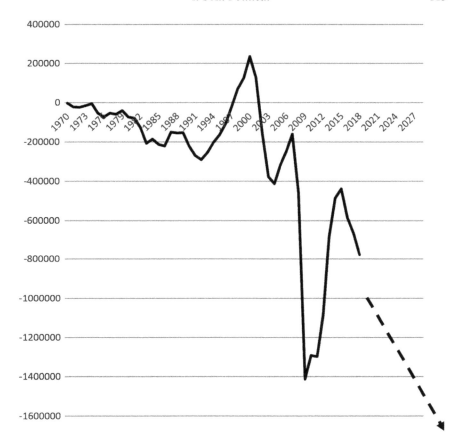

Figure 5.3 US Surplus/Deficit High Spend. Author Generated from "Federal Surplus or Deficit," U.S. Office of Management and Budget, Accessed July 22, 2019, https://fred.st louisfed.org/series/FYFSD.

politicians and many who support them suffer from a problem of "incomplete knowledge." While most of us attribute abject stupidity to the wayward politician that we can't see ourselves ever agreeing with, as discussed previously, it's impossible for a policymaker to have perfect information about any particular policy in a world where they are expected to have general knowledge about every policy. But, this lack of knowledge leads to an opportunity for *deficit bias*. Heterogeneous knowledge between the direct short-term and the indirect long-term effects of fiscal policies gives societal preference toward and satisfaction in the former. If a government spends like a lottery winner in Vegas, families *might* get more benefits, the educational system may help more children reach their potential, and infrastructure may improve intra- and inter-country trade. If taxes are also cut like the government has the ability to operate *pro bono*, those same families and businesses have more money in their pockets, are also cognizant of this direct effect, and *might* use that money to provide their own social benefits. But the costs of a reduction in a government's ability to spend in the future (because they've already spent everything) or the need to jack up taxes on everyone down the road (because they've got to raise enough fund to pay for services and general operations in the future) allude most of us.[7] Since the indirect long-term costs aren't so apparent in contemporary debates, or we are somehow convinced that additions to the debt will somehow take care of themselves, we ignore, forget about, or put off concerns about the future. When you got your first Capital One Visa card as a teenager, you probably experienced a feeling that leads to the same deficit bias problem in countries. Unaware of the consequences of the future, it's easy to go out and have some fun spending to our heart's content today.

Perhaps politicians aren't the benevolent actors that we always assumed? Maybe they aren't too different from anyone, and we should learn to assume that they are rational actors that work hard to get the most benefit for themselves (or even their particular segment of constituents) within the confines of normal economic limitations (resources, time, information, etc.). And maybe, just maybe, the voters that elect them do just the same, attempting to maximize their own personal benefits, to heck with the rest of the country, or to future generations when today's voters are no longer around. This might be a cynically tinged explanation, but it does help to describe how *political economy theory* attempts to combine the political world with the economic one and explains the inefficiencies that come about when politics have a hand in fiscal policy.

A vastly different line of thinking has been advanced by a number of political scientists, concluding that we have so misdiagnosed our fiscal problems that we are forever doomed to mismanage the solutions unless we change our political way of thinking. Mark Blyth's famous work[8] countered the common conclusion that governmental overspending has been the grand issue that has created all of our woes. Governments weren't the problem that caused the financial and fiscal crises that led to recessions everywhere; the private sector markets were to blame, per Blyth.[9] Therefore, the solution also rests, not in applying FCs to what we thought were the poorly managed finances of a particular country, but should instead face the banking sector or the private sector in general. Yet somehow, political motivations have veered away from placing blame where blame is due. The debate about which type of consolidation fares the best is irrelevant and misapplied; the real debate should be whether we need austerity at all. The argument is significant in that the presumption is that FCs usually result in costs being borne by those who need the most assistance (e.g., spending cuts will cut back on transfers, while tax increases hit the middle class). Blyth, Summers, Krugman, and many more would rather that the private sector (not the government) pay to repair the mess it created. This divergent line of thinking has attracted a substantial following over time and is increasingly considered by policymakers around the world.

Economists may counter with an "incentives"-based argument, reminding Blyth and similar thinkers that increasing costs to producers of wealth will likely diminish a percentage of the tax base that society depends on or needs. Considering politics, still others place the blame firmly in the lap of the politicians and the regulations and taxation system that they created. Companies focused on profit, after all, can only operate within the boundaries laid out for them and the incentives they create.

While politics and economics often seem worlds apart, they do intersect in important ways that have an impact on which policies are championed and eventually enacted across governments. Whether the private sector or governments have been to blame for the global crisis may be less relevant, given that policy trends favor FCs. But how did FC theories become so popular and trendy after the crisis in the first place? The next section discusses how unknown theories found prominent places for themselves on the desks of policymakers around the world.

NOT SO EXPANSIONARY FISCAL CONTRACTIONS

Pagano and Giavazzi's *EFC theory* had an amazing run for a couple of unknown academics (unknown outside of academia). What started as a theory based on a few European case studies ended up running wild throughout academia and perpetrated the world of policy like few other ideas have. EFC theory's attraction was that it demonstrated how the implementation of fiscal austerity may actually lead to an unexpected and unheard-of result—that an economy can *expand* in the face of severe deficit cuts. If these anti-Keynesian heretics were telling the truth, policymakers could finally have their cake and eat it too: getting the fiscal house in order would also mean that you can add a positive shock to economic output, a win-win for all involved. Policymakers dead-set on austerity, finally, had the research to back up their claim that *it's all good, not just for the future, but for the right now too!*

Unfortunately, their data didn't entirely hold up to posterity's (annoying) affliction with scrutinizing elder academic statesmen, nor did their own subsequent findings. Later research validated some aspects of EFC theory,[10] but also negated the crux of it. In fact, few studies today hold that cutting back on spending necessarily begets economic growth in the near term, though some do (while a number of others holds that it can be quite expansionary in the long run). Even EFC theory's creators have had some second thoughts about the original definition:

> Governments should commit to future spending cuts large enough to stabilize debt levels over the medium term. But, once future sustainability is locked in, they could afford to take some risks with current deficits. They could delay removal of the fiscal stimulus, or even add some additional stimulus if private demand is slow to recover.[11]

But, EFC theory's prominence in the policy world at the time, as well as the continued carryover of some of its basic concepts, provides an interesting example of how the ostentatious world of politics can combine with the traditionally clandestine back offices of academia to propel an idea into prosperity and accepted wisdom.

Whether EFC theory holds in reality was irrelevant, as the counterintuitive idea at the time began to transform the way academics, think tanks, policy experts, and then policymakers began to think about FC policies. When faced with a fiscal crisis, policymakers intent on doing something to instigate macroeconomic stabilization were chomping at the bit for something that could curtail out-of-control deficits while also stabilizing and eventually improving economic growth opportunities in the future and economic performance in the short to medium term. EFC may not have been the precise answer, but its inventors shifted the dialogue to something uniquely attractive that took the rare leap that transcended academia to make a dent in real-world policy decisions.

While Giavazzi and Pagano may have kicked off the party, Alesina and others from the University of Bocconi (Italy) elevated the stature of EFC-related ideas to notoriety. Being part of the NBER's well-respected research team,[12] the Italian Stallions of academia bolstered the credentials of their research methods and results, while simultaneously publishing in some of the world's top academic journals and doubled as affiliates at world-renowned research universities like Harvard. While a Harvard University affiliation commands broad worldwide respect, getting published in the journals *Economic Policy* and *American Economic Review* provides unprecedented validation (and guarantees that you'll never have to buy your own drinks at the Harvard Club). With unparalleled credentials, the Bocconi team was able to disseminate the case for their ideas on expansionary austerity with ease, or at least the possibility of the phenomenon if not the guarantee of its existence in every case of FC policies. With a team of experts in tow, Italy's finest ensured that the rest of academia paid attention. While they were on the offensive, winning the battle of ideas, others were left defending what became viewed as the antiquated policies of yore.

After gaining some ground among academic peers, Sebastian Dellepiane-Avellaneda described how a second stage developed, which allowed for the ideas emanating from Bocconi to be taken up, supported, and debated by a knowledgeable bunch with wide social influence. Having published papers on the differences between FCs based on government spending cuts instead of tax adjustments at the IMF (*IMF Staff Papers* are well read and known by high-level policy experts around the world), the IMF and the OECD both placed consideration of the ideas in a place of prominence, publishing the new proclamations of austerity policies within their most notable publications that are must-reads for anyone in policy, economics, or the world of finance: the *World Economic Outlook* (IMF) and the *OECD Economic Outlook*.[13] Later publications of the two renowned institutions systematically considered the existing literature on fiscal policy and consistently addressed the ideas that were advanced by Bocconi's progeny, some even conceding that fiscal multipliers (that which indicates the effect of an increase in spending on economic output) can actually be negative, meaning that an increase in government spending can lead to a decrease in the average response in private consumption, or aggregate demand—a phenomenon that can be due to simultaneous increases in interest rate risk premiums and/or high debt.[14]

Noting how "key institutions" couldn't help but take up these newly embedded ideas on fiscal policies, Dellepiane-Avellaneda noted how widely accepted the Bocconi-led views had become.[15] A 2000 EMU report even opened with confirmation of how important it was to ensure fiscal stability through the government spending channel: "Achieving and sustaining sound positions in public finances is essential to raise output and employment in Europe. . . . Expenditure-based budgetary adjustments send a strong signal of a government's commitment to fiscal consolidation and are likely to generate positive expectations."[16]

With articles, publications, and conferences having various titles such as *Expansionary Fiscal Consolidations in Europe: New evidence*,[17] *Lessons from Successful Fiscal Consolidations*,[18] and *Received Wisdom and Beyond: Lessons from Fiscal Consolidations in the EU*,[19] the European Commission, World Bank, IMF, and the OECD had combined with prominent academic journals and think tanks to support the academics who began with a simple idea that austerity can, in some cases, be a very good thing. Doing so, they successfully assured the solidification of similar research, ideas, and philosophies in their place of prominence across the world of policy.

Successfully framing the debate among policy discussions, assured that their preferred research questions enlightened future investigations, and solidified its place in politicians' agendas, the policy prescription preference that leaned toward FCs became the accepted wisdom. But don't take my word for it. The European Commission itself claimed that a comprehensive examination of the empirical studies on FCs made this a known fact:

Alesina and Perotti (1995) find that successful adjustments are mainly expenditure based, with a focus on primary current expenditure. This result has been replicated and confirmed by a series of later studies (for instance Alesina and Perotti 1997; Alesina and Ardagna 1998, von Hagen et al. 2002, Briotti, 2005, Lambertini and Tavares 2005) and is by now accepted as *received wisdom.* (Emphasis added)[20]

When your life's work is deemed the "received wisdom" of the day, you know you've won over a lot of hearts and minds, including those in the political world.

Having won the championship for the wisest of wise policy solutions, it was hard to ignore the contribution that this field of research had on an increasingly obvious ideological shift. Anyone who had doubts about the fiscal policy mechanisms that flowed from Keynesian-dominated philosophy had an immense and growing swath of empirical studies and new data ready to support them, and the satisfaction of knowing that they may no longer be the heterodoxical pariahs at their annual policy wonk gatherings, but instead accepted, mainstream participants in what then became a heated dialogue.

How did these ideas filter down to the political powers of the world to be advanced in practical proposals around the globe?

Policy solutions that claim to reconcile conflicting goals, in this case "austerity without pain," are music to the ears of politicians, as brilliantly argued by Paul Krugman (1995) in *Peddling Prosperity.* Politicians, from both left and right of the political spectrum, are always eager to buy "magical" solutions to economic problems. The commitments of expansionary contractions have naturally served the interests of the conservative coalition. It also appealed to third-way social-democrats interested in signalling economic competence in the age of global markets, like central bank independence. Both conservative and progressive leaders could build on these increasingly "common sense" ideas to legitimise fiscal consolidation, not least in the run-up to EMU. More generally, the expansionary-austerity narrative has been a powerful discursive weapon for accommodating the electoral and coalitional imperatives of the neoliberal era.[21]

Politicians always want a solution to their constituents' concerns, but they never want to pay for it at the polls. How do they reconcile this? They find policy ideas that target the problem (or attempt to), but cause little pain (or they hope it won't). In this case, as it became obvious to political leaders that something has to be done to correct a country's or region's fiscal path—especially in light of the growing debts and deficits post-2008 global crisis—cutting back on spending or increasing taxes to improve fiscal conditions under the normal Keynesian transmission of fiscal policy would only cause more harm to an economy. In fact, conventional fiscal policy demanded the opposite, supposing that only stimulus could bring back fiscal alignment, or that a fiscal correction wasn't necessary at all. Given that the latter idea is hard to digest politically, the search for a solution that captured the best of both worlds had already taken place prior to the release of this new line of research. Once politically palatable fiscal solutions were found, the temptation to implement them was impossible to overcome. Likely unbeknownst to the political implementers at the time, historical hindsight may have vindicated many of these decisions, as contemporary research has confirmed the necessity of FCs, though not always the precise chosen pathway for implementation.

Yet, without the benefit of hindsight and today's research data, knowing and believing were one thing for a politician; applying said beliefs to promote the advancement of those policies in the face of election accountability is another. Political policymakers who have come to accept that an FC is a necessity, or furthermore realize that they will become a necessity whether they like it or not, have an even tougher decision to make. Should one still impose an FC knowing that there could be political consequences?

The next section discusses how some policymakers have feared that implementing FC may lead to certain political death. If newly minted evidence on FCs holds up, implementing the counterintuitive policies should make policymakers heroes. But, will an electorate reward a brave public servant with early retirement regardless?

AUSTERE POLITICAL CAREERS

Imagine being a politician. You are one of the benevolent, well-intentioned, and honest kind, and you've come to the firm belief that FC is best for your homeland. Perhaps you are the democratically elected president of Aldovia and you've just come out of a frightening meeting with the appointed treasurer. Unfortunately, he hasn't been so forthright with you and has hidden a bit of bad news over the years. Just after submitting his resignation, he drops a binder on your desk that serves as a truth bomb on the country's finances. After analyzing the books you discover a dreadful trend: government revenues have run inverse to spending for the last five years, digging the country into a deficit that would put *The Emerald Isle*[22] to shame. Unfortunately, the previous chancellor was an incompetent, who misdirected the majority of the country's finances to corrupt public works projects that benefited the country's future little, but added to the national debt a lot. Now you see that, at the current rate, Aldovia won't be able to pay the interest on its debt within the next couple of years unless something dramatic is done. On top of everything, investors have grown concerned about the political stability of Aldovia, as well as the possibility of higher taxes that will be needed to cover the cost of the debt and are increasingly choosing to relocate to the greener pastures of neighboring countries.

After a previous bout of austerity in another administration, you believe that your countrymen are wary of another wave of FCs. However, your deputy treasurer, who just graduated from the University of Bocconi, has convinced you that a particular type of austerity has been implemented successfully in a country with characteristics that match Aldovia's nearly perfectly. An FC of a particular type will work, you are convinced. Nonetheless, you are up for reelection next year. Since you don't think your political career can survive an onslaught of Aldovian consolidation policies, you withdraw your fiscal policy proposal to the legislature and concede that you are too chicken to do what you know is right.

Though part of this mythical scenario may seem absurd, it does mimic the real reactions present in the mind of many policymakers today. Political wisdom has long held that cutting a budget deficit by cutting spending and benefits, and/or raising taxes, can only lead to voters reciprocating with their own form of austerity, one that puts a harsh limit on one's political career. Tighten the budget too much, and you can kiss reelection goodbye.

Since the increasing debts and deficits of the 1970s, 1980s, and now in the 2000s (especially after 2008-led recessions), politicians wondered if they could even implement an FC and survive. If they are trying to do what they perceive as the right thing by cutting the deficit and consolidating some finances, voters will reward them with a cozy retirement from politics. If they spend to appease every constituency until they have distracted the country enough to forget about growing deficits, it will all eventually catch up to them—maybe sooner than later.

This scenario is a real concern in an age where high deficits from years of care-free fiscal policy combined with the global recession of the 2008 era. Worse, global demographic shifts toward a more aged population make it more expensive for governments to support citizens (and more politically costly to take away those benefits). Higher social security, pensions, and healthcare costs plus fewer young people earning an income[23] will equal some interesting fiscal obstacles in the near future. Figure 5.4 gives us a taste of the worldwide demographic direction. Figure 5.5 provides an overview of where healthcare expenditures are headed.

Despite the seeming improvements in recent years to some countries' fiscal bottom lines, these trends will only increase the necessity of, or propensity toward, FCs of some degree.

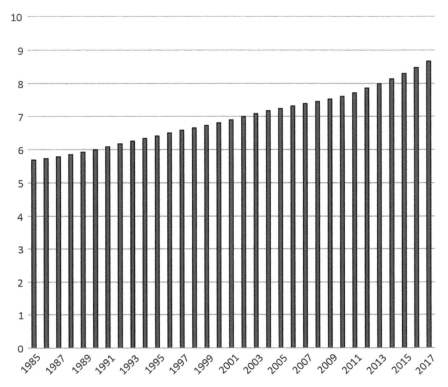

Figure 5.4   Population Older than Sixty-five. Author Generated from "Population ages 65 and above (% of total population)," World Bank, Accessed July 22, 2019, https://da ta.worldbank.org/indicator/SP.POP.65UP.TO.ZS.

Buchanan and Wagner[24] (1977) first supposed that voters are wary of any policies that promise a long-term benefit, for a number of reasons. Perhaps they don't believe that the policy will provide the benefit in the future that is promised today or might even have scant understanding of how a policy may benefit them in the future. Maybe they think that someone else will come along and change the policy before a benefit is attained. Or maybe voters are just "money in the bank" kind of people, who just don't believe they're getting anything until they see it hit the account. On the other hand, wary voters do tend to reward policies that offer something tangible today.

The "conventional wisdom" that was first articulated in Buchanan's famous work has a similar implication for fiscal policy. *Give me something today and I'll reward you for it, regardless of the future cost (which I may not understand anyway)*, says the voter who may not care too much about the growing debt or deficit, but cares a whole lot about his or her benefits and tax rates from the government today. On the other hand, a voter that has to live

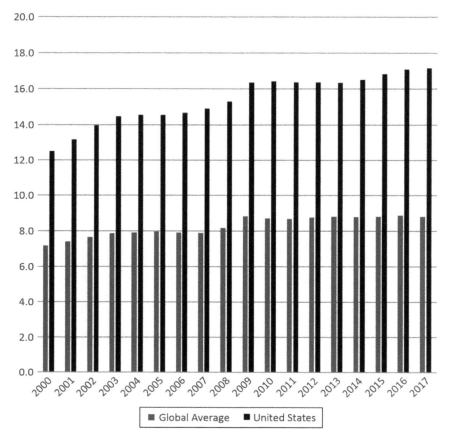

Figure 5.5   Healthcare Spending. Author Generated from "Health spending," OECD, Accessed July 22, 2019, https://data.oecd.org/healthres/health-spending.htm.

through a period of FC and undergoes a reduction in benefits or lower take-home pay will make sure the policymaker knows it at the polls. Conventional thinking seems to line up with the common sense attained through life experience. We humans tend to be a bit impatient and are wary of future guarantees, especially those promised by politicians.

Policymakers have since begged for an out. In a world in which the uninformed voter gets to decide future fiscal policy, how can an elected leader do what he believes to be right, without suffering subsequent electoral losses? Recent research may have provided empirical evidence in contradiction to this traditional way of thinking. In fact, similar to the counterintuitive results advocated for by expansionary austerity believers, there have been instances when even the harshest of terrible FC policies have been implemented and a party, politician, or individual policy official known to be responsible for the policies have been able to convince voters that the policies were necessary and will be beneficial. Though not entirely one-sided, recent studies often demonstrate that electability prospects of politicians advocating for austerity as a central part of their campaign, or reelectability prospects of those who have implemented them, are much higher than previously thought. Per the Bocconi-Italians, "there is no strong correlation between the tightness of fiscal policy and a government's probability of being elected,"[25] offering renewed hope to a number of developed world leaders who see the FC writing on their future walls.

Before getting too excited future or current leader of Aldovia, the research is far from reaching a consensus. Much like the world of macroeconomics in general, there are often too many factors at play that influence the political environment, making it nearly impossible to create methodologies for testing the electoral repercussions to austere policy implementers. Perhaps a particular incumbent with a hardcore FC resume is so much more attractive than anyone running against him or her because of policies other than those related to fiscal policy. Maybe voters don't put a lot of weight onto preferences related to country-level finances, but instead vote more heavily based on other factors. In the United States, for example, polling organizations tend to find that the national debt rarely breaks into the top five most important issues; Gallup polling recently found that only 2 percent directly cited fiscal policy as a concern that motivated an election decision.[26] The United States, however, hasn't had to undergo Greek-like measures of austerity (though it has had its share of FCs) and has yet to undergo the type of fiscal crisis present in so many other countries, but the example should serve as an indicator of how public interest may not be sufficient enough to supplant an incumbent based on his or her fiscal policy decisions or proposals.

A number of other possibilities (related more to OECD countries, ignoring extreme outliers of the developing world) may have an influence over the electorate's response to a legislator that is known to be favorable to austerity policies. Noting the impossibility of measuring the dominant party of a government based on the personalities of its leaders, style of the party leadership, or more, it can be hard to find a way to establish a relative ability to withstand political criticism. It is also tough to test the political strength of seemingly weak governments, as the coalitions predominantly found in European political systems can sometimes be stronger than a government dominated by a single, splintered party. Combining these intuitive speed bumps to usual empirical testing methodologies, Alesina pronounced that "austerity does not systematically lead to an electoral defeat."[27]

Some of the techniques applied by Alesina and others to attempt to analyze the electoral consequences or benefits of supporting FCs are important to study and understand, for the sake of knowing why it is so tough to understand the implications for elections. A classic 1998 example compiled data from nineteen OECD countries to consider whether FCs led to a penalty at election time. To do so, the authors examined the ideological bent of the parties in power in government at a particular point in time through a new variable that accounted for the dominance of a particular party, as well as the change in the head of government. Theoretically, if there is a shift in either, then the incumbent party (also represented by their ideological beliefs) was voted out of office due to disagreements over the results of their proposed and implemented policies (or lack thereof). If the ideology of the government is aligned with the ideology of the head of state, and there is a shift in government following a period of FC, then there is strong evidence that voters chose against reelection due to those policies. On the other hand, if reelection correlated with an FC or fiscal stimulus than perhaps voters rewarded incumbents for their efforts. In order to attempt to ensure that the FC was a dominant issue, the authors studied only consolidations that were of a significant magnitude (in this study they had to be at least 1.5 percent of GDP). The results seemed to align with those of more recent times: letting the fiscal policy reigns free doesn't necessarily mean a bonus at the polls. Voters don't always see fiscal extravagancy as a benefit and therefore don't vote like they agree with those that impose such policies. In fact, the opposite may be true. A government that tightens the fiscal reigns may be rewarded with *more* time in office.[28]

Throughout history incumbents have used economic indicators (the ones that were favorable during their term) to convince the voter that the economy is on a swell ride to happy town, all due to the efforts of the public servant. Sometimes, though more rarely in increasingly transparent government statistical organizations (especially across the developing world), statistics have even been manipulated to present a rosier outlook than may be the case otherwise[29] to extend a perceived advantage based on the conventional knowledge that voters pay attention to macroeconomic statistics and give credit to incumbents when they improve. Yet, across developed countries, economic growth has had little impact on the probability of reelection success.[30] In fact, in some cases, unexpected economic growth in an election year can cause suspicion (see previous note on shifty, pre-election GDP indicators in the United States), thereby having a negative effect on the voting tendencies of at least a segment of the electorate. Those who trust the validity of government statistics with newly updated methodologies precariously close to an election season are likely supporters of the incumbent in the first place, while those who are suspicious of the positive improvement in the macroeconomic environment were likely already suspicious of the candidate for reelection.

Due to the unfortunate lack of evidence supporting the influence of macro-indicators on election outcomes, Brender and Drazen took a stab at trying to find a causal effect in the midst of the 2008 global recession.[31] By studying both developed and developing country political situations, "new and old democracies," governments run by presidents and parliaments, "countries with proportional or majoritarian electoral systems," and countries with "different levels of democracy" (350 election campaigns in 74 countries), the examination focused on the question of whether fiscal expansion policies (aka fiscal stimuli) raise the chances of an incumbent getting reelected. Conclusion? There is zero evidence[32] that increasing a deficit during an election year makes for a good campaign plan and an improvement in the probability of election success. In fact, voters were found to be a bit more sophisticated than politicians anticipated and voted less often for an incumbent in situations in which the deficit increased during an election year. It turns out that intentionally worsening a country's fiscal position in an election year—ostensibly to offer your constituents some sort of perceived benefit—isn't the strategy for success that some have previously thought.

In the wake of prominent and widespread FC plans in the last decade, others have taken a more direct look at how "politically destabilizing" austerity plans are for those that choose to implement them.[33] His examination concurred that FCs don't necessarily beget political losses. While a negative political response is expected and can be prevalent following austerity, savvy political leaders often find a way to mitigate the potential losses that have been theorized in previous research, instead of guaranteeing reelection.

Given the real-world practice of implementing fiscal plans over multiple years, how have elected officials fared? Are these plans affected by the political cycle? Policymakers may be more likely to pass and execute a plan when they don't have the worry of a pending election hanging over their heads. In fact, the data seems to show that governments push for an FC as far away from the next election as possible (or as close to the previous one).[34] This is either a smart, intentional strategy—politicians are cunning enough to know that even if all works very poorly for the policymaker, voters may forget about the tragedy by the time elections roll back around again—or a newly elected group of political leaders were elected to put into place a plan that they campaigned on and they realize that the momentum compels immediate action in order to guarantee policy success. Regardless, it does seem that politicians have a bit of a fear of reprisal, attempting to enact FCs early on so that the kinks can be worked out long before the next election day. A various array of compounding variables within an economy may work in favor of macroeconomic correction, no matter how bad the outcome may have been in the face of the austere policies alone. Even if the economy doesn't improve as promised, early implementation may also allow a party or individual to diffuse blame for poor economic results across other policy choices, or other politicians (*it was my predecessor's fault* is a lasting classic).

While there is little evidence that FCs are harmful to elected officials that implement them, there is evidence of a trend in the types of plans advocated for. Despite the clear indication that there is a consistently more positive benefit with regard to economic performance from FCs based on government expenditure cuts, governmental leaders still pick tax-focused policies as their favorite. Furthermore, historical data, especially since the most recent global recession, shows that taxation-focused FCs are strongly correlated with high turnover in governments. This is part of the original paradox stated in the beginning of this book: even knowing the benefit of a spending-focused FC, whether due to better GDP performance or electoral outcomes, policymakers often favor raising taxes as their policy of choice for correcting fiscal imbalances.

Though seemingly paradoxical, there are rational reasons behind policymakers actions (though not always correct or justified). First, given policymakers' and voters' lack of patience, it's easier to visualize and obtain a quick response from a tax hike. If a revenue boost is needed, a tax increase can have an immediate effect (regardless of the disproportionate magnitude in response anticipated, i.e., a tax increase of a certain percentage will not increase tax revenues by the same percentage). A broad-based standard increase in tax rates is easier to understand than cutting government spending, which inevitably leads to the fight over which cuts are laid on which government functions. Even if voters disagree with a tax increase, the direct nature of most tax adjustments is easy to understand and allows a voter to gauge the impact it will have. But the effects of government spending cuts are less apparent, leading to confusion and an opportunity for detractors and competing parties to develop effective counterpoints. A general statement that government spending will be cut by X percent is meaningless in the eyes of many, but when voters notice—or if opposing parties are convincing enough—that those cuts will be applied to medical benefits, there may be an adverse reaction at the polls. Oftentimes the fear of the unknown is worse than other policy solutions.

Second, the effects can be better targeted to specific groups through tax channels. Most call these distributional concerns, whereas a policymaker is worried about which segments of society (various socioeconomic groups, for example) may be affected by revenue adjustments. If government spending–focused austerity measures lead to the least-bad effect on economic output, the spending cutbacks that will have the largest effect on total spending are often within programs that benefit lower income individuals. Considering the U.S. example, various social security and health entitlements are projected by the CBO to grab a much larger percentage of total budget over the next twenty years.[35] A more effective plan to cut government expenditures would surely focus on the largest drivers of spending, such as these Social Security and Medicare programs. Yet, very few policymakers have the appetite to face the angry granny lobby, or risk being featured in political attack ads that pit the elected official against a low-income family. It's just terrible politics.

If you never thought that politicians and economists could get along, well, you were mostly right. But, quite often, they find an intersection in which their work collides. Even though few politicos have backgrounds in economic theory, with experience putting together empirical analyses with real-world data, they nevertheless are required to make decisions based on the best information they can gather. Economists are tasked with making the most compelling cases for their research in language that the average elected official can understand, which is generally outside of the natural range of the academic. Voters and privately acting advocates thereby serve an important and irreplaceable function. Civil engagement in the face of fiscal crises may require more than picking the most well-liked candidate, but educating policymakers on the best policies and/or choosing the one that will most likely follow the path that you know to be most suitable. This can be a daunting task, but for democratic institutions to work most efficiently, politicians can't be swayed by uninformed voters who misunderstand issues, but should be motivated and free to apply the policies that are best supported by the data. A well-oiled democracy doesn't require just a congenial relationship between academia and politics, but a well-informed intermediary that can serve as the information liaison between the two.

NOTES

1. Barry Weingast, Kenneth Shepsle, and Christopher Johnsen, "The Political Economy of Benefits and Costs: A Neoclassical Approach to Distributive Politics," *Journal of Political Economy* no. 89 (1981): 642.

2. Weingast, et al., "The Political Economy," 643.

3. Signe Krogstrup and Wyplosz, Charles, "Dealing with the Deficit Bias: Principles and Policies," in *Policy Instruments for Sound Fiscal Policies*, eds. J. Ayuso-i-Casals, S. Deroose, E. Flores, and L. Moulin (London: Palgrave Macmillan, 2009), 23–50.

4. Krogstrup and Charles, "Dealing with the Deficit Bias."

5. In a famous U.S. example, President George H. W. Bush, the forty-first president of the United States, campaigned on a famous line from a 1988 speech, "Read my lips: no new taxes." Of course, we all know what happened next—new taxes.

6. David Romer, *Advanced Macroeconomics* (New York: McGraw-Hill, 2012), 605.

7. Romer, *Advanced Macroeconomics*, 606.

8. Mark Blyth, *Austerity: The History of a Dangerous Idea* (Oxford: Oxford University Press, 2013).

9. Blyth, *Austerity*, 52–53.

10. See previously discussed work on Alberto Alesina. There have been cases in which austerity can be expansionary, especially when reliant upon spending cuts instead of tax increases. However, that is not the norm. Alternatively, Alesina advanced the idea that government spending cuts were the best type of austerity because they are less harmful to economic performance than hiking taxes, but aren't necessarily expansionary.

11. Francesco Giavazzi, "The 'stimulus debate' and the Golden Rule of Mountain Climbing," *VoxEU*, July 22, 2010, https://voxeu.org/article/stimulus-debate-and-gold en-rule-mountain-climbing.

12. The NBER, based in the United States, is one of the world's most respected economics research institutions, has been home to 29 Nobel Prize winners, 13 presidents of the U.S. president's Council of Economic Advisers, and 1400 leading professors at academic institutions across North America. They also have a powerful little committee that decides when recessions have commenced or ended in the United States.

13. Sebastian Dellepiane-Avellaneda, "The Political Power of Economic Ideas: The Case of 'Expansionary Fiscal Contractions,'" *The British Journal of Politics and International Relations* no. 17 (2015): 396.

14. For example, Ilzetzki, et al. find negative multipliers in highly indebted countries. The logic? If you already have a lot of debt and you decide to spend more, you may have a big tax increase coming, along with some pesky free-market risk premium hikes from creditors, which can impede the propensity to consume and invest. Ethan Ilzetzki, Enrique G. Mendoza, and Carlos A. Véghc, "How Big (Small?) Are Fiscal Multipliers?" *Journal of Monetary Economics* 60, no. 2 (March 2013): 239–254.

15. Dellepiane-Avellaneda, "The Political Power of Economic Ideas," 396.

16. European Commission. "Public Finances in EMU 2000," *European Economy 3/2000*, Brussels: European Commission (2000).

17. Antonio Afonso, "Expansionary Fiscal Consolidations in Europe. New evidence," *Applied Economics Letters* 17, no. 2 (2010): 105–109.

18. European Commission, "Public Finances in EMU 2007," *European Economy 3/2007*, Brussels: European Commission (2007).

19. Martin Larch and Alessandro Turrini, "Received Wisdom and Beyond: Lessons from Fiscal Consolidations in the EU," *EC European Economy* (2008): 320.

20. Larch and Turrini, "Received Wisdom and Beyond."

21. Dellepiane-Avellaneda, "The Political Power of Economic Ideas," 399.

22. Remember Ireland's 32 percent deficit to GDP ratio?

23. As of 2019, Italy, Spain, and Greece all have youth unemployment rates (eighteen- to twenty-five-year olds) that exceed 30 percent. Who is going to pay Grandma's hospital bills?

24. James A. Buchanan and Richard E. Wagner, *Democracy in Deficit: The Political Legacy of Lord Keynes* (New York: Academic Press, 1977).

25. Alberto Alesina, Carlo Favero, and Francesco Giavazzi, *Austerity: When It Works and When It Doesn't* (Princeton: Princeton University Press, 2019).

26. "Most Important Problem," *Gallup*, accessed February 18, 2019, https://ne ws.gallup.com/poll/1675/most-important-problem.aspx.

27. Alesina et al., *Austerity*, 175.

28. Alberto Alesina, Roberto Perotti, and Jose Tavares, "The Political Economy of Fiscal Adjustments," *Brookings Papers on Economic Activity* no. 1 (1998): 199.

29. Just before a recent presidential election in the United States, for instance, the methodologies for measuring GDP were revised to include research and development expenditures. Since research and development became part of the big "I" (which stands for "investment") in the equation that captures aggregate economic output, the methodological shift gave current and future GDP growth the perception that it improved more than anticipated. Informed individuals noticed and accounted for the difference, but how many voters really paid attention to what was happening behind the scenes?

30. Adi Brender and Allan Drazen, "How Do Budget Deficits and Economic Growth Affect Reelection Prospects? Evidence from a Large Panel of Countries," *American Economic Review* no. 98 (2008): 2203.

31. Brender and Drazen, "How Do Budget Deficits and Economic Growth Affect Reelection Prospects?"

32. If you love the excitement of the more climactic moments in life, economics may not be your thing. "Zero evidence," which is often stated as "failed to reject the null hypothesis" in statistics, is the most common conclusion in most studies.

33. Paul L. Posner, "The Politics of Fiscal Austerity: Democracies and Foresight," *Indiana Journal of Global Legal Studies* no. 2 (2015): 433.

34. Alesina, et al., *Austerity*, 181.

35. "Social Security," Congressional Budget Office (CBO), accessed February 19, 2019, https://www.cbo.gov/topics/social-security.

Part Two

SOME INTERESTING CASES

WHAT HAPPENED WHEN, WHERE, AND WHY

Chapter 6

Hellenic Hellions or Heroes of Hellas?

The Greeks are an exceptional people. Resting at the crossroads of three continents, some say they are also at the crossroads of human development. Having given birth to the first civilized societies in Europe, it also gifted democracy to the world and all of its abundantly amazing ramifications—with a few exceptions, of course. Its influence on Western civilization, and hence the entire world, in the culinary arts (who doesn't like a good Gyro?), literature, political science (though we might regret this one), sports, and mathematical and scientific advances is indisputable, while one of the longest and most beautiful coastlines in the world exemplified by Santorini's ever-present contribution to computer screensavers and home calendars has brought pleasure to millions through today. The field of economics today likely wouldn't exist had the Greeks not first considered how mathematics, philosophy, and science interact in the real world (another advancement we might regret).

The Hellenic Republic, however, isn't good at everything. In fact, in recent years, they have been flat terrible at managing their country's finances.

Not long ago they proved to be a booming society of competent fiscal managers, providing for a strong economy that wasn't weighed down by structural limitations and monies owed to the rest of the world. Before its famous recent crises, the Greek economy became a well-developed, advanced, high-income country that ranked among the middle of the pack of European nations in terms of GDP. Per the *Human Development Index*—a UN composite of life expectancy, per capita income, and education levels—Greece has improved substantially between the period 1990 and 2017, increasing its composite index score by more than 15 percent, putting it in the top 31 in the world. With a service sector–based economy, long, healthy life spans, and a knowledgeable citizenry that earns a comfortable living, Greece hasn't done that terribly for itself.

But something happened when Greece joined the Economic and Monetary Union (EMU) of the EU that seem to make its economic planners go a little crazy. Many will say that the subsequent financial, fiscal, and humanitarian crises were a result of the imposing requirements of the EMU, while others say incompetent leadership led to the major hiccups of the 2010s. In the following I will discuss some of the events that led up to the Greek crises and some of the causes for its inception, while also considering how Greece's deficits and debt combined with a worldwide recession to put it out of its misery (temporarily). Did the required FC policies put into practice in Greece force it into an economic doomsday? Or, was it a result of its own "creative" accounting and profligate government spending?

THE GOOD TIMES

By most accounts, Greece's economy was steamrolling ahead nicely prior to joining the EU and undergoing an onslaught of attacks by multiple crises from just about everywhere, as they might describe it. In 1980, Greece wasn't significantly differentiated from the EU or advanced country averages in GDP per capita (see figure 6.1, *Greece vs. World*), coming in at around 68 percent of the Euro average and around 60 percent of the advanced country

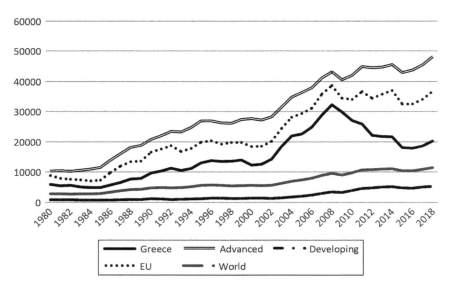

Figure 6.1   Greece vs. World. Author Generated from "GDP per capita, current prices (U.S. dollars per capita)," International Monetary Fund, Accessed July 22, 2019, https ://www.imf.org/external/datamapper/NGDPDPC@WEO/OEMDC/ADVEC/WEOWORLD.

average, respectable for a relatively small Mediterranean country.[1] Its GDP per capita was also nearly seven times that of the developing world and more than twice the world's average. Its public debt-to-GDP ratio was also a *very* impressive (compared to the world, as well as nearly any other country today) 21.4 percent in 1980, which was lower than almost every other European country at the time. Consider that today, Denmark, known as the stingy scrooge of the advanced world, has a 34 percent ratio, while the EU average is 79 percent. Though some will argue that the average Greek lives better today due to increased living standards, on the books they looked pretty good back in 1980.

In relation to its closest economic allies that help make up the GIIPS countries (see figure 6.2, *Greece vs. P(P)IIGS*), it was nearly on par with Spain and Ireland, trailing behind the economic powerhouse (believe it or not) of Italy (at least compared to other GIIPS) in 1980. As you'll see in figure 6.2, I throw in an extra *P* for Puerto Rico, just for an interesting developmental comparative analysis between Greece and its Caribbean Compatriot that is often made today between the two countries due to their vast indebtedness, lack of full economic autonomy, and the timing of recent debt defaults not long after the 2008 global shock. We will discuss this more here as well as in the next chapter, but in 1980, Greece's GDP per capita was more than 30 percent higher than Puerto Rico's.

But the EU economy took a shellacking in the early 1980s, bringing Greece down with it. Both the EU average GDP per capita and Greece's GDP per capita fell almost 20 percent by 1985 after a worldwide recession(s) of the early 1980s that hit the EU especially hard. Interestingly enough, Ireland, noted for its harsh FCs of the 1980s, only took a GDP per capita dive of approximately 6 percent. Puerto Rico, on the other hand, underwent an economic boom (while the United States also had a recession in the early 1980s), growing its GDP per capita by one-third over the same time period. As you'll see in the next chapter on Puerto Rico, both have been plagued by recessionary periods imparted by the economies within which they are integrated or connected, but to a significantly greater magnitude (Puerto Rico experiences recessions at the same time as the United States, but always much worse, while Greece has experienced a similar phenomenon versus the EU). In the particular case of the early 1980s, Greece's deep recession took a back seat to Puerto Rico's growth.

But in the late 1980s, Greece's economy experienced a revival. Again spurred by massive growth across the EU, Greece averaged 15 percent GDP per capita growth in the late 1980s, surpassing Portugal and Puerto Rico with ease by 1990. However, its growth still paled that of Spain, Italy, and Ireland, which all grew at a faster rate over the same time period. By 1990, Greece's GDP per capita was only 70 percent of Spain's, 47 percent of Italy's, and 71

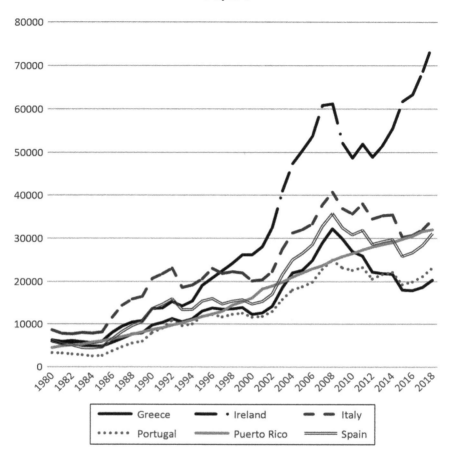

Figure 6.2   Greece vs. P(P)IIGS. Author Generated from "GDP per capita, current prices (U.S. dollars per capita)," International Monetary Fund, Accessed July 22, 2019, https ://www.imf.org/external/datamapper/NGDPDPC@WEO/OEMDC/ADVEC/WEOWORLD.

percent of Ireland's. Notwithstanding a second half turnaround, debt-to-GDP went through the roof in the 1980s, going from 21 percent (lower than almost all the GIIPS) in 1980 to well over 90 percent by the early 1990s, the second highest rate among the GIIPS. This was the beginning of the unhappy ending that we know today.

From 1990 to 1995, Greece again turned a significant growth corner. Despite being undercut by a 7 percent GDP fall in 1993, it averaged GDP per capita growth of 9 percent over the period, a staggering pace that every grow-ing country wishes to maintain over its lifespan (but that darn business cycle just won't allow). Over this pre-European Zone entry time period, it managed to improve from a paltry 70 percent of Spain's GDP per capita to 84 percent in 1995, stayed well above Portugal and Puerto Rico, and grew from 47 to 63 percent of Italy's GDP per capita, but fell slightly behind Ireland's growth (was 71 percent in 1990 and 68 percent of its GDP per capita in 1995). Overall, Greece's performance was a good showing for the EU, putting in strong contention for the highly coveted award of being accepted as a full member into the monetary union that would become the Eurozone (EZ).

Between the early 1980s and the mid-1990s, Greece was merely part of a customs union in Europe, originally created by the *Treaty of Rome*. While the removal of borders for the purposes of trade and migration movements helped to economically integrate Greece into the rest of the European community—where smaller countries like Greece were able to benefit from larger markets, lower cross-continental costs, simpler taxation systems, and the overall opportunity to tap into the vast wealth across Europe—the temptation of being part of the oft-discussed monetary union that was to be the EU was too great to ignore. If Greece wanted to continue to dip its toes into the profitable waters that ran through Europe, it had to consider a full partnership with the newly formed EU.

As far as Greece was concerned, it was already dependent upon the economies of its neighbors and had nothing to lose, only to gain, by lobbying for and eventually joining the EU under the new *Maastricht Treaty* of the early 1990s, which is generally considered the EU's founding document. Greece's decision to get a little bit more involved in the EU's business was supported by failures in fiscal and monetary policy in the early 1990s. With an inflation rate of 20 percent in 1991, the Greeks were way out of balance with the proposed cap of 3.9 percent of the Maastricht Treaty. Maybe the EU could teach it a thing or two about monetary policy? With a budget deficit of 11.4 percent against the Maastricht's target of 3, perhaps it realized that it also wasn't a good fiscal policy manager and needed a good mentor. Whatever the reason, Greece and all its vast and impressive history was willing to give up a little of its autonomy and culture to take another step toward greater fiscal integration and full monetary policy integration with the rest of its friendly neighbors in the EU.

After 1995, Greece's decision and public support for all things Euro had a substantial economic impact. Though it failed in an early attempt to go so far as to adopt a European Constitution (they really wanted to show their love), they did however further their economic and social integration by beginning a process to comply with the "convergence criteria" set forth by the Maastricht Treaty. If Greece wanted to be a full member of the Economic and Monetary Union of the EU, this was the ticket. Be like everyone else (or at least try really hard to and act like it in public). Given the vow of monogamy that the

Greeks took toward their beloved at the EU, they eventually were given the prize, allowing them to eliminate the Drachma and take on the Euro as its one true love.

During this period of enhanced integration and promises to be good little EU children, Greek's economy began a sustained path of decent growth marked by increased investment. Its GDP per capita continued to improve, while investments into its economy were the real story of the late 1990s. The Greeks were fairly adept at wooing corporate dollars, bringing in corporate investment to the tune of 10 percent of its GDP in the late 1990s, an increase from its 1995 levels beat out only by Portugal.² Overall investment broached 23 percent, topping the pre-1996 level of 20 percent. Greece's seemingly inevitable entry into the EU seemed to provide a bit of a confidence boost to investors.

Over the same window of years that comprised the late 1990s, Greece's external indebtedness also increased. From the mid-1990s to the early 2000s, its *net foreign assets* (the total value of assets that Greece owned outside of Greece minus the total value of Greece's domestic assets owned by foreigners, including other EU members or wanna-be members) declined substantially, indicative of equally substantial *current account deficits* (a measure of Greece's foreign trade; a deficit indicates that it was importing more than exporting). Its net exports fell substantially, averaging −9.1 percent of GDP from 1996 to 2000, which led to a current account deficit that fell as a percentage of GDP by 5.7 percent over the same time period. As EU subsidies began to subside, so did Greece's net current transfers and primary income. The driving force that seemed like a significant boom to Greece's economy of the late 1990s (corporate investment) did lead to an increase in *productive capacity*³ as well, but may have begun setting the stage for the Greek government to consume and invest its own resources, while the support it thought it had from the EU economy may not have been enough to curtail what became wildly out of sync spending.

When Greece was finally allowed to kick the Drachma to the curb in 2001, growth in GDP per capita peaked at 31 percent in 2003, then averaged 13 percent between 2001 and 2008. Throughout the entire 1990s GDP per capita grew by 22 percent, but in the eight years since becoming a Euro slinger, the same indicator grew by 156 percent. Spain was the next closest GIIPS country at 140 percent over the same time, but even the next one down the list (Ireland) only got to 118 percent growth from 2001 to 2008.⁴ Greece's trade balance also floundered, deteriorating at a rate of −10.6 percent (related to GDP), across these years, contributing to its quickly growing current account deficit and external indebtedness.

Prior to entering the Eurozone, its fiscal outlook was beginning to improve in accordance with the "convergence criteria" mandated to new entrants.

Greece had to fall within certain inflation, budget deficit, debt-to-GDP, exchange rate, and interest rate targets in order to pass the EU's strict entrance exam. To do so, it tightened its fiscal belt a bit and, aided by falling interest rates, was able to stabilize the growing debt over the decade of the 1990s and land on a soft 88.5 percent debt-to-GDP ratio by the end of the decade.

Greek policymakers couldn't wait until the EZ sent over its first load of Euros so it could reverse course and bulk up on spending plans, however. With such amazing growth in Greece, its economy could have floated back toward that optimal fiscal policy path that has eluded so many for so long. It was finally their chance to get its fiscal house in order and show the world what made it so amazing back when it was known as the center of the world. But policymakers just didn't have it in them to wait it out. While they may very well have thought they were doing great things for the Greek future by borrowing to invest in its people (the debate about what was to show for that "investment" is still ongoing), from 1999 to 2009 Greece's debt ratio increased by 43 percent (from 88.5 percent debt-to-GDP in 1999 to 126.8 in 2009). The biggest jump happened between 2007 and 2009—right in the belly of the 2008 global crisis and beyond—when it increased its debt-to-GDP ratio by 23 percent in a matter of just two years.

Greece's aggregate output was booming in the years from 2000 to 2007, fueled by investment growth, consumption increases (savings fell by 6.7 percent and corporate investment also dropped a bit), and extremely loose fiscal policies. What could go wrong? A better question may be, how was the government able to borrow so much and grow its debt so quickly without anyone noticing, caring, or doing anything about it?

BIG FAT GREEK CRISIS

Looking back on the historical record, it's still difficult to know exactly how Greece got itself into the mess that quickly snowballed after the global recession. Many question whether its circumstances were entirely self-induced, one that was imposed upon them by a less friendly than expected Eurozone accomplice, or a combination of the two. Irrespective of who is to blame, there are some indicators that started to show how, when, and where Greece was able to borrow so much.

Since Greece was preparing to join one of the most powerful economic unions on the planet, while incorporating its required fiscal and monetary discipline, Greece's fiscal credibility received an instant boost in the eyes of the rest of the world. As internal demand for goods and services increased throughout the 2000s, the world (mostly the rest of the EU) was happy to offer a helping hand in the form of an extension of credit, presuming that

Greece was a safe bet—or at least much safer bet backed by the grander EU. The subsequent blow to its current account over the decade amounts to more than 6 percent of GDP, a larger decrease than Italy, Ireland, Portugal, or Spain. Lender confidence was booming across the EU, and relative improvement in the GIIPS was substantial enough to justify such lending, forcing banking sector loan rates to fall to all-time lows, keeping the spigot open for Greece's spenders.

Pre-Euro/EMU, the GIIPS had to borrow at rates in excess of 20 percent, stifling the ability to spend and invest in their economies. Intending to justify the perception as an equitable partner in the Eurozone experiment and all its Maastricht Treaty glory, the GIIPS and its EU advisers wanted to make it easier for its new economic partners to borrow, invest, and grow. To do so, it simply offered itself as a guarantor to lenders that were willing to take a risk on Greece, offering terms acceptable enough to induce as much lending as Greece was willing to borrow. Since banks had nothing but upside, some say the moral hazard that was created wasn't too different from that which developed during the U.S. financial crisis when policymakers tried to improve housing ownership with incentives that decreased lending standards. Countries with current account surpluses, such as Germany, were flush with cash but were conservative lenders. With the backing of the EU, the partnership between fiscally tight Germany, along with other core EU countries, and Greece seemed like a win-win. Not only could successful countries invest in Greece with little risk, the resulting benefits from the investment could lead to a Greek revival that would have the added bonus of Greece consumers purchasing and importing more and more from its benevolent EU partners.

Unfortunately for Greece, and all its lending partners, Greece's "investments" didn't pay off exactly as expected. As is the plight of many developing countries, aggregate economic growth led to wage growth that combined with tighter labor market reforms to make Greece far less competitive; productivity growth just couldn't keep up. Internally, the Greeks were feeling good as the government kept spending, borrowing, and offering greater benefits, a sign that inappropriately signaled to consumers that it was okay to keep borrowing as well. But, without a swift and immediate structural shift to the economy, the return on investments had little chance of turning positive.

Even before the crisis began, Greece was in an awkward and progressively perilous position. With a current account deficit of 16 percent, a government deficit of almost 7 percent, and total government debt over 103 percent, it was in a worse position than the other GIIPS; however, combined with sovereign debt exposure larger than in Italy, Spain, Portugal, and Ireland, Greece stood more vulnerable to a significant negative economic shift than the others.[5]

To boot, it was beginning to miss the fiscal targets that the *Stability and Growth Pact*[6] of the EU had laid out for its newest members. Trying and trying as it might, Greece just couldn't keep up with such strict demands as a 3 percent of GDP deficit. After closer scrutiny of Greece's finances in later years, it was noted that it was nowhere near the 3 percent standard. "When it was admitted into the Eurozone in 2002, Greece's (later revised) budget numbers showed a budget deficit of 6% of GDP. Systematic waste in spending, tax evasion, and overly optimistic revenue projections were the main causes."[7] Greece was growing, but government debt was growing much, much faster, and Greece's accountants became adept enablers that failed to alarm anyone who might have been able to help the fledgling country.

In the lead up to the crisis, the world's giant investment banks (check out the European Court of Justice's *Goldman Sachs v. Greece*, as an example) were on a tear, inventing new financial products to "help" its fine clients, while mostly helping themselves to nearly risk-free profits. While such devices as the derivative-inspired CDOs were especially rampant in the United States, the JPMorgans of the world thought it prudent to lend a hand to poor Greece by creating products that kept loans off the books and out of sight from the Stability and Growth Pact's all-seeing eye. In essence, large lenders gave Greece a lump of cash (not a loan, just don't call it a loan whatever you do) that had liens on future cash flows. It seems like a simple oversight that perhaps the EU intentionally turned a blind eye to, but for some reason the accounting standards of the Eurozone couldn't quite keep up with the trickiness of investment banks, nor the malintent (or ineptness) of a country like Greece.

Since Greece promised to comply with certain fiscal standards as part of its new club of Euro friends, it couldn't afford to be forced into fiscal discipline, so it also did what it could to "save" Greece from the Eurozone's heavy hand as they might have put it during their defense trials. Fudging the books was a necessary means to a much better end to the Greek saga. After the crisis, Greek finance lords were finally forced (under the gunpoint of more, this time seriously necessary, loans from the IMF and others) to revise their fiscal records and get a tighter grip on the truth. Instead of that required 3 percent deficit that the Eurozone mandated to get Euro access in 2001, Greece's deficit surpassed 6 percent. The 2009 government debt was also revised to show that it owed far more than it previously certified, with a deficit of around 12 percent of GDP. In 2010 its deficit was again revised to 13.6 percent of GDP—almost the highest in the world.

Greece's calculated misrepresentation of the truth took some significant intestinal fortitude, which would have all worked out well had it not been for the ensuing economic crises. The Greek economy, however, began to take it on the nose during a simultaneous pounding from three different foes.

Described as "The Three Shocks," the trifecta of pain began in 2007 with the global financial crisis.[8] Given the first hints of worldwide headwinds, foreign investors began to realize that Greece may not be able to make good on its loans. Even the fudged accounting ledgers available for public consumption couldn't hide the fatal flaws of Greece's high public debts. Greece's unwillingness and inability to self-regulate spending forced investors to doubt that they would receive the promised return to their substantial investments, leading to a sovereign debt crisis. The subsequent banking crisis didn't help as outsiders also became suspicious of the sector's solvency. Predicting massive losses, banks doubted whether it was worth the risk to continue financing operations and lending to other businesses, or even to each other. With a stalling banking system, it became difficult for economic activity to continue. A similar crisis prevailed in the United States after the housing bubble burst, when banks (unaware of who had bad mortgage loans on their books) began to cease lending to ensure they wouldn't lose too much to deadbeat borrowers.

The last crisis, that economists call a *sudden stop*, took place when foreign investors decided to leave Greece altogether. No one wanted to lend to Greece's government, banks, or private sector anymore, so all lending activity suddenly stopped. When lenders stopped lending to the government, banks stopped lending to banks or to borrowers within Greece, and everyone pulled out of Greece, things got really bad, real fast. Worse, Greece's advancing stages of development meant that it would have a harder time recovering than an emerging economy, similar to how adults recover more slowly from an ailment in later stages of life. Kids (emerging market economies) bounce back much faster from an early childhood illness; adults, like Greece, often suffer advanced complications.[9] With advanced development and outstanding debt held by businesses, consumers, and the government, the interconnected and interdependent nature of the Greek economy ensured that it would be impacted to a far greater extent and further into the future than some of its less developed neighbors.

WHAT NOW?

Just like any person who finds themselves in over their heads with debt, Greece had a few options. If an individual or company finds itself on the brink of insolvency, one can file for bankruptcy to simply wipe the slate clean (while giving a small return to borrowers from the proceeds of a few asset sales). The option is tedious, but highly useful for putting an income statement back in the black. But, the downside is a negative credit report that will likely stymie or slow any future lending, probably a good "punishment" for someone who hasn't been so good with their finances. Or, if banks are willing and perhaps significantly indebted enough and believe in a proposed turnaround plan, they can lend you more money to help get you through. For the case of a country, the same is virtually true. Scrapping the whole debt lot and defaulting on loans is sometimes the best option for a developing country with relatively small amounts of debt. Such a restructuring doesn't make lenders very happy, but in the end, they tend to get some return on their initial investment through such an orderly restructuring.

Unfortunately for Greece, the idea of an orderly restructuring didn't win the vote of the EU overseers who wanted what's best for the Greek economy (most likely because members and their financial sector friends had so much to lose in Greece). The EU stoked public fear when it suggested that the Greek economic contagion would just be too powerful to overcome, infecting the rest of the continent like the Black Plague. If Greece defaulted, so would the other GIIPS who wanted to quickly dig themselves out of their own holes, leading to an economic tidal wave that would ruin the fiscal houses of every member of the EU. Saving Greece would prove that restructuring wasn't necessary (though, repeating history, their actions would create another issue: the moral hazard).

Others, however, saw the rejection of the restructuring option for what it more likely was. Though multiple governments would suffer from an alternative bailout process, banks and the financial system were sure to benefit. Germans and French banks were especially exposed to Greek debt; in total, their loans to Greece were higher than those among any other set of countries. Under a new lending scheme, a significant loss to these loans and arguably to the economies and banking sectors of the two largest economies in Europe could be avoided.

J. Paul Getty, once the richest man in America, was known to have said this pertinent gem, "If you owe the bank $100 dollars, that's your problem; if you owe the bank $100 million, that's the bank's problem." Greece's massive debt load seemed like more of a problem for other people than the Hellenic Republic. Nearly ambivalent to its future fiscal path, political pressures skewed Greece's preferences toward a bailout.

The bailout came with conditions, however, that Greek would have chosen against with the benefit of hindsight. Given the prevalence and popularity of severely austere fiscal policies at the time, the EU joined with the IMF and the ECB (referred to as the "Troika") to offer a giant pile of money, in return for a bout of severe FCs that the Troika assumed would make everything better.

TROIKAN AUSTERITY

Critiques of the Troika reflect the severity of its disciplinarian hand. In Greece, it intended to implement some of the roughest FCs known to man, demonstrable of a willingness to do nearly anything to avoid restructuring, banking system losses, and contagion. Unfortunately, this was their first foray into the fun of austerity, and signs were suggesting that they weren't very good at it. Some have argued that communication and negotiations across the process were so poor that the fiscal adjustments plans forced upon Greece were set to fail from the beginning.[10] Others say that they were so firmly rooted in politics, avoiding any application of sound economic advice, that decision-makers couldn't possibility have had the best interest of Greece in mind.[11] To put it bluntly, the planning was poorly done, overly optimistic, and entirely unrealistic (source: the IMF itself).

Without experience, but full of gumption with a mix of bankers and do-gooders prodding from behind, the Troika chiefs laid their best "consolidate or else" plans at the feet of the Greeks. The first step in the financial aid process was the signing of a Memorandum of Understanding between the IMF, ECB, the European Commission (EC), and Greece. The 110 billion euro "loan" was supported by the Eurogroup and the IMF's Stand-by Arrangement program for member countries in serious need. The Greeks, for their part, merely had to actually (no this time, seriously) bring down their deficit to 3 percent of GDP. With a deficit topping out at about 13.6 percent of GDP in 2009, this wasn't going to be easy. Even the IMF had some doubts about Greek support for the FC plan, citing, among other probable objections, the existing, entrenched, and culturally accepted practice of paying government employees two extra months-worth of salary at the end of every year.[12] Cutting back would likely end these sorts of popular practices, making for a grumpy set of voters at the next election.

The real question is how Greece aspired to undertake the demands of the Troika's MOU. Many have attempted to analyze the precise composition of Greece's fiscal plans that were implemented in 2010 and expected to cover the period from 2010 to 2014, but the "innumerable revisions, discussions, and data adjustments resulting from the exhausting confrontations between Greek authorities and the Troika" have made it a challenge, to say the least.[13] In 2010, for example, Greece announced that it would be rolling out tax increases that were approximately 3.7 percent of GDP, with spending cuts totaling 5 percent over subsequent years of the plan. It was expected to impose zero FC in this first year, but actually pushed through tax increases of 0.5 percent and spending cuts of almost 2 percent of GDP. *Surprise!* The following year was more reliant upon tax increases to cut the deficit, but then surprised us all again by leaning more toward spending than expected, and so the process went on. All told, the plan was to cut the nasty 13.6 percent of GDP deficit to a fiscal surplus that actually surpassed 4.5 percent.[14] Such a turnaround required an equal and opposite slicing and dicing of taxes and spending mechanisms. If all went as planned—which as noted, it did not—it would be the miracle turnaround of the century.

With a firm dedication to overly optimistic planning, the Troika and Greek planners were faced with a problem when Greece's true fiscal situation was finally outed and growth ensued more slowly than projected. If the economy didn't grow as expected, they couldn't raise the revenues it planned without further consolidation. If debts were higher than they thought, the entire initial set of assumptions would have to be adjusted in order to fulfill the terms of the MOU and make the Troika, the Germans, the French, and lenders and investors everywhere a bit less uneasy about the prospects of their investments in the Greek economy. While some suggested that the solution was to take it a bit easier on Greece, perhaps relaxing the expected outcomes so that Greece didn't have to have such harsh austerity, the IMF concluded that "larger consolidation efforts" were needed.[15]

In the updated Troika agreement, Greek policymakers committed to continue with its initial plan to achieve a deficit of only 1 percent in 2012, but cut back on its plan for a 4.5 percent surplus in 2014. Its first plan consisted of government spending–focused FCs that made up more than half of the total plan. Those nice little thirteenth and fourteenth month bonuses were cut, as were some transfers and investments by the government. Taxes were increased with a higher VAT, as fees were increased on vice goods (alcohol and cigarettes, which Greeks probably needed the most at this very moment), along with a surprise assessment on the one group of productive members of society—firms that were still, somehow, able to make a profit.

Did it all work? Did the FCs turn out to be profitable for the Hellions of Hellas? Did the citizenry turn from its angry ways and eventually congratulate the IMF? Well, all of this is yet to be seen. But in the years after the FC plan's initial implementation, Greek GDP per capita began to dive. In 2009, it lost 9.5 percent of its GDP per capita. In 2011, 4 percent, and in 2012 14 percent. GDP fell and fell fast.

As the Troika's agreement terms were based on Greece's ability to achieve deficit levels as a percentage of GDP, the faster Greece's GDP fell, the more difficult it was for a deficit to catch up. For example, what if Greece's current deficit is 3 billion euros and its GDP is 100 billion euros (made up numbers to keep it simple), which equates to a 3 percent debt-to-GDP ratio. If the new austerity measures cut the GDP to 50 billion euros and the deficit remained at 3 billion euros, the debt-to-GDP ratio jumps to 6 percent! Greece would have to cut its deficit in half at the same time that its GDP fell, in order to maintain the desired ratio. As the GDP fell over the years after the plan's implementation, the Troika failed to consider just how much of an effect the austerity would have on Greek economic growth. Given the politics involved and the lack of economic foresight, the plan never had a chance to succeed.

Greece's subsequent defaults, plan shifts, and eventual economic turnaround have been discussed more thoroughly in recent news than is worth reiterating here. The real question as it relates to this book is whether earlier estimates based on past FCs were so incorrect as to improperly choose and apply the FC plans that the Troika and Greece chose. The Troika, with all its faults, seemingly attempted to impale Greece with only the harshest set of austerity measures that it could handle. Since it set out to save Greece, when earlier Greek defaults and restructuring might have helped it save itself, it can be implied that it never meant for the ruins of Athens to be a metaphor for its future economy.

For its part, the Troika also underestimated the dynamic macroeconomic effects caused by other variables which likely led to imperfect predictability. Olivier Blanchard, former chief economist at the IMF, conceded in 2014 that the timing for and application of Greek FCs was just all off, for several reasons.[16] The monetary policy applied to the suboptimal monetary union[17] that is the new Eurozone had already called for Zero Interest Rate Policy (ZIRP by its much more catchy acronym), leaving few tools to help the likes of Greece and its friends in the GIIPS. Blanchard furthered that FCs were so intense that the predictive power of prior modelling wouldn't hold true under these unique conditions. Others suggest that one of the real reasons for the mistaken predictions was that falling output correlated with an increase in long-term interest rates, exacerbating the need for austerity as aggregate output would fall as a result.[18]

The threats by the Troika for harsher austerity and fewer loans were met with threats of Greek defaults and all out total Grexit. To date, it's not easy to decide who was ever really right, if anyone at all was. Greece was able to eventually turn fiscal deficits into surpluses, improving from a 5 percent debt-to-GDP deficit in 2015, to a 0.5 percent surplus in 2016 and 1.10 percent in 2018, with a current account nearly balanced. While some point to this as success, the people of Greece have suffered tremendously as the country has lost growth opportunities, suffered under untenable debt loads and constant threats of another recession, maintained high unemployment (most notably reaching 28 percent, with youth unemployment approaching half of those aged under twenty-four, potentially losing a generation of worker experience), and untold additional social consequences.

The faults run deep and wide, while the resulting lessons and conclusions are vast and compelling. While Greece and its counterparts across the EU were all impacted, the lessons on FCs for economic researchers will continue to confound data and results, leading many to the conclusion that there is no single, righteous model of best practice when it comes to repairing a nation's fiscal condition. Every country is different.

Though it may seem to some that Greece's style of FC didn't bode so well for the Hellenic Republic, others contend that it would have held under certain conditions and point to examples of how that may have looked. In the next section, I delve into Puerto Rico's finances, a unique case altogether for a number of reasons, but altogether more similar to Greece than many other countries. Does Puerto Rico support the Greek case, or demonstrate an alternative path the Greece could have taken?

NOTES

1. All of the following macroeconomic indicators are courtesy of the International Monetary Fund, unless otherwise noted, and can be found on its website. "Datasets," International Monetary Fund, accessed January 10, 2019, https://www.imf.org/exter nal/datamapper/datasets.

2. Pierre-Olivier Gourinchas, Thomas Philippon, and Dimitri Vayanos, "The Analytics of the Greek Crisis," *NBER Macroeconomics Annual* 31, no. 1 (2017): 1–81.

3. Productive capacity is another mythical indicator established by the economics community, which attempts to measure the maximum amount of economic output that a country can have. Here, I am suggesting that Greece's productive capacity was increased due to drastic increases in investment, output per worker, and so on. However, in the aggregate, I call it "mythical" because there is no agreed-upon method for measuring how much an economy is "able" to produce; we can only attempt to measure what it actually does. The rest is more or less a theoretically based best guess.

4. "GPD Per Capita, Current Prices," *International Monetary Fund*, accessed July 22, 2019, https://www.imf.org/external/datamapper/NGDPDPC@WEO/OEM DC/ADVEC/WEOWORLD.

5. Gourinchas, Philippon, and Vayanos, "The Analytics of the Greek Crisis," 14.

6. The Stability and Growth Pact was created as sort of a fiscal Big Brother, monitoring countries' finances to ensure that fiscal discipline was maintained across the EU.

7. Alberto Alesina, Carlo Favero, and Francesco Giavazzi, *Austerity: When It Works and When It Doesn't* (Princeton: Princeton University Press, 2019), 149.

8. Gourinchas, Philippon, and Vayanos, "The Analytics of the Greek Crisis," 14.

9. Gourinchas, Philippon, and Vayanos, "The Analytics of the Greek Crisis."

10. Sylvia Ardagna and Francesco Caselli, "The Political Economy of the Greek Debt Crisis: A Tale of Two Bailouts," *American Economic Journal: Macroeconomics* 6, no. 4 (2014): 291–323.

11. Alesina, Favero, and Giavazzi, *Austerity*, 152.

12. What may seem crazy to the average American is actually a fairly customary practice across Latin America and even in Europe. For your holiday bonus, you get a month's pay. Then generally, the second month of pay is disbursed two other times throughout the year. Even in Puerto Rico, part of the United States but still part of Latin America in many ways had something similar, but call it a Christmas bonus. Today, Puerto Rican employers, including the government, are required to pay 6 percent of annual salary (up to a max) to its employees, a point of strong contention

with bondholders who haven't been paid a dime by the Puerto Rican government since 2014.

13. Alesina, Favero, and Giavazzi, *Austerity*, 152.

14. Alesina, Favero, and Giavazzi, *Austerity*, 153. The authors attempted to construct a chart that followed the expected, unexpected, and announced FC plans for Greece over the years of the plan. Even these economists and experts on austerity had to admit that the plan was "entirely outside the realm of good economics."

15. European Commission, "The Economic Adjustment Programme for Greece," *Occasional Paper no. 72*, European Commission (December 2010).

16. See Olivier Blanchard and Daniel Leigh, "Learning About Fiscal Multipliers from Growth Forecast Errors," *IMF Economic Review* 62, no. 2 (2014): 179–212.

17. Google Scholar "asymmetric monetary union" to learn more about how the EU's monetary policy may be "suboptimal" for Greece and others.

18. Alesina, Favero, and Giavazzi, *Austerity*, 158.

Chapter 7

The Enchanted (and indebted) Island of Puerto Rico

Think you had it rough during the recent housing, financial, or fiscal crises? Your afflictions likely don't compare to the economic woes of Puerto Rico (unless you are Greece). Starting as a colony of Spain, then choosing to become a semiautonomous territory of the United States, Puerto Rico had a path of economic development that diverted from most successful countries, including those of the EU. Confined to the economic boundaries (its successes and policy limitations) of the United States, one of Puerto Rico's biggest hindrances has always been its inability to decide whether to get out of its parents' basement, or shack up as a permanent and contributing member of the household.

After deciding that the agrarian life wasn't the most profitable, Puerto Rico built a dependency upon the U.S. economy, which seemed like a good idea—at first. When Congress repealed a set of tax incentives that helped make it a manufacturing center, a decade-long shrinking economy ensued that subsequently led to an unprecedented run-up in government debt. Still struggling to escape the shackles of a depression—an economic catastrophe amplified by recent natural disasters—Puerto Rico has made nearly every austerity choice available in a policymakers' toolkit, only to fail to cover its debt obligations just a few years after the Global Crisis of 2008, eventually filing for a form of "bankruptcy." Today, Puerto Rico has a new series of FCs being considered at the direction and discretion of a Congressionally mandated fiscal control board. Will new austerity help it to right its fiscal ship, or will Puerto Rico need other, more substantial reforms?

Some have long-questioned whether its status has served as an impediment to economic growth. Should the island continue to succumb to the monetary and fiscal policy (with some degree of leeway on the latter) that Uncle Sam bestows, in order to guarantee a basic level of guaranteed support

151

and benefits? Should it become an island-state (i.e., a separate country) that risks it all on the prospects of greener economic pastures, in the hopes that it becomes more like Singapore than Cuba? Or should it leverage an already integrated society to further establish itself as one that is fully American by becoming state number 51, with all the benefits and pleasures (and costs) that come with statehood? It's an important decision that will have vast economic implications for Puerto Rico for the foreseeable future, while also affecting revenues to the U.S. treasury and other Americans in a number of other ways.

Questioning how they have fared to date, as well as speculating on how things will turn out for the little Caribbean island, makes for quite the interesting case study. Considering simultaneously the differences between Puerto Rico and other nations with similar debt concerns (PIIGS/GIIPS of the EU come to mind) also calls for some entertaining analyses related to FC policies.

HOW IT ALL GOT STARTED

Puerto Rico was founded by Spanish expeditions in 1493 when Spanish ships were cruising for a cool spot to hang out. Realizing that the island had lovely, untouched beaches, Spain decided it was theirs, and made it a colony of the Spanish crown for more than 400 years (they *really* liked the beaches).[1] When the United States romped Spain in the Spanish-American War of 1898, it acquired a number of territories, including Puerto Rico. The United States introduced a government that was subject to its federal laws, but provided a range of latitude and autonomy in setting local policies. After a series of Supreme Court cases, known as the *Insular Cases*, it was held that because Puerto Rico is an unincorporated territory, it would not be subject to the revenue clauses of the Constitution, yet would still maintain a number of fundamental rights. Interpretation: Puerto Rico doesn't have to pay U.S. federal taxes, but still gets to act like someone that does. Puerto Ricans were granted U.S. citizenship in 1917 and the territory officially became a "Commonwealth" under its constitution in 1952, a status that it maintains today.

Although afforded some autonomy, Puerto Rico has never had full authority over its own economy and government. A 1917 law gave Puerto Rico the right to levy its own local tax policy, yet, in 1920 they were seemingly stripped of the privilege of having any direct trading routes when a law was passed that forced ships to first go through mainland U.S. ports before heading to Puerto Rico, inflating the costs of all goods brought to the island. Some have put the cost for this process in today's dollars at somewhere in the billions of dollars to the local economy, or approximately 1–2 percent of GDP.[2] Puerto Rico is also required to maintain the U.S. federal minimum wage—which some have estimated to be nearly twice what the prevailing equilibrium wage rate actually is, limiting the total number of employed individuals on the island—and has to apply the same labor and environmental standards as the rest of the United States.

Given the prominent place in fiscal policy literature related to the simultaneous influence of trade and monetary policy, it is useful to also note that Puerto Rico does not have the ability to adjust either according to its local needs. It must fully comply with the trade policies of the United States and is under the monetary umbrella of the U.S. Federal Reserve. With a disparate and unique history and economy, the monetary union that captured both Puerto Rico and the rest of the United States is similar to the asymmetric and inefficient union that covers both the core countries of the EU and Greece.[3] The correlation between the business cycles of Puerto Rico and the rest of the United States are sometimes negative; applying the same monetary policy that the United States applies to the rest of the country often does more harm than good in Puerto Rico. For instance, as the U.S. economic growth rate turned positive in the third quarter of 2009, Puerto Rico was just hitting the bottom of its recession. When U.S. monetary policy began to tighten, the island's economy was pushed further into a recession. If Puerto Rico had its own sovereign monetary policy and central bank, it would likely have maintained expansionary policies for a longer period of time.

Despite these impairments, the United States did attempt to leverage Puerto Rico's tax autonomy to the advantage of both Puerto Rico and the rest of the United States. In 1921, the United States sought to boost economic growth by providing corporate tax exemptions for all U.S. corporations with income derived in Puerto Rico, while Puerto Rico doubled down with its own local income and other tax incentives. For corporations, the benefit was a new "U.S.-based" location that provided for a lower tax bill. Along with a source of cheaper labor and the advantages of being a U.S. territory, labor-intensive manufacturing boomed in Puerto Rico. Between 1950 and the mid-1970s, output per employee grew by nearly 5 percent per year, similar to the rapid growth seen in East Asia over the same time period.

In 1950, GDP per worker broached 30 percent of the U.S. average, while in 1980 it peaked near 74 percent, making Puerto Rico one of Latin America's most developed societies and one of the fastest economic turnarounds the region has ever seen. Today, GDP per capita in Puerto Rico is about half (approximately 30,000 dollars per year) of that of its U.S. benefactors (about 60,000 dollars), but is still higher than any other Latin American country (Panama is broaching 29,000 dollars per capita, while the next contender, Chile, is butting up against 27,000[4]).[5] Despite its historic developmental concerns, it seems that the U.S. affiliation was still an unprecedented advantage.

Even in the face of strong macroeconomic growth—at least as measured by sheer GDP power—labor force participation has remained far below 50 percent since 1960, compared to the U.S. rate, which has climbed to above 60 percent.[6] Gross National Income (GNI) has also declined as a fraction of

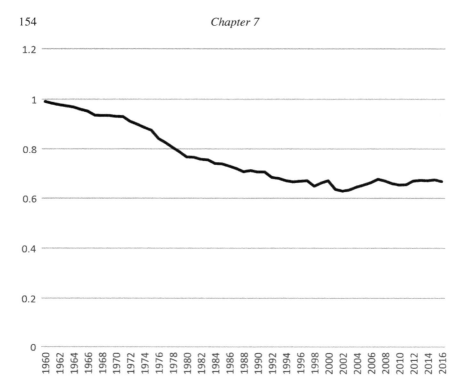

Figure 7.1 Puerto Rico GNI. Author Generated from "Puerto Rico," World Bank, Accessed July 22, 2019, https://data.worldbank.org/country/puerto-rico.

GDP during this time period (see figure 7.1, *Puerto Rico GNI*), demonstrating a propensity for foreign corporations and individuals to transfer the economic benefit of their output to areas outside of Puerto Rico. No, this wasn't what Congressional tax experts anticipated.

As of 1976, U.S. government tax incentives were found to contribute to lower federal tax revenues and sparse employment growth in Puerto Rico. What did legislators do? Some suggested they just remove any tax advantages and let the Caribbean colony fend for itself. Puerto Rico had the same opportunity to let the private sector work its magic as any other country in the world (or U.S. state for that matter), according to this line of thinking. The government will likely do more harm than good by implementing policies that are certain to have even more unintended consequences.

Others objected, suggesting that it was the obligation of the most developed country on the planet to take care of its dependents. Not ready to kick Puerto Rico out of the house, many argued that Puerto Rico's condition was the result of U.S. hegemony in the first place (though the comparison to the rest of Spain's former colonies suggests that it is still better off than it might have been had the United States not taken it as a spoil of the Spanish-American war). Plus, Puerto Ricans were—and still are—*American* citizens. Popular opinion in the United States has always leaned strongly in favor of offering a helping hand to fellow Americans, regardless of their location or whether any perceived wounds are self-inflicted. U.S. legislators decided, therefore, to replace the tax exemption policy in favor of one that allowed Puerto Rico to create domestic tax credit incentives for U.S. corporations already paying "foreign" taxes to Puerto Rico. For the purposes of taxation, Puerto Rico is now considered a foreign entity to the United States.

The new tax scheme seemed successful at first, contributed to the vast growth of wholly owned subsidiaries in Puerto Rico. However, the modification of incentives led to a shift from economic development in industries that required local labor, to those capital-intensive industries that moved high volumes of dollars, but made substantially smaller contributions to the local economy. Laxed employment growth led to decades of Congressional scrutiny over the real benefits of federal tax laws related to Puerto Rico. Were the tax laws benefitting Puerto Rico's long-term economic development or American corporate bottom lines at the expense of the American taxpayer? Uncle Sam wanted his money, or at least wanted to see some return on his investment. With neither in hand, something else had to be done.

Over the six decades since becoming a "commonwealth" of the United States, Puerto Rico has effectively transformed from an agriculturally based economy to one based on industrial manufacturing to the knowledge-based economy of today, yet it is still directly reliant on the U.S. Federal Government. Given the economic ties, but historically weaker and mercurial economy, Puerto Rico has been more greatly impacted by the contractionary episodes of the U.S. business cycle than the rest of the country, making for a not-so-fun economic rollercoaster ride since the 1970s. During oil crisis–led shocks that led to U.S. recessions in the 1970s and interest rate–based shocks of the early 1980s, Puerto Rico's economy was crippled by longer and vastly deeper contractionary periods, aggravated by the ever-changing minds of U.S. policymakers who, quite frankly, just didn't know what to do with the tenuous economy that is now home to millions of American citizens. Without a clear plan, poor growth continuously demanded haphazard spending and investment, which more often resulted in high debt than a sustainable path to economic success.

RISING DEBTS OF THE 1980s

Prior to the 1980s, the focus was on incentives that attracted large, export-oriented, U.S. multinationals that operated manufacturing facilities in pharmaceuticals, electronics, chemicals, and more, all of which flourished on the island. After Congress replaced Puerto Rico's corporate tax incentive scheme with a new one in 1976,[7] along with a local corporate tax adjustment in 1978 that further reduced the percentage of revenues that corporations had to send to the tax man, Puerto Rico's development began to focus on the high-tech and finance sectors. Puerto Rico's GNP[8] doubled between 1980 and 1990, from 11 billion dollars to nearly 22 billion, though its real GDP growth rate had fallen to a paltry 2.3 percent.[9]

Despite what seemed like an economic revival, something was askew on the *Enchanted Island* (a nickname given to the island, because its natural beauty will enchant even the most angry of debtors). After Congress closed several previously advantageous loopholes, corporations began a notable shift in manufacturing that took advantage of the new laws as written. Whereas previously it was more beneficial to bring labor-intensive manufacturing to the island, the new law incentivized corporations to bring only intangible property, leaving large re-investments (such as research and development or capital improvements and expansions) behind in their mainland U.S. operations. Instead, products were only "finished" in Puerto Rico so as to apply tax breaks that were applicable only to goods ready to be sold, significantly reducing the number of employees required in the manufacturing process. Pharmaceutical companies were among the most adept at implementing these tax policies, as more than 80 percent of the most prescribed drugs in the United States were manufactured in Puerto Rico by 1990.[10] While industry boomed, employment and domestic entrepreneurship, small business development, innovation, and overall industry diversification did not.

Being American citizens, with the ability to travel to any part of the United States and find alternative work opportunities and conditions in the most prosperous of areas, fewer and fewer Puerto Ricans chose to remain. During the 1980s, an average of 13,000 citizens left Puerto Rico for the U.S. mainland every year (a population decrease of 0.3 percent per year). Though not a dramatic shift, the continuous emigration of middle- to upper-income families and individuals (those that left tended to be the ones that could afford to leave and had the training, education, and skills that employers seek within the rest of the United States) to greener pastures brought with them a disproportionate amount of income-producing skills and consumption-inducing income.

The Federal Government also greatly improved the amount and efficiency of transfer payments and other public assistance to Puerto Rico during the late 1970s and 1980s. For the first time, Puerto Ricans became eligible for the U.S. Food Stamp program in the 1970s, while other public assistance doubled during the 1980s. However, with high poverty rates (per the U.S. Census Bureau, nearly 60 percent of the population of Puerto Rico was under the federal poverty line in 1980), a disproportionate number of Puerto Ricans (as compared to other U.S. locations) were allotted some level of social/transfer benefits based on means-testing standards. With so many citizens eligible for federal and local benefits, combined with a lower cost-of-living, the incentive to join the labor force fell precipitously. By 1980, unemployment rested at 17 percent (down from a high of 20 percent in the mid-1970s) and labor force participation fell below 45 percent.[11]

High unemployment,[12] combined with low labor force participation, supported by little employment growth and opportunities and buttressed by social programs that incentivized leisure over work made for a terrible recipe for increased productivity, and one that didn't bode well for its economic development future.

Given the continued disadvantages, Puerto Rican legislators began to shift their own resources to support the population. "By throwing enough money at the problem it might go away" was the philosophy of the day (both in Puerto Rico and across Latin America, it turns out). Through a number of significant reforms, the local government increased investment in programs that were intended to promote economic development. It leveraged its *Banco Gubernamental de Fomento para Puerto Rico*[13] (Government Development Bank) to help promote infrastructure improvement and expanded investments in programs that facilitated regional exports produced by local businesses—all via the sale of general obligation bonds, guaranteed by the full faith and credit of the Government of Puerto Rico (whose "faith and credit" later became meaningless).

Even in a place as enchanting as Puerto Rico, government investment still costs money. Because of the substantial investments, deficit spending and debt made a strong showing during the 1980s, doubling the public debt from approximately $6 billion to more than $12 billion by 1990.[14] But, given the increased GNP, the debt-to-GNP ratio for Puerto Rico was kept at a reasonable 54 and 56 percent, respectively. The island managed to keep growth ahead of debt, so far.

DOUBLING DOWN IN THE 1990s

The 1990s was a wonderful time for Americans in general. Winning Miss Universe and a bunch of boxing crowns might have been enough for the beauty pageant and lightweight fighting aficionados of the Puerto Rico, but a growing economy that benefited from a U.S. economic boom was a nice cherry on top. Real GDP growth doubled from the average 2.3 percent of the previous decade, to 4.6 percent throughout the 1990s (or approximately 5.8 percent GNP growth, year over year, which turned out to be a 37 percent from 1970, a hint of things to come). The level of educational attainment rose (approaching average OECD levels), as did labor force participation, while poverty rates continued the slow decline from the previous two decades, and the official unemployment rate fell by more than 20 percent. By a lot of measures, it seemed as though Puerto Rico was improving, possibly even headed toward a long-term trend of growth.

Puerto Rico's economy also became increasingly dependent on the tax incentives afforded by special exceptions in the tax code for companies investing in the territory. Since 1970, the percent of GDP which was attributed directly to manufacturing jobs (those that were supported by the favorable U.S. tax laws) grew from 30 percent to 40 percent in the 1990s, supporting more than 172,000 jobs in 1995. Though the manufacturing sector greatly improved overall growth, it didn't support the island's domestic output, nor did it serve as an investment in future growth.

This is where the difference between the macroeconomic indicators that represent GDP and GNP (see previous note for more on this) can help shed light in Puerto Rico. Since so many of the corporations in Puerto Rico were continental U.S.-based corporations that invested in the island in order to get a tax break, the revenue from those operations were sent back to corporations outside of Puerto Rico (i.e., the earnings were those of non-residents), GDP as an aggregate indicator just didn't capture the real output as it pertained to the benefit it afforded to the citizens of the island. If looking only at GDP, it seemed as if Puerto Rico was still growing at a respectable rate throughout much of the last few decades. But, if you consider that roughly one-third of Puerto Rico's GDP was returned to the bank accounts of the major manufacturers on the U.S. mainland in 1997,[15] it is easy to see how little of it went to benefit the average Puerto Rican or Puerto Rico's future economic prospects. The divergence in GNP and GDP is oft-cited by economists as a reason why the tax breaks were ineffective as an economic stimulant, while also failing to dramatically improve employment in Puerto Rico and costing taxpayers more in benefits per worker than employees were compensated.

Given the low ratio of benefits to expenditures to the U.S. Treasury, Congress—which was in the midst of a cost-cutting FC of its own in the mid-1990s—decided it was time to phase out the Section 936 tax incentives over the next ten years, beginning in 1996. Combined with a cut to transfer benefits led by an extensive welfare reform plan, the government-dependent island of Puerto Rico received a significant shock to its economy.

Several additional factors exacerbated Puerto Rico's problems. First, it has spent little time, money, and effort diversifying its own economy. As an example, nearly every other Caribbean nation receives more than a third of its annual income through tourism, while tourism contributes less than 10 percent to Puerto Rico's economy. Policymakers often refused to focus on those sectors in which it had a comparative advantage, and instead relied upon and emphasized promotional efforts to develop sectors that were built upon the tax incentives from the federal government. The largest sector by far was manufacturing, representing nearly half of the economy's output, but it was almost entirely built upon the financial advantages Puerto Rico had to offer. Taking away the drivers that incentivized its largest sector was not going to go well for the island.

Second, Puerto Rico's federal and municipal governments accounted for an increasing percentage of the economy, reaching more than 60 percent by the 1990s (more than twice the U.S. average at the time).[16] With such a large percentage of the GDP being consumed by government, the private sector incentive (and ability) to reinvest and grow the economy was restricted. During a brief period in the 1990s, policymakers did attempt to privatize some of these assets, including selling a government-owned shipping line, its state-owned telephone company, and attempted to privatize a large portion of its prison systems, but privatization of inefficient and expensive government-owned entities halted in the early part of the following decade, allowing many to remain even today.

Lastly, despite seeing the writing on the wall and already beginning to feel the effects of the proposed phase out of the tax incentives, Puerto Rico kept spending, maintaining a fiscal policy trajectory that did nothing but add fuel to the pending fire. With various public works initiatives and other investments, administrators funded an urban train system, a new "superaqueduct" water system, a new coliseum, and a new convention center, to name a few. Well-intentioned legislators proposed that the public spending would stimulate the economy and improve economic returns (unfortunately, these types of projects have yet to produce the expected ROI). Combined with reduced tax revenues from a slowing economy, Puerto Rico's deficit began to rise, doubling outstanding public debt from 12 billion to 24 billion (nearly 60 percent of GNP), an increase that accelerated in the latter part of the decade.

PUERTO RICO'S LOST DECADE

The 2000s didn't treat Puerto Rico so well. The capital flight subsequent to the tax credit wind down was joined by two recessions to ensure that Puerto Rico got kicked while it was down.

By the year 2000, more than 60 percent of the working age population was either unemployed or not actively pursuing a job (not in the labor force). Federal transfers accounted for nearly 31 percent of the island's total GDP, and most of the rest could be attributed to manufacturing that was headed for a slow demise. Its underdeveloped private sector left little room for growth opportunities, had few industries that employed lower educated, lower income individuals, and had no growth in domestic businesses of virtually any size that could counter falling employment from foreign corporations leaving the island behind. Bureaucratic impediments of "red tape" made it difficult for entrepreneurs to build a business and crippled an otherwise competitive economy. The government accounted for 30 percent of non-farm employment and its expenditures accounted for more than 48 percent of GNP.[17]

Without dramatic and immediate structural economic development shifts, any exogenous disturbances to its economy would likely begin a death spiral for Puerto Rico and its nearly 4 million American inhabitants. Unfortunately for the island, just such an incentive to spiral out of control began with the first U.S. recession of 2001, brought about by the dot-com bust of the late 1990s.

In the early 2000s, the local economy (as measured by real GNP) averaged close to 1.7 percent growth, with unemployment shrinking from 17 percent to 10 percent. Yet, Puerto Rico's economy was disproportionately impacted by U.S.-wide recessions, causing GDP to turn solidly negative after the first recession of the early 2000s, remaining in the red the entire decade.

But policymakers didn't have time to pout and wonder what could've been; instead, they got busy trying to spend their way to prosperity. Austerity researchers around the world began salivating at the opportunity to study the fiscal fiasco that was Puerto Rico. From 1990 to 2005 or so, revenues to the tax man rose at a compounded rate that was 30 percent lower than the growth rate of its borrowing. Deficits were winning the fiscal battle, and Puerto Rico's debt was beginning to pay the price.

In a single fiscal year (2003–2004), outstanding government debt increased by 24 percent. Between 2000 and 2006, debt rose by more than 75 percent, a pace of growth that was among the fastest in its history. The government did everything in its power to put off economic catastrophe. It invested more than 1 billion dollars (more than 10 percent of the yearly budget) in self-managed community projects to decrease poverty, in massive infrastructure projects, and in the creation of new programs to reduce poverty and government dependence, all of which drove the growth of public employment by nearly 12 percent in just the first half of the decade.[18] The Puerto Rican government's spending spree had no end in sight.

Then came the global recession that pummeled the Earth in 2008, whose contagion spread to Puerto Rico before the recession was officially underway in the United States in 2007. Puerto Rico wasn't ready, was entirely dependent on others, and thought it had no choice but to keep its current fiscal discipline out of order, for the good of its people. Would we have another case study that proved high debt to be untenable, titillating the sense of the Bocconi researchers of the world? Or would Krugman finally prove, once and for all, that the bond boogeyman doesn't exist?

IN THE MIDDLE OF A CRISIS

Despite all of its efforts, the government just couldn't fight the economic battle. The phase out of tax incentives—which officially ended in 2006, just in time for a massive recession in the United States that pushed Puerto Rico into a depression—coupled with a large and growing deficit and public debt to prompt even more drastic policy changes. It's never fun when your hand is forced.

Public employees' salaries were frozen and twenty-eight public agencies were consolidated (which resulted in a two-month government shutdown with an estimated economic impact of more than 2 billion dollars, or a couple of GDP percentage points), major utility subsidies were eliminated, taxes were increased on the banking sector, and an island-wide sales and use tax was created.[19]

In 2009, a new administration took the wheel in Puerto Rico, promising to right the fiscal track. With a 3.3 billion-dollar deficit, nearly one-third of total yearly revenues to the government,[20] liquidity problems were so rampant that one of the new governor's first acts was to take out an immediate loan to cover the first public employee payroll under his administration. You know you're on the brink of disaster when you have to take out a loan just to pay the bills. The following several years heralded a drastic structural adjustment period. More than 20,000 public employees were laid off (more than 10 percent of the workforce), government spending was cut by 10 percent, taxes were raised in some sectors and on high-end real estate and earners, contract negotiations and pay raises were frozen, corporate tax rates were flattened and reduced, toll roads and the island's biggest international airport were privatized, and more than 4 billion dollars was borrowed through the sales of now famous Puerto Rican bonds to cover the government's liquidity needs. The government also enacted two major laws intended to boost foreign investment and re-invigorate some of that enchanted feeling that foreign investors once had for Puerto Rico: income taxes on certain types of income, as well as capital gains from real estate were dropped to zero. As Puerto Rican residents were already exempt from U.S. federal income taxes, there was a real opportunity for new residents to pay nothing in income tax in perpetuity. Bring on the billionaires.

What kind of effect did all of these austerity measures, structural shifting, and re-investment have on the fiscals of the island? Giavazzi, Pagano, Alesina, and the rest of the Bocconi boys would be proud to hear that their contention that the possibility of expanding austerity still lived. In 2012, Puerto Rico saw its first return to positive economic activity (as measured by real GNP) since 2006.

Had a spending-focused FC, combined with certain structural reforms, proved the contention that it could lead to growth, or at least, better economic outcomes than those led by tax-based policies? Perhaps, but voters were so skittish that they didn't give policymakers a chance to find out. The governor that implemented all of the consolidation policies was voted out at the end of his first term, just before the positive effects of his administration's policies had taken effect. Citizens didn't like the cuts and didn't see the positive benefit they would receive (at least in terms of a growing economy, not including other distributional concerns, etc.) and couldn't wait to try someone else.

THE GOOD OL' DAYS

Starting in 2013, a new administration brought about a major shift in economic policy. Deficits and employment remained major issues, while a mass exodus of professionals to the mainland U.S. reduced the number of economic contributors, and the new group of policy minds had to do what they promised the voters they would do, even if it was clear that the past leadership's policies had a positive effect on aggregate demand.

In order to counter the deficit, the new governor let his Keynesian-aligned policy advisers dominate his policy agenda. While austerity was still required, it was decided that cutting government spending didn't do for the population what they might have liked, and instead chose the opposite path: tax the heck out of anyone who could afford to do so. Major tax cuts from the previous administration were overturned, effectively increasing taxes by as much as 60 percent on high-income, domestic earners, while some spending reforms continued, including funding cuts for schools and other social investments, public employee salary reductions (and sometimes downright freezes were enacted), public employee pension reform was passed to privatize pensions, and major reorganizing initiatives were enacted on some of the more inefficient utilities, with an increase in incentives to attract foreign direct investment.[21]

In 2014, many considered Puerto Rico to be on the brink of absolute collapse and ruin. With a deep budget deficit that compiled aggregate debt for more than a decade, few places have experienced debt growth in the way Puerto Rico did. Total public debt quickly surpassed 100 percent of its GNP (more than 150 percent outstanding debt to the public including liabilities of its wholly owned public corporations).[22] Unemployment ran wild, butting back up against 15 percent (not including the large informal sector, which is estimated to comprise nearly 40 percent of the economy), while labor force participation remained low at nearly 40 percent. Puerto Rico's economy had been contracting for nearly a decade.

Credit analysts Moody's, Standard & Poor's, and Fitch saw the writing on the wall. It was time to downgrade the Puerto Rican government bonds to "junk" status, while also reducing its credit rating substantially. Yet, many continued to buy Puerto Rico's bonds because they were the only triple-tax-exempt bonds that could be bought from anywhere, by anyone in the country. High rates of return should have been a disincentive to investment, but merely increased the intrigue for investors as most believed that Puerto Rico would either continue complying with its obligations or the U.S. government would back them up.

When it became clear that the debt load was too high for the government to sustain itself, another territory-linked legal quirk compounded Puerto Rico's problems as it discovered, unlike every other debt-dealing municipality in the United States, that it wasn't allowed to file for bankruptcy. High returns, tax exemption, U.S.-backing, and no recourse for a government who didn't want to pay was the too-good-to-be-true scenario that the world was waiting for. Everybody wanted in.

But, with steep credit rating drops and little opportunity for growth, there would be no more borrowing to finance government operations. Discovered through judicially sanctioned investigations, we now know that much of the borrowing (through bond market sales) in later years was used to pay existing debt, a move that courts have held to be an illegal use of revenues from the sale of government-issued bonds.[23] The debt spiral had begun, and this Ponzi scheme of borrowing to cover borrowing had nowhere to go but a quick demise.

In August 2015, the Puerto Rican government officially called it quits and defaulted on its debt. Bondholders, who weren't just zillion-dollar hedge funds, but millions of Americans across the country—including owners of teacher's pensions, 401k-backed mutual funds, and individuals alike—were finally starting to see that perhaps they should have paid a little more credence to the fiscal and economic track of Puerto Rico. It wouldn't be making good on its promises anymore.

Legislators in Puerto Rico had proven their fiscal ineptitude, compelling Congress to listen intently as their constituents begged for someone to help. PROMESA[24] was passed in 2016, which created a Fiscal Oversight and Management Board (FOMB) to oversee Puerto Rico's fiscal policies and attempt to get it back on track. Legislators in Puerto Rico benefited from being able to malign necessary FC policies and accredit them to their American overseers, while bond owners would (hopefully) get a return on what may otherwise have been a lost bond battle.

Right after the creation of the FOMB created a bit of positivity and a sigh of relief that something may finally be changing the fiscal crisis on the island, Hurricane Maria gave the economy the biggest single day economic setback it had ever seen, causing billions in lost output over the next year alone. In recent years, the combination of significant economic losses, the dependency on U.S. taxpayer funds and assistance, the lack of economic growth and potential investment, continued emigration to better opportunities in other parts of the United States to the tune of 48,000 citizens per year since 2010 (peaking at an estimated more than 100,000 in the year following the hurricane), endless lawsuits between Puerto Rico's bondholders and the government, and what seems to be an ineffectual fiscal oversight board[25] have made for a difficult combination of economic obstacles that will be hard to overcome. So far, forced change has brought about some glimmers of economic revival and diversification in entrepreneurship, energy, telecommunications, and real estate, while the continuance of attractive personal and business tax incentives have combined with cheap assets to offer what many see as an opportunity to get in before Puerto Rico turns its tide. Others, however, think that Puerto Rico is merely doomed to repeating the trials and tribulations of its hard lessons, if it doesn't make a change to its status.

RESISTANT TO NECESSARY CHANGE

With its fiscal status in limbo (once again) and slow economic growth (yes, it's still slow), most Puerto Ricans, and now the rest of the United States, have come to realize that its existing status as a semiautonomous territory of the United States is no longer best for its long-run economic well-being. In recent plebiscites, Puerto Rican voters overwhelmingly voted to change its status in 2012,[26] then again in 2017 in a hotly contested vote.[27] Though the outcomes of these contests will forever be debated, polling has consistently found that voters in Puerto Rico now favor becoming the fifty-first state of the United States over its existing status, or even a Brexit-style referendum (Prexit).

Going independent would be a seriously risky venture. The intention would be for the new island-state to become more like the powerhouse move of a Singapore, but, unfortunately the leaders of Puerto Rico's independence movement have different ideas. First, they suggest invalidating all of Puerto Rico's debt, which couldn't make Moody's, Fitch, and S&P dislike them anymore. It would be quite difficult to fund this new venture, with no way to borrow. Second, they seem to have their sights set more on a decidedly socialistic path than the capitalistic one that has brought prosperity to its neighbors in Latin America and the Caribbean. Given the combination, an independent Puerto Rico would likely be more like a Cuba (whose GDP per capita is 7,600 dollars USD, one third of the world's average), than a Singapore (with its amazing turnaround success story and impressive near 60,000 dollars GDP per capita, more than three times that of the world's average).

Yet, a clean-slate and fresh ideas have been known to turn around a country or two throughout history, but it remains that independence is the riskiest economic route. The status quo hasn't worked out at all for Puerto Rico. No one serious seriously considers this as an option, though it is the most likely outcome for the foreseeable future. Investors tend to see "political risk" in perpetuity as a con to potential projects, which is part of the reason for the limited amounts of foreign direct investment Puerto Rico receives, even with amazing tax incentives. Its economy will likely never get out of its slump without a dramatic shift.

Finalizing its long-storied American status with a star on Old Glory is likely the best option for the island, and for the country as a whole. If Puerto Rico is allowed to become a state, political certainty will lead to an investment boom with implications for the entire U.S. economy. Not only will the substantial reduction in political risk incent greater foreign investment from around the world, but there is a lot of data to submit that Puerto Rico would likely follow in the footsteps of Hawaii, benefiting from its new status and quickly developing a substantial service and tourism sector due to its new connection to the United States and all of the wonderful free press and marketing resulting from the statehood process (years of *positive* headlines in the media would do well to change its image, much like headlines since hurricane devastation in 2017 in Puerto Rico has helped propel a tourism boom).[28] With a growing economy, fewer transfer payments will flow from the U.S. Federal Government to Puerto Rico, while individual and corporate contributors will be less likely to leave the island for greener pastures on the mainland.

As investors gain new confidence in Puerto Rico's future, the stifled economy will be able to remove a burden that has been building for decades, allowing the island to reach its full economic potential. Even under the recent conditions of high debt combined with a shrinking economy, estimates suggest that corporate and individual taxpayers in the new state will contribute 6–10 billion dollars more to the U.S. Treasury's bottom line.[29]

Further considering the market dynamism of an improved economic climate, and it is easy to see how many more billions of dollars of profits, individual income, and taxpayer revenue can be produced. Combine increases in corporate and individual entrepreneur investment with Puerto Rico's positive trade balance, the expectation of rapid growth in an already productive tourism sector (imagine a state as beautiful as Hawaii, but takes only one-fifth the time to get there from the highly populated East Coast of the United States), and an opportunity for improved intrastate commerce (sorry Miami, Puerto Rico is poised to take over as the gateway to the Americas), and the new state's economic productivity will be a welcomed addition to the U.S. economy.

Fiscally, economic growth can but add to the stability of incoming tax dollars. It is impossible to predict how political forces will handle those new funds, and whether they will implement prudent fiscal policies that keep Puerto Rico from becoming the "Greece of the Caribbean," "the Debt Spiral of the Deep South," "the Burgeoning Borrower of the Barrel's Bottom," or whatever unpleasant moniker one may want to allot a frivolous governmental spender.

Puerto Rico does present an interesting case study of exciting ups and downs for a population of millions of Americans. Its fiscal policy path hasn't always been the optimal one—many will argue that it never has—but its choices provide an opportunity for a close analysis of the effectiveness of the policies suggested throughout this book, within the context of an understanding of Puerto Rico's current association with the United States and all of the impediments therein. Given its integrated philosophy of spending-focused FCs of the early 2010s that begat a very short stint of growth, it may have proven a point for those who propose that an FC with government spending reductions is best—especially in light of a subsequent policy shift to taxation consolidation and the resulting economic downturn. However, the confounding effects of many variables throughout the micro and macro environment make for an intricate and complicated analysis, that policymakers the world over need to better understand.

NOTES

1. Puerto Rico, meaning *rich port* in Spanish, was the original name of its capital city that is now called San Juan—San Juan was the name intended for the island. Somewhere along the lines, a cartographer switched the two and didn't realize that Rich Port didn't make a lot of sense as the name of an entire island. Epic prank, or were extra rum rations given out that day?

2. Caribbean Business. "Studies Peg Cost of Jones Act on Puerto Rico at $1.5 billion," *Caribbean Business*, February 21, 2019, https://caribbeanbusiness.com/studies-peg-cost-of-jones-act-on-puerto-rico-at-1-5-billion/

3. Consider reading up on Robert A. Mundell's work on Optimum Currency Areas, for example: Robert A. Mundell, "A Theory of Optimum Currency Areas," *The American Economic Review* 51, no. 4 (September 1961): 657–665.

4. Figures are based on Purchasing Power Parity and are in International Dollars. Don't know what an "International Dollar" is? In an attempt to find a currency that could be used across countries, they developed this new money that "would buy in the cited country a comparable amount of goods and services a U.S. dollar would buy in the United States." "What is an international dollar?" World Bank, accessed March

20, 2019, https://datahelpdesk.worldbank.org/knowledgebase/articles/114944-what-is-an-international-dollar.

5. International Monetary Fund. "Report for Selected Countries and Subjects," *World Economic Outlook Database*, October 2018, accessed February 18, 2019 from https://www.imf.org/external/pubs/ft/weo/2018/02/weodata/.

6. "Local Area Unemployment Statistics: Puerto Rico," Bureau of Labor Statistics (BLS), accessed July 22, 2019, https://data.bls.gov/timeseries/LASST72000000 0000003.

7. For reference, you may see this referred to as the Section 936 law, referring to a section of the U.S. tax code that allowed for the preferential tax treatment for Puerto Rico–located corporations.

8. GNP is the preferred measured of aggregate income in Puerto Rico, given that much of its output is created by foreign-based corporations (including those from the continental United States). Since a large percentage of its GDP is sent back from whence its corporation came, it doesn't make sense to count it in an indicator which attempts to calculate the total effective output that benefits Puerto Rico. GNP, therefore, is calculated as GDP net of payments that are sent abroad.

9. Alexander Odishelidze and Arthur Laffer, *Pay to the Order of Puerto Rico* (Fairfax, VA: Allegiance Press, 2004).

10. Government Accountability Office (GAO), *Pharmaceutical Industry: Tax Benefits of Operating in Puerto Rico* (Washington, D.C.: GAO, 1992).

11. BLS, "Local Area Unemployment Statistics."

12. For a developed country, 17 percent is a high unemployment rate, though not for an emerging economy, necessarily. With its Latin American–style proclivity toward small business and off-the-books jobs, unemployment is generally estimated to be higher than official statistics.

13. *El Banco* wasn't so *bueno*, however, and has been forced to shutter its windows as of 2019.

14. Gustavo Vélez, *Reinvención boricua: Propuestas de reactivación económica para los individuos, las empresas y el gobierno* (San Juan, PR: Inteligencia Económica, 2011).

15. John Mueller and Marc Miles, "Section 936: No Loss to Puerto Rico," Lehrman, Bell, Mueller, and Cannon econometric consulting (1997).

16. Odishelidze and Laffer, *Pay to the Order*, 133.

17. Sergio Marxuach, "The Puerto Rican Economy: Historical Perspectives and Current Challenges," Center for the New Economy (2007), accessed February 18, 2019, from http://grupocne.org/wp-content/uploads/2012/02/FLMM.pdf.

18. Vélez, *Reinvención boricua*.

19. Vélez, *Reinvención boricua*.

20. "Monthly Indicators," Government Development Bank for Puerto Rico," accessed February 14, 2018, http://www.gdb-pur.com/economy/latest-information-monthly-indicators.html.

21. Robert Slavin, "Puerto Rico Plan Aims to Reboot Economy," *The Bond Buyer*, accessed May 10, 2014, from http://www.bondbuyer.com/issues/123_90/puerto-rico-plan-aims-to-reboot-islands-economy-1062350-1.html.

22. Government Development Bank for Puerto Rico, "Monthly Indicators."

23. Mortgage lenders don't allow individuals to pay their housing payments with a credit card, so how did Puerto Rico get away with paying debt with debt over any given period of time? Desperate times call for desperate measures.

24. The Puerto Rico Oversight Management and Stability Act just happens to have the acronym that means "promise" in English. Do all political offices have at least one staffer dedicated to finding clever and memorable acronyms for their bosses' bills?

25. In 2019, a U.S. court found the appointment of the FOMB's members to be "unconstitutional," rendering them invalid and the status of the one entity that can oversee the island's fiscal status in limbo. Well, this can't be good.

26. In 2012, the majority of voters in Puerto Rico answered "no" to the first of a two-part question of whether it should remain a territory of the United States, then "statehood" in answer to the question "No? Then, what do you suggest we do?"

27. In 2017, a follow-up plebiscite was conducted because the United States deemed the first extralegal. In this version, more than 97 percent of those who voted chose the "statehood" option. However, those who were against statehood decided that abstention was better than actually voting against it. This interesting tactic may have paid off as many see the second vote as also invalid.

28. Andrew E. Gerow, "Shooting for the Stars (and Stripes): How Decades of Failed Corporate Tax Policy Contributed to Puerto Rico's Historic Vote in Favor of Statehood," *Tulane Law Review* 88, no. 3 (2014): 627–650.

29. Government Accountability Office (U.S. GAO), "PUERTO RICO: Information on How Statehood Would Potentially Affect Selected Federal Programs and Revenue Sources," *U.S. GAO* (March 31, 2014).

Chapter 8

Nipponomics

Being a nation of stalwart survivors post-World War II, the Japanese must have thought life was getting too easy in the decades prior to the 1990s. With multiple periods of hyper-growth under its belt, the island nation decided to change directions when it celebrated World War II's platinum anniversary with a spending spree that made sure it would become the world's most indebted. Now having lost two decades to a flat economy, Japan has succeeded in giving the rest of the world a fighting chance to catch up. Catch up they have, but the country has recently decided enough is enough, now trying every trick in the book to dig itself out of its new, downgraded position to the lower tier of the world's elite economies, which has it placed firmly among the world's slowest growing. With an array of potential fiscal and other policy solutions, distinct cultural considerations, and unique outcomes to study, Japan makes for another interesting case on the effectiveness of FC policies in the face of an inimitable economic dilemma.

BRIEF ECONOMIC HISTORY

The Japanese economic story would put the recent Greek tragedy to shame. Prior to World War II, most of us think of Japan as being an isolated archipelago that few Westerners had the opportunity to visit or influence. At least, that is what Hollywood has taught us. The reality, however, has been a bit different.

While Japan has always been a nationalistic society—partly, if not mostly due to its geographic isolation—it began opening itself to the influence of the West even before World War II. Realizing that the best way to catch up with the booming economic growth of the Western World was to be more like them, Japan adopted a national motto of *fukoku kyōhei*, or "Rich State, Strong Army," during the *Meiji* period of the late nineteenth century up to World War I. The policy shift placed a strong focus on nationalism, but opened its economic doors in order to support its long-term vision. Deviating from its feudalistic past, Japan sent thousands of students to Western universities, created its own Western-based education system at home, and set up vast infrastructure revitalization initiatives to lay the foundation for modern development. While it allowed for a private sector to develop during this period, the government maintained tight controls over which industries developed and how, and insisted on a certain degree of economic isolation. Economic seclusion paid off in the 1930s as the Great Depression had a much weaker impact on Japan than most nations around the world. In fact, it was one of the few future behemoths that continued to grow throughout the decade. Economic liberalization policies propelled Japan to broad-based success by the end of the 1930s,[1] but its leadership wasn't ready to let go of the reigns yet, nor its beef with Western society.

The Empire of Japan picked a fight that would have repercussions for the rest of its economic history. Though it didn't seem like a good idea after Hiroshima and Nagasaki, joining forces with Nazi Germany and the fascists of Italy in the 1940s said a lot about where Japan stood in its beliefs about Western philosophies of democracy and economic freedom. Bolstered by booming jingoism and supported by the military powers of Germany and more, their egos got the best of them when they decided to take on America. Attacking Pearl Harbor in 1941 was the single worst decision Japan could have made at the time, but also the single best thing that could have ever happened to its future economy. Before its surrender, the war had a significant toll on Japan: inflation was out of control, domestic production couldn't meet demand, trade was impossible due to maritime restraints, the currency devalued dramatically, and some estimates suggest that 40 percent of infrastructure and economic capital were completely wiped out (not to mention entire cities and losses of millions of contributors to the labor force).

When the United States began its occupation in 1945, Japan immediately democratized and put to good use the billions that America offered to help it rebuild. GDP growth topped 9 percent in the 1950s and 1960s as its economy shifted from agrarian to one focused on manufacturing and eventually the service sector. Japan was on the way to becoming the booming industrialized nation the Meiji had always dreamed, but it took its demise to finally make it happen.

Due to a robust investment in education, its growing labor force was able to contribute to the diversification of its economy, especially within the service sector and other knowledge-based industries (they were early investors in consumer electronics and computers, as we are all aware today), as well as booms in productivity growth. After adjusting to overcome the oil crises of the 1970s, Japan leveraged its investments in economic infrastructure to propel growth in the 1970s and 1980s to average 5 percent, solidifying it as one of the world's strongest economic superstars.

Japan's rapid growth has been one of the few great success stories the world has ever seen, yet there have been some bumps along the way (oil crises of the 1970s and a large housing and asset bursting bubble of the late 1980s and early 1990s, for instance). Yet, since the 1990s, the Land of the Rising Sun has been plagued by setting price levels. Noting immense and perhaps overblown fears of inflation, the economy instead instigated a period of deflation that has now run rampant in Japan for nearly three decades today.

Chapter 2 briefly introduced the concept of deflation and how it can be a worse hazard than inflation. Inflation may spiral out of control, but monetary authorities generally have the ability and tools to reign it in, though not always the will to do so. On the other hand, deflation cannot always be contained or overcome. As I previously noted, the problem with deflation, or even the possibility of deflation, is that consumers realize that the goods they want to buy are going to be cheaper tomorrow, so why buy today? While you may think you need a new car today, have a pile of Yen stacked up on your kitchen table, and have the tacit approval of your significant other to buy the car you want, it makes little sense to walk down to the car lot today if rapid deflation is going to give you a discount tomorrow. In fact, unless you are certain that deflation has stalled, you really don't know when your daily discounts will stop rolling in making it very difficult to pull the trigger on a major purchase. The same can be applied to the consumption decisions of millions of Japanese every day, who have a disincentive to make a purchase under the same circumstances.

For the policymaker, fighting deflation can be nearly impossible. During inflationary periods, a central bank can jack up interest rates and yank money out of the banking system overnight, effectively killing inflation, but with deflation, policymakers have to find ways to prod the consumption choice. It's much easier to take away an option to purchase than it is to compel individuals to consume. Just ask any economic development economist.

Since deflation has been synonymous with Japanese economics since the 1990s, every head of state's objective has been to reverse course and get Japan's economy roaring again. Currency devaluations, central bank QE, low (and now negative) interest rates, and vast governmental spending programs have been packaged as new policy tools to overcome the problems of falling asset prices, insolvent private sector corporations, banking default risk, the fear of continued deflation, and even now a crisis of demography with little to show for it. Now famous papers by noted economists from around the world have criticized the Japanese for their ineptitude and inability to prompt the inflationary pressures necessary to reverse Japan's stagnating economy.[2]

Japan is still the third largest economy in the world today, but its bumpy economic road has obliged policymakers to throw FCs, fiscal stimuli, expansionary monetary policy, and the kitchen sink at the problem. The following will discuss some of those attempts, the results, and what may lie ahead for Japan in the near future.

FISCAL CONSOLIDATOR-IN-CHIEF

If there were ever an award given for the top fiscal consolidator in the world, Japan would certainly be a frontrunner. The tightfisted Japanese have been passing and implementing austerity measures since we were all still learning where the country of Japan is on the globe. The results of Japanese economic policies haven't always lined up with other FC episodes however, often diverging from expected outcomes that would have been expected in other OECD countries. After all these centuries, the Japanese are still trying to do everything as only Japan can.

Inflationary 1970s

Despite what the last thirty years of history may tell us, Japan is quite capable of experiencing inflation. In fact, there was a time when Japan faced severe inflation to the point where it had to do something dramatic to change its trajectory. In 1973, an oil crisis beset the world, brought on by an OPEC embargo—OPEC's Middle Eastern–based members didn't like the rest of the world being friendly with Israel during the Yom Kippur War, so they created an embargo to "punish" the West. While this particular oil-embargo had an intentional, direct, and deep impact on the United States, where inflation rose to 11 percent in 1974, the effects were negligible compared to the levels of inflation bestowed upon Japan. Having become strongly reliant upon the importation of petroleum for its manufacturing sector, combined with its failure to diversify the regions that it imported from, Japan's economy was rocked by inflation. In 1974, inflation peaked at 23 percent (see figure 8.1, *Japanese Price Boom*). Increasing costs didn't only put fear in the minds of consumers, but without a cheap source of petroleum industrial production declined for the first time since World War II.

Since Japan had invested earlier in one of the best educational systems in the world, its current leaders were pretty smart and learned lessons quickly. The powers in charge weren't too keen on promoting dependence on any industry that relied on resources from other countries, so it began to diversify. Industry diversification required massive investment ensuring that government spending went up substantially; however, even in 1980, debt had yet

Figure 8.1 Japanese Price Boom. Author Generated from "Consumer prices for Japan," World Bank, Accessed July 22, 2019, https://fred.stlouisfed.org/series/FPCPITOTLZGJPN.

to cross the 50 percent debt-to-GDP threshold (at the time, 50 percent was considered the point at which fiscal regulators needed to start worrying).[3] But the Japanese had become a fiscally prudent bunch and were deeply concerned that the new historic levels of budget deficits and debt payments were going to be detrimental to economic growth. Officials were so concerned that both were growing at alarming rates that they initiated a plan for "the restoration of fiscal discipline" in 1979.[4] Given the original causes of this particular debt "crisis," their first go at FC was composed of some interesting tax hike choices—most of the proposed fiscal austerity over the following three years was based on gasoline and aviation fuel tax increases.

Austerity and Growth in the 1980s

But as inflation grew and the economic outlook continued to have a cloudy forecast, preserved by another oil and inflation crisis of 1979–1980, Japan took a page from an old-Keynesian textbook and decided to continue cutting the deficit via the taxation channel. Prior to this, Japan's investment in diversification was beginning to pay off, and its monetary policy regimes combined to control for the pending doom of petroleum cuts. OPEC wasn't going to win this round. Peak inflation for Japan topped out at around 8 percent, while soaring to 14 percent in the United States.

At this point, Japan had learned how to grow and was growing well. With economic tailwinds, some surmised that it could afford the one option rarely offered to countries to control for high debt: let growth do all the work of digging out of the debt hole. But, Japanese officials are a worrying bunch and have always been adamant about staying ahead of the business cycle and other foreseeable hurdles. In 1980, they sought to cut the deficit with another round of tax increases twice the size of the 1979 version, doubling again in the 1981 fiscal year.[5] Despite a period of higher than normal inflation, Japan demonstrated its ferocious adhesion to fiscal discipline by increasing taxes that would only add to inflationary pressures. Reminiscent of the long-term planning schemes of periods gone by in Japan as well as in other Asian countries, policymakers clearly preferred a correction and a bit of discomfort today over future fiscal imbalance.

Unfortunately, the tax-focused austerity measures didn't pan out the way Japanese officials expected as economic growth slowed and the deficit began to increase at a faster pace than they wanted. Tax hikes put downward pressure on economic expansion, negating any expected benefit to the debt-to-GDP ratio from increased tax revenues. Sluggishness on top of growing deficits was enough justification for a change in course. So, in 1982 it decided that perhaps spending cuts would work a bit better than the previous tax hikes had, at least in terms of cutting the deficit. While dominant economic theory of the time might have dictated that both actions would be recessionary, new contrarian evidence that there may be benefits to cutting back on spending over relying on tax hikes was enough to convince Japan to give the policy shift a try. Regulators weren't ready to let go of tax increases altogether, however, as they did push through their biggest FC yet, but with a combination of both types of fiscal adjustments.

After some success, it doubled down and implemented another FC in 1983, 86 percent of which was based on proposed spending cuts. Gross debt subsequently grew by 10 percent from 1982 to 1983, but it leveled in 1983 as a palpable 3 percent growth rate also set in. Policymakers were excited that growth was again on a rapid upswing, and even more excited that they may have found the fiscal policy solution to their debt problems. Over the late 1980s, Japan's success continued as it grew by more than 5 percent per year and its debt-to-GDP ratio also fell from 77.3 percent in 1987 to 63.5 in 1991.

Budding EFC/expansionary austerity advocates had another point of support for their newest research angle.

Have You Seen My Decade(s)?

Japanese policymakers were clearly still experimenting with their optimal economic path when the 1990s rolled around. Unfortunately for the Japanese, prior policies didn't translate to continued success, as Japan somehow misplaced the entire decade. If that weren't enough, even after a decade of stagnation, they couldn't figure out which policy mix would reverse course, doing it all over again in the 2000s. *The Lost Decade* is not a term bestowed upon 1990s Japan because they were partying so hard they don't remember where it all went; the decade was one that many a Japanese wish they could return to and call "mulligan." Unfortunately, they don't have a redo option, but can merely look back at the couple of fateful errors of the late 1980s and hope to not repeat the same mistakes that shocked the economy into submission and led to an eventual *Lost Score*.

The opposite economic pattern developed in the U.S. economy, which may have helped to assure Japan's downfall at the end of the 1980s. After a severe recession pinned the U.S. economy in the early part of the decade, stagflation prompted the U.S. Federal Reserve to hike interest rates to unprecedented levels, and the dollar appreciated considerably against foreign currencies (the dollar's value improved by about 50 percent against the yen, for instance[6]). U.S. exporters weren't happy about the impact on sales from an appreciated dollar. As political pressure mounted, the United States began lobbying for a plan that would help its exporters, reduce its burgeoning current account deficit, make its products more competitive on the world's stage, and hopefully (fingers crossed) improve the overall U.S. economy. *The Plaza Accord* of 1985 did just that, depreciating the yen over the next two years by more than 50 percent, returning the United States to its state of prominence.

While all was swell on U.S. soil, the rapid appreciation of the yen meant that its own products were now more expensive. Heavily reliant upon exports, the BoJ had to put in extra work to expand monetary policy to counter the effects and heat up the economy. The economy did heat up, but so quickly that asset price increases rapidly turned into a massive bubble. Much like what happened in the United States before its recent housing crisis, the BoJ encouraged banks to lend to less qualified buyers, prompting demand to outpace housing stock leading to intense overvaluations. Krugman famously critiqued the Japanese for this failure,[7] but seemed to have less to say when the United States did the same in the 2000s (in fact, in a 2002 article he suggested the United States *needed* a housing bubble, going so far as to ask Federal Reserve Chairman Greenspan to create one[8]).

To counter what was becoming an increasingly clear and obvious asset bubble based on speculative practices, along with the fear of another spike in inflation, the BoJ let interest rates fly. The knee-jerk reaction was practical in its attack on asset prices, and partly justified given Japan's experience with inflation in the 1970s, but most macroeconomists and central bankers today argue that Japan was overly hawkish. Consider figure 8.2, which illustrates Japan's inflation "problem" building in the late 1980s. Yes, there was a clear upslope in the inflation curve prior to 1989, but the rate of inflation had barely hit 2 percent when the BoJ pulled the rate trigger.[9] The decision to push interest rates as high as 6 percent over a short period of time was sure to have some negative ramifications.

Figure 8.2   Japan Late 1980s Inflation. Author Generated from "Consumer Price Index," Bank of Japan, Accessed July 22, 2019, http://www.stat-search.boj.or.jp/.

The consequences quickly became concern for the long-term future economic wherewithal of one of the Earth's most successful economies. As the asset bubble burst and prices came tumbling down, the *Nikkei 225* followed. More importantly, however, was the way in which banks, insurance companies, and individual and other institutional asset owners and investors were left hanging. With a significant dip to the price of assets, banks and insurance companies were especially overleveraged in the same manner in which U.S. banks were after the housing crash in 2006. With a ton of bad debt on their books, the banking system in Japan threatened to spread its debt disease to the rest of the economy, likely resulting in a sudden stop similar to Greece and Puerto Rico in the 2010s. With far greater resources than Greece or Puerto Rico, Japan chose to bail out banks by pumping yen.

The girth of the asset bubble had eluded policymakers, however, as debts were so massive the government couldn't print enough yen to circumvent the inevitable zombie banking apocalypse. Massively indebted, worthless banks were turned into zombies by government lending, which turned around and created their own zombie companies (*zombie banks* and *zombie companies* are called such because they have a negative net worth and are supported by some external lender of good faith who feels that it is necessary to keep them open, i.e., the government), none of which could operate efficiently or create the economic growth that Japan needed. When policymakers finally saw the folly of their ways, they pulled the plug to allow the embedded problems to work themselves out through banking sector bankruptcies and consolidation. Credit retreated and eventually halted, giving pause to economic growth. The government's policymaking professionals were unable to reverse the trend before an entire decade slipped away.

The next decade of economic malaise did have one positive outcome for economics professional everywhere. Without a decade of stagnation in one of the world's strongest economies, it wouldn't have created one of economics' most interesting indicators today: Japan's government indebtedness (figure 8.3, *Japan's Debt*).

After dipping to a 63 percent debt-to-GDP ratio in 1991, the lowest level since 1982, Japan's debt ratio—encouraged by government spending and slow growth—skyrocketed and approached 100 percent of its GDP in just *four years*. Of course, policymakers were well aware of what was happening and slowly began making plans to help alleviate some of the debt concerns with some down-home fiscal austerity.

When debts were on the rise in the early 1980s, inflation was booming and things weren't looking rosy on the growth side of the economy, but Japanese policymakers rarely proposed deficit reduction measures greater than 0.5 percent of GDP. But in 1997, the future of its indebtedness was getting so out of sorts that policymakers knew something far more drastic has to be

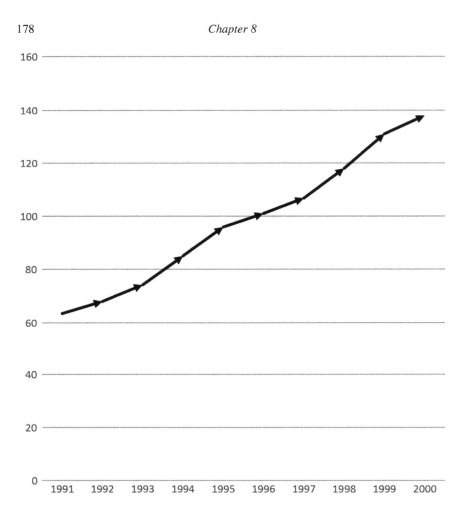

Figure 8.3   Japan Debt. Author Generated from "Central Government Debt," International Monetary Fund, Accessed July 22, 2019, https://www.imf.org/external/datamapper/ CG_DEBT_GDP@GDD/.

considered. With "widespread public and political support for consolidation" in hand, authorities pushed forward an "essential first step in the process of restoring fiscal health" with an FC that equaled almost 2 percent of GDP.[10] While still not over-the-top dramatic in the scheme of the world's deepest deficit cutting plans (remember the Greeks), given that this was considered part of a medium-term plan to cut into the foreseeable future, it has to be considered in full context. Policymakers were fully aware of the fact that it was in worse fiscal condition than any developed country in the world, with a demographic trend toward an aging population that wasn't helping. The multiyear plan was composed of a first-year FC plan that totaled 1 percent of

GDP via tax increases and another 0.5 percent in government spending cuts (attempting to protect the social security safety net as much as possible), but followed that up in 1998 with another round of tax increases to the effect of 0.5 percent of GDP.

Japanese debt, however, didn't seem to slow much from the opening bout of austerity. After peaking at nearly 15 percent growth in 1994, debt slowed to 5 percent growth in 1996 and 1997, but then increased to 11 percent Y-O-Y growth in both 1998 and 1999. The year 2000, however, saw a return to a mere 5 percent debt-to-GDP growth, finally reacting to austerity. Following the successful turnaround of the 1980s and flirting with a respectable increase to its GDP in 1990, Japan's economy instead took a turn for the worse, averaging less than 1 percent of real GDP growth over the decade of the 1990s. Japan should have learned the lessons of the late 1980s and instead focused more on governments spending reductions as the primary driver of austerity (figure 8.4).

The preferred end to this story would have been the fairy tale "happily ever after" sort that turned economic malaise of the 1990s into a giant boom of the 2000s. At this point in history, the rest of the world was beginning to route for the Japanese underdog, hoping that such a turnaround would be true for *Land of the Rising (but economically discouraged) Sun*. Regrettably, the 2000s weren't just a repeat of the 1990s; things actually managed to get worse. With real GDP struggling to grow past a single percent (real GDP per capita fell to an average of 0.8 percent in the 2000s) and debt continued its epic rise to the point of crossing the unheard of 200 percent debt-to-GDP threshold (number one in the world; see figure 8.5, *World's Best Debt*). Policymakers decided it was finally time to start chopping again. For more than half the decade, Japan operated under a policy of FC.

In 2002, Japan made the announcement that it had come up with a multi-year FC that would eventually lead to a "primary budget surplus by the early 2010s," quite the ambitious objective for a government with the world's highest debt.[11] In an attempt to do so, it implemented a 0.48 percent spending-focused FC in 2003, another 0.6 percent based mostly on spending in 2004, more government spending cuts of 0.22 percent in 2005, then reverted to the taxation stream to cut the deficit by 0.72 percent of GDP in 2006 (two-thirds of which was tax-focused) and another small round of tax hikes in 2007, extending the expected term of a primary surplus to the middle of the 2010s.[12]

Plans are, of course, all well and good, but the unexpected is inevitable. In spite of a respectable glimmer of growth hope in the early 2000s (Japan averaged 1.4 percent real GDP per capita growth through 2007, see figure 8.4), the Global Crisis of 2008 rippled throughout the world. Japan wasn't immune or insulated this time. After nearly two decades of stagnation, deflation, huge debts resulting from ineffective stimuli, and a whole host of struggling

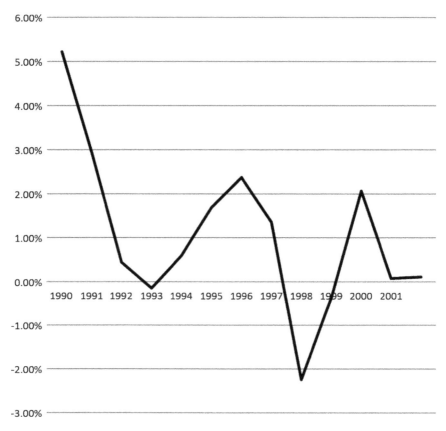

Figure 8.4 Real GDP Growth. Author Generated from "Real gross domestic product for Japan," The Cabinet Office of Japan, Accessed July 22, 2019, https://fred.stlouisfed.org/series/JPNRGDPEXP.

macroeconomic indicators, Japan entered its own recession, losing 1 percent of GDP per capita in 2008 and another 5.4 percent in 2009.

WAS AUSTERITY THE CURE?

Japan's debt has since leveled off at a mere 250+ percent of GDP, but the economy is on the long road to recovery. *Abenomics* has been the leading philosophy for Japan's future economy since Shinzo Abe took over in 2012 as prime minister, which was composed of easy money policies to leave behind deflation, more fiscal stimulus to give a shot of adrenaline to Japan's growth rate, and structural reforms that it hoped would help boost private investment.

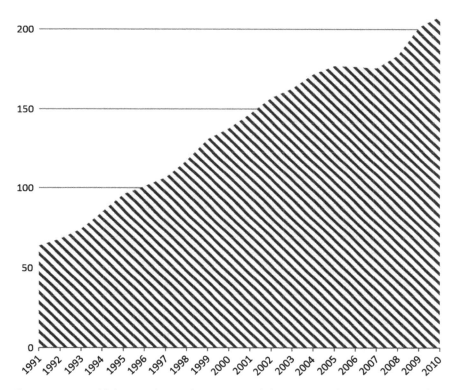

Figure 8.5 World best Debt. Author generated from "Central Government Debt," International Monetary Fund, accessed July 22, 2019, https://www.imf.org/external/d atamapper/CG_DEBT_GDP@GDD/.

Falling from its graceful place as the second grandest economy to fifth—behind the United States, China, the EU, and India—the Japanese economy was nearly dead-flat in 2018. Still strongly dependent on manufacturing (especially automobiles) the economy will likely continue to suffer as demand shifts toward electric vehicles, unless Abenomics diversification strategies start to work. Japan is also heavily reliant upon government investment, led by the BoJ. Unfortunately, fiscal austerity (via tax hikes) has taken too much money out of the economy for too long and will only hurt economic growth prospects, so Japan instead relies upon the BoJ to implement QE through a flood of yen in return for a massive amount of government bonds on its books, to the tune of 60–70 trillion yen per year (approximately 650 billion dollars). The BoJ has also maintained interest rates at record lows, entering into the negative in 2016 hoping that charging commercial banks to make deposits will incentivize them to instead seek alternative investments in the market.

The nation of islands, nevertheless, is still staunchly dependent upon expansionary monetary and fiscal policy, both of which may have ineffectively combined to create a classic *liquidity trap*.[13] Its current economic development has become so addicted to new money, with few prospects for investment, that it requires a growing debt; austerity has no place in Japan's economy. Thankfully for Japan, and Modern Monetary Theorists (previously referred to as MMTers) everywhere, inflation also has no place in Japan, so the flooding of yen has yet to have an obvious negative effect on its economy. MMTers will, say, spend away as long as inflation doesn't take over and hope that the economy recovers (and no other bubbles or other economic calamities disturb the process). Since Japan is also its own biggest debtor, perhaps policymakers will just decide that Japan will never pay itself back, or maybe even write off what they owe. For now, Japan appears to have no choice but to agree to take the bait of MMT.

While there are a number of core and splinter issues that have led to Japan's economic condition, demographics and growing debt will continue to be long-term impediments. As the Japanese age, there are fewer and fewer productive members of the labor force who have to somehow pay for the old-age benefits to take care of the growing class of elderly. Older citizens, by the way, also don't consume as much, further damaging growth potential. With an isolated society that shuns immigrants like the plague, the expectation that it will have 30 percent fewer people in 2065 than today means it will have to undergo impressive structural reforms and fiscal and monetary policy adjustments in the future that will make the Troika blush.[14]

It's yet to be seen whether FCs will continue to be necessary as MMT advocates continue to advocate the idea that being indebted to oneself in the face of low inflation is essentially harmless. In the academic world, some have proclaimed Japanese austerity to be ineffective anyway, but others argue that it has been absolutely necessary in not advancing complete and total ruin for Japan. Perhaps Abe and his successors will eventually agree with MMTers and turn off the fiscal austerity spigot altogether? Or will Japan continue with planned austerity in order to keep the debt's growth to a trickle, knowing that the super debt it has incurred is already set to eventually come back to haunt them?

Given the contemporary nature of its debt growth and polices intended to counter, Japan will be an interesting case to study for many years to come.

NOTES

1. Though with price levels nearly half of those in the United States and nominal wage rates that were one-tenth of the average U.S. wage rate, the newly minted yen didn't go as far as they might have liked. For a good summary on PPP between the United States and East Asia at the time, see Kyoji Fukao, "Real GDP in Pre-War East Asia: A 1934–36 Benchmark Purchasing Power Parity Comparison with the U.S.," *Institute of Economic Research Papers*, Hitotsubashi University (February 2007). Retrieved March 6, 2019, from http://gpih.ucdavis.edu/files/Fukao_Ma_Yuan.pdf.

2. See, for instance, Ben S. Bernanke, "Japanese Monetary Policy: A Case of Self-Induced Paralysis?" Princeton University (1999), accessed March 6, 2019, from https://www.princeton.edu/~pkrugman/bernanke_paralysis.pdf.

3. "Central Government Debt," International Monetary Fund, accessed July 22, 2019, https://www.imf.org/external/datamapper/CG_DEBT_GDP@GDD/.

4. International Monetary Fund, "IMF Recent Economic Developments," *IMF* (1980): 34.

5. Pete Devries, Jaime Guajardo, Daniel Leigh, and Andrea Pescatori, "A New Action-Based Dataset of Fiscal Consolidation," *IMF Working Paper No. 11/128*, Washington: International Monetary Fund (2011).

6. Anne-Marie Brook, Frank Sedillot, and Patrice Ollivaud, "Channels for Narrowing the US Current Account Deficit and Implications for Other Economies," *OECD Economics Working Paper* 390 (2004): 1–29, https://doi.org/10.1787/263550547141.

7. Paul Krugman, *The Return of Depression Economics and the Crisis of 2008* (New York: W.W. Norton Company Limited, 2009).

8. Paul Krugman, "Dubya's Double Dip?" *The New York Times*, August 2, 2002, accessed March 6, 2019, from https://www.nytimes.com/2002/08/02/opinion/dubya-s-double-dip.html.

9. Interest rate and inflation information on Japan are based on data from the Bank of Japan. "Statistics," Bank of Japan, accessed March 10, 2019, from http://www.boj.or.jp/en/statistics/index.htm/.

10. International Monetary Fund, *IMF Staff Report for Article IV Consultations* (Washington: International Monetary Fund, 1997), 22.

11. Organization for Economic Co-Operation and Development (OECD), *OECD Economic Survey* (Paris: OECD, 2003), 15.

12. Devries et al., "A New Action-Based Dataset," 58–59.

13. Liquidity traps happen when money floods the economy and is easily accessible for investments, but there are few tenable investments to be made. Therefore, capital isn't used for productive purposes and instead is hoarded for, well, nothing. This is the main reason that the BoJ has implemented negative interest rates. Surely, there is something out there better than having to pay someone to hold your money?

14. Tomoko Otake, "Japan's Population Projected to Plunge to 88 Million by 2065," *The Japan Times*, April 10, 2017, https://www.japantimes.co.jp/news/2017/04/10/national/social-issues/japans-population-projected-plunge-88-million-2065/#.XIFNDChKjD4.

Chapter 9

The Paradox of Argentine Austerity

Japan's attempt to blow away its competition in the decade-losing competition was impressive. By upping the ante and losing growth for, not one, but two entire decades, it has truly become its own unique story. So how do you beat that without extending the pain over an additional decade? Well, some might say that Japan was simply attempting to take attention away from Latin America, which, just before Japan began doing so in the 1990s, threw away its own entire decade of growth in the 1980s. Yes, not just one country, but an entire region of lost economic potential befuddled researchers as Latin America's economy just sat there, doing nothing . . . for a decade.

You can't help but be impressed by a region's ability to lose an entire decade. From Brazil to Uruguay to Mexico and beyond, there are simply a basket full of fun examples of what to do—and not to do—when facing fiscal crisis (emphasis on the *not to do*). Notwithstanding all of the potential economic follies (and, let's be fair, the amazing turnarounds and triumphs as well), this chapter will more closely consider the amazing ups and downs that have led to innumerable Argentinian anxieties. Historical factors that characterize the region, and the economic history that led to Latin America's debt crisis of the 1980s, as well as Argentina's own debt crisis (then another, and one or two more for good measure) will be considered and scrutinized, along with the Argentine Republic's eventual outcomes and issues today (there are many). Not to be too much of a depressant, it is important to acknowledge some of the country's success stories, despite the fatal mistakes and contrarian responses to its economic conditions that notable economists have chided Argentina for, apologized for, then scolded again. Unsurprisingly, many of the same economic errors made in Argentina have a strange similarity to the Greece, Puerto Rico, and Japans of the world, and are the same mistakes that will likely continue to be made for all eternity.

LATIN AMERICAN ECONOMICS

If you live within the borders of the largest economy on Earth, there is good reason why you should understand Latin American history, especially as it relates to its economic development (and if you live anywhere else, there is good reason why you should understand what impacts the U.S. economy, because it impacts you). The United States imported roughly 406 billion dollars from Latin America in 2017, which is roughly one-fifth of total U.S. imports.[1] Since U.S. exports total around 12 percent of the economy, it's also noteworthy that an even larger percentage of exports go to the region, while Mexico continues to be one of our top two trading partners in the world (right alongside Canada). Since most U.S. immigrants are from Latin America (more than one-third come from the region), what impacts migration in the region also impacts the U.S. economy. Latin America's economy is intricately tied to the world's largest economy, which is intricately tied into the world's aggregate economy (just ask anyone who lived through the U.S. financial crisis of the late 2000s).

Politically the region has historically favored more control by the state, which has impacted its development potential and economic activity today. Throughout its history it developed a semi-honorable tradition of black-market activity, as its citizens attempted to circumvent the control of their unfriendly colonial overseers sent by the Spanish and Portuguese crowns, while those in power today have solidified off-the-books activity by continuing it through politics own accepted system of patronage. Whereas other regions have delved into fascism (Europe), Latin America's top-down style of control has been marked by the influence of interest groups and their influence on particular political parties, giving more power to those on the bottom. Today, most of the countries of LA have become liberalized democracies, but the tendencies toward government providing for the welfare of the public remains.[2]

Economically, the region's richest are the relatively well-to-do countries of Uruguay (GDP per capita of 18,000 dollars), Chile (16,000 dollars), Mexico (10,000 dollars), and Argentina (9,000), with poor Nicaragua and Honduras earning an income that no American or European would even get off of the couch for. Compared to the rest of the world, Latin Americans live in the middle of the income pack, with a quality of life in a similar range resulting from a broader economic development bent that has leaned on the production of primary products and the use of policies such as *import substitution industrialization*—a protectionist trade policy that gives a hand to domestic imports, in order to build out a country's home-grown industries. The region generally hasn't grown that quickly in terms of GDP per capita, averaging 2.5 percent in the 1960s, 3.2 percent in the 1970s, a big goose egg (−0.3 percent) in the 1980s (teaching Japan how to lose a decade before Japan knew it was possible), then turning the corner in the 1990s with 1.1 percent growth and a 2.4 percent economic "boom" in the 2000s.

WHERE THE SILVER COUNTRY FITS IN

From the late 1800s until the early 1900s Argentina looked like it was going to become the economic superpower on par with the United States. Argentina took advantage of fairly open trade policies across the world to combine with its high levels of agricultural production to become one of the world's great exporters. Macroeconomic growth led to personal wage growth as Argentinian wages rose from 76 percent of UK wages in the 1870s to 96 percent in the early 1900s—or 80 percent of U.S. wages—on par with some of the largest economies in the world.[3] All told, Argentina was looking marvelous.

But World War I and the ceasing of foreign investment, as well as the economic catastrophe that the Great Depression bestowed upon the world, led to significant economic malaise that Argentina never recovered from. The Peron coup d'état of 1943 ushered in Argentina's own lengthy period of corporatism that ensured import substitution industrialization would be the focused economic policy over the coming decades. It didn't work out as well as Peron might have anticipated—despite a worldwide economic golden era of booming greatness, Argentina experienced pretty slow growth. By 1970 import substitution was a known failure and a price/wage spiral combined with expansionary monetary policies to beget, you guessed it, uncontrollable inflation.

Before and partly through the 1980s, Latin American countries tried to borrow and spend their way through its development concerns. Excess liquidity in global markets prior to the 1980s helped to feed the region's insatiable appetite for borrowing. However, in 1982, Paul Volcker (U.S. Federal Reserve Chairman) created a policy of giant interest rate hikes that led to a region-wide debt crisis in Latin America. Immediate bankruptcy might have been better than kicking the inevitable can down the road, but Latin America accepted difficult restructuring plans instead, perpetuating the debt burden on its countries, adding to the economic concerns that held back growth that eventually ended up being entirely lost during the 1980s. While they tried to hyperinflate their way out of the debt (more on this in a minute), the combination merely turned into a suicide mission.

Being so incredibly lost, yet so intricately tied to the U.S. economy (and inevitably the rest of the world's), America had to take action. *The Brady Plan* that began in 1989 with Mexico and started what is now known as the *Washington Consensus* exchanged the old ubiquitous bad bank debt for new bonds with extended maturities (at the price of a "haircut"[4]), while also offering new loans to Latin American countries, with conditions. Greece learned what these "conditions" were and eventually didn't like them—neither would Latin America.

Argentina eventually signed on to the deal in 1992, getting a haircut that has been estimated to be between 20 and 35 percent. This wasn't the only consequence. After the deal, sovereign bonds ownership (as a percentage of total Argentinian debt) increased from 27 percent to 70 percent within a year. This meant that Argentinians no longer had control of or ownership over their own debt problems, but instead handed it over to a group of outside investors—including hedge funds and anonymous bondholders from around the world—that had their own sets of goals and distinct incentives to achieve those goals.[5] On top of this, Argentina was being molded to regain access to the credit markets, something a number of analysts today say only set up a moral hazard for a country that had nothing to lose and everything to gain by borrowing a lot more. In other words, by eliminating the concerns that countries had about the old debt and guaranteeing Latin America and Argentina again, the Brady Plan essentially gave birth to and permission for an entirely new round of borrowing. Rehashing a question that seems to precede many of the debt crises of the world, *what could go wrong?*

So, debt grew, and it grew immediately. Between December 1992 and December 1993, Argentina's outstanding debt grew by 13 percent. Yet, the GDP growth simultaneously improved as well (in fact, GDP grew at a rate of over 10 percent in 1991 and 1992 and over 6 percent in 1993; see figure 9.1) meaning that debt-to-GDP only grew by a couple of percentage points over the same time period (from a respectable 26 percent to 28 percent; see figure 9.2). Debt-to-GDP was a misleading indicator in the early years of Argentina's re-debting regime, although its pace would accelerate in the very near future. Looking more closely at figure 9.1, you'll notice just how volatile Argentina's GDP growth was between 1980 and 2016. Any given snapshot in time is just as likely to capture what may look like a booming economy as it would show economic growth being overtaken by even developing world economies.

To control for hyperinflation that reached over 3000 percent and 2300 percent per annum in 1990 (you read that correctly), Argentina's Central Banker-in-Chief was one of the few public servants in the world willing to give up his job and resign (really, he just did something different within government, like any good public servant would). The Argentinians had no choice. While their hyperinflation was becoming the example du jour for every new textbook, providing a lot of free marketing and press, it wasn't so practical for the average Argentinian. So, Argentina pegged the peso to the U.S. dollar and Argentina gave up its monetary policy autonomy and authority and ceded another part of its economic tools to the Americans (figure 9.3).

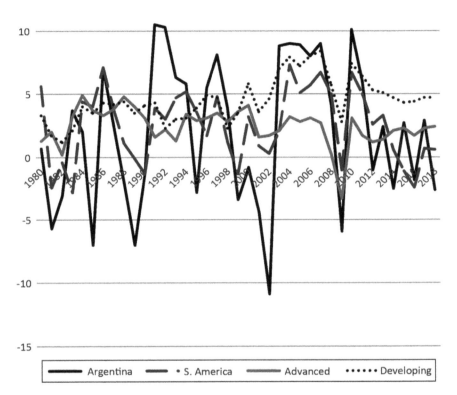

Figure 9.1 Argentine vs. World. Author Generated from "Real GDP growth," International Monetary Fund, Accessed July 22, 2019, https://www.imf.org/external/datamapper/NGDP_RPCH@WEO/OEMDC/ADVEC/WEOWORLD.

Debt + Austerity = 1990s Argentina

A quick glance at some select macroeconomic indicators throughout the 1990s would make even an amateur economist wince. The magnitude of some of the fluctuations in GDP growth (6 percent growth in 1994, 3 percent decline in 1995, 8 percent growth in 1997, 3 percent decline in 1999, etc.), the high levels or growing unemployment problem (Argentina averaged over 15 percent unemployment, not including underground economic activity or various broader measures of unemployment), fluctuations in the capital account that went from 14 billion dollars (1999) to −5 billion (two years later), and fiscal deficits combined with interest rate payments that increasingly remained in the negative, all combined to make for an ugly picture that was sure to end in painful FCs.

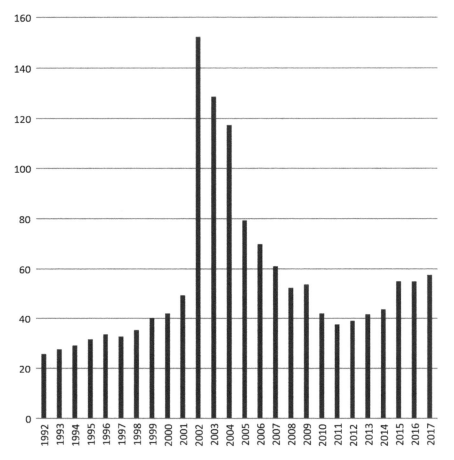

Figure 9.2   Argentine Indebtedness. Author Generated from "Central Government Debt,"
International Monetary Fund, Accessed July 22, 2019, https://www.imf.org/external/d
atamapper/CG_DEBT_GDP@GDD/.

Set off initially by the overvalued Mexican peso and capital flight from
Mexico in 1994 (now called the Mexican peso or *Tequila Crisis*), Argentina was also maligned with concerns about its currency valuations and the
convertibility regime that it previously set up, which greatly impacted production, employment, and aggregate output. The episode was merely demonstrable of the underlying fragility of Argentina's economy and prompted the
high unemployment and deficit concerns previously noted. Without improving revenues, interest payments on all of the new loans that the Argentine
government had acquired were becoming more and more expensive. An
overvalued peso combined with FC to worsen the current account and its
substantial deficit throughout the entire decade.[6]

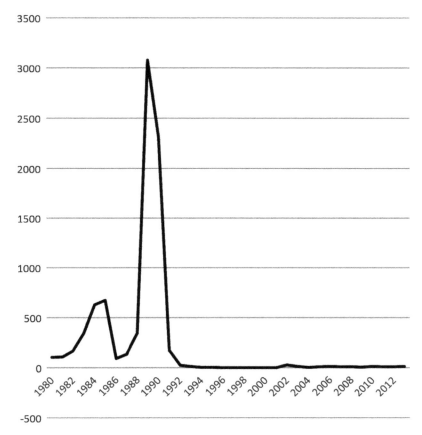

Figure 9.3 Argentine Hyperinflation. Author Generated from "Inflation, consumer prices for Argentina," World Bank, Accessed July 22, 2019, https://fred.stlouisfed.org/series/ FPCPITOTLZGARG.

After the Tequila Crisis, foreign direct investment began to wear thin. Without these expected flows of capital, the currency board was going to have a very hard time keeping up with the Argentine peso's peg to the dollar, making it increasingly dependent upon borrowing to do so. Whether an individual, company, island territory (Puerto Rico), or country, borrowing just to cover your obligations is not just contemporaneously dangerous, but is a clear sign to external observers that something is awry. Not only did outstanding public debt have to increase to cover its peg as shown in figure 9.2, but private sector debt increased sevenfold over the decade.[7]

Emerging market contagion was just plain bad luck for Argentina.[8] The combined effects of the 1997 Asian financial crisis that started all the way over in Thailand, Brazil's self-imposed financial crisis after a significant currency devaluation in 1999, and the Russian Flu financial crisis of 1998 that led to devaluation and default on debt all made countries like Argentina look really bad. Because they were all in the same class of emerging economies, investors saw them for the similarities they had. Capital flew off the shelves of developing countries back home to the safety and security of its advanced country places of birth. Since debts in emerging markets now leaned toward pending default, investors demanded higher risk premiums on public and private debt, which increased interest debt payments and made it much more difficult to find (or at least to afford) new lenders as old bonds matured. With the addition of a recession that began in 1999 (the economy shrunk by 3.4 percent that year and continued shrinking through a peak of 11 percent in 2002), it was impossible for the country to fulfill its debt obligations. It had no choice but to reconvene the big guns in Washington and beg for mercy.

With the help of the IMF and World Bank, the tricky threesome put together some patchwork to keep the economy turning, fueled by even more lending via much more expensive channels. Consider the new loans akin to what a loan shark might offer to a desperate gambler who just knew he was going to hit it big on the next spin of the roulette wheel; Argentina was certain its economy would turn with enough time and band-aids. All that policymakers had to do was implement a few fiscal cuts here and there, including major cuts to salaries and pensions (which never works out well for the politicians involved).

Despite the patchwork, Argentina was en route to a major default for a major country. With a last second Hail Mary, the IMF offered another debt swap in 2001. Of course, the long-term costs of the newly held bonds were gigantic, so the plan was either going to work, or make Argentina's default, restructure, and next step toward economic Hades that much more difficult for everyone involved.

Despite all the swaps, restructures, currency pegging, and secondary market begging, nothing could stop the doom that would become the largest default in human history. One hundred billion dollars-worth of loans would be declared worthless in 2001 when Argentina formally stopped making payments on its debt. The next years would be marked by some of the toughest courtroom fights that debtors ever had to undergo to attempt to force Argentina to pay something . . . anything. The price eventually paid wouldn't just be the time and resources of lenders and the Argentine government—the average citizen in Argentina was likely to bear the biggest burden of all.

WHY DIDN'T WE DO THIS THE FIRST TIME?

After the default and immediate peso devaluation, debt as a percentage of GDP jumped to Japan levels, far surpassing 150 percent. Interestingly enough, both Japan and Argentina had almost the exact same debt ratios in 2002. Japan, however, saw their debt fiasco through and kept on riding the debt train. Argentina, given its much smaller size and inability to access credit markets, even in its own country, decided that (i.e., was forced to) it would take another path. After all, Argentinians were suffering immensely under levels of poverty that surpassed half the population, unemployment beyond a quarter of the population, and few prospects for economic opportunity that wasn't off the books.

Simultaneously, Argentina began to realize that the IMF and World Bank, though they may have wanted to help save and revive Argentina, may not have had the best interest of the country in mind as much as the best interests of global bondholders. Or perhaps their restrictions for Argentina or understanding of the needs of the South American country were just outside of the expertise of the IMF, World Bank, or the United States. Since typical forms of fiscal austerity were no longer a possibility without growth and unnecessary since it wasn't going to pay its debts anyway, policymakers skipped the formalities and took a big chance by offering its debtors whatever Argentina felt like it wanted to pay. This doesn't mean that they completely ignored the calls of all of its creditors and just went in another direction. Argentina knew that it eventually (and very soon) would need their capital once again. But this time, it was going to restructure on its own terms.

Through a voluntary exchange, Argentina offered its old, not-worth-the-paper-its-printed-on bonds in exchange for new ones with new terms that were much more amenable to future economic growth in Argentina. By telling the IMF and World Bank to "go jump in a lake" while Argentine policymakers figured it all out, they thereby avoided any conditions that the institutions would force upon them, such as the harsh FCs placed upon Greece before and after its own defaults in 2014. Argentina had learned its lessons of the past and now, under the nothing to lose scenario that it was in, decided to make a series of low ball offers to creditors that would cut between 65 and 75 percent of the face values of loans, and elongate maturity dates.

With the ball in its court, Argentina had to make the tough choice between choosing to succumb to the pressures of the global investment community and offering terms that were much more to their liking. It hoped a quick, direct process of the latter would be favorable to debtors who would respond with faster future access to the markets and not punish them further with high debt premiums; but if not, a big cut in its payment terms would at least make it easier for Argentina to pay its debts and grow its economy. The Argentine government made the argument that if it did not invest more heavily in its own people and economy there would be no point in having access to new loans that it couldn't afford, so it decided to risk it all, and slap the financial market with a final "take it or leave it."

When growth-indexed payments were offered to sweeten the pot, more than 75 percent of bondholders accepted. Subsequent swaps helped to push down the debt-to-GDP ratio from 106 percent in 2004 to 52 percent in 2006, further reduced by a 2010 swap that dropped the ratio to 36 percent debt-to-GDP. Growth, which some argue was prompted by investments in domestic markets and programs for "social inclusion," averaged 8 percent from 2003 to 2008, had a relatively minor hiccup after the Global Crisis of 2008, then resumed its torrid pace, pushing to 10 percent in 2010.

Fiscal austerity be damned. The Argentinians had seemingly found a glitch in the matrix and took advantage of it by cutting debt-to-GDP in half, without being forced by anyone to stall government spending or raise taxes through the roof. Income distribution was also improving, unemployment fell from 15 percent in 2003 to 6 percent in 2015, and wage growth continued to outpace inflation. Argentina had beaten the beast that is the global lending community and lived to tell about it.

THEY'RE BAAAAAACK

Did you think that billion-dollar investment funds from around the globe would simply give up that easily and let Argentina walk all over them? After the country's initial default decision, groups of bondholders began suing Argentina and kept suing them for a decade. A small group of bondholding "holdouts"—not necessarily those that refused to accept the exchanged, value-reduced bonds that Argentina offered in 2002, but were more likely *vulture funds* that bought out debt that no one wanted anymore for huge discounts—kept suing and suing until they finally won a victory in 2014.

After a couple of years of negotiations and proceedings, and a change in the presidential administration in Argentina, the legislature decided that it was more worthwhile to issue a load of debt to pay off these vulture victors than it was to continue fighting them. New lenders have noted how Argentina initially refused to pay in the first default, but eventually gave in. If Argentina tries to default again, bondholders will stage a much more aggressive battle.

THE NEW, OLD ECONOMICS OF ARGENTINA

With Mauricio Macri's inauguration in 2015 came a shift in economic policy that left the heterodoxy of the Kirchner's in the dust. This new model rejected the idea that it could simply tell creditors to "hit the road" and make up its own terms, and instead offered a neoliberal worldview that complies with original agreements, implements FCs when necessary, and combines those with certain structural reforms to improve the growth outlook.

After an immediate currency devaluation, interest rates were also hiked by more than a third, and speculators began building up practices that accumulated returns as high as 38 percent betting on the fluctuations in the peso. Domestic and foreign investment taxes were reduced, while domestic prices were allowed to increase, putting inflationary pressures on the economy. Domestic production also took a hit, reversing the growth of 2015 to put 2016 in the red.

After borrowing to pay off old debt loose ends, the country commenced borrowing to cover the budget. To boot, the economy began contracting at a rate of 3 percent in 2018. Between 2012 and 2017, Argentina's debt-to-GDP ratio increased by nearly 20 percentage points,[9] a fate that it would not likely outgrow. Traditional FC was right around the corner.

BACK TO THE AUSTERITY DRAWING BOARD

Facing a 2018 peso crisis (what's new?), Argentina went back to its old nemesis in the IMF to ask for a loan. Knowing the IMF would put austerity conditions on Argentina, the Macri Administration still decided to pursue international help. Regardless of the economic implications anticipated by some (and despite, or in light of, failures in Greece), the IMF still insists on lending to countries that are willing to accept the type of fiscal reform that IMF researchers prefer.

In order to accelerate deficit reductions, the government swiftly pushed forward with cuts in spending and an increase in taxes, hitting the deficit from both sides. With a 2018 deficit of 1.3 percent, cuts to government employment were expected to combine with export taxes to balance the budget by 2019.[10] At the time of writing this book, inflation is holding at 30 percent, while central bank rates were jacked up to 60 percent to contain or drive it down. Strong FCs have been combined with hawkish monetary policy in the hopes that Argentina's new form of austerity will only beget short-term pain and will eventually put Argentina on the righteous long-term path toward economic growth, but this time with eyes set strongly on fiscal prudence. As of mid-2019, the IMF seems to be pleased with the outcome, noting that fiscal and current account deficits have fallen or turned positive. Most now see recovery on the horizon.

It has been a long, winding road to fiscal and economic recovery for Argentina, but it does seem that, while the prior shunning of FCs had little long-term benefit, those implemented today have combined with structural adjustment reforms in recent times to finally bear economic fruit.

NOTES

1. According to the U.S. Census Bureau, the official source for U.S. trade statistics. "Trade in Goods with South and Central America," *U.S. Census Bureau,* accessed June 10, 2019, from https://www.census.gov/foreign-trade/balance/c0009 .html.

2. Patrice Franko, *The Puzzle of Latin American Economic Development* (Lanham, MD: Rowman & Littlefield Publishers, 2007).

3. Blanca Sánchez-Alonso, "Making Sense of Immigration Policy: Argentina, 1870–1930," *The Economic History Review* 66, no. 2 (November 2010): 601–627.

4. The price wasn't two bits. The "haircut" part was a return on the bonds that was less than the original face value, which was essentially a debt restructuring with the guarantee of payment by the full faith and credit of the strongest economy in the world.

5. Pablo J. Lopez and Cecilia Nahon, "The Growth of Debt and the Debt of Growth: Lessons from the Case of Argentina," *Journal of Law and Society* 44, no. 1 (March 2017): 102.

6. Lopez and Nahon, "The Growth of Debt and the Debt of Growth," 103.

7. Lopez and Nahon, "The Growth of Debt and the Debt of Growth," 105.

8. The following sections, unless otherwise credited, rely upon Lopez and Nahon's description of the Argentine crisis of the 1990s and 2000s. Lopez and Nahon, "The Growth of Debt and the Debt of Growth."

9. "Central Government Debt," *International Monetary Fund,* accessed July 22, 2019, from https://www.imf.org/external/datamapper/CG_DEBT_GDP@GDD/.

10. Richard Pardington, "Argentina Launches Fresh Austerity Measures to Stem Peso Crisis," *The Guardian,* September 3, 2018, accessed March 8, 2019, from https ://www.theguardian.com/world/2018/sep/03/argentina-austerity-peso-crisis-macri.

Conclusion

Is There Really a Paradox?

The next economic crisis is right around the corner. This isn't doomsday speak; it's just as much of a fact of life as saying, "you will get hungry later today." Economic crises happen from time to time, and, while sometimes they are caused by factors outside of our control (e.g., natural disaster, attacked by a crazy group of terrorists, recession within borders of major trade partners, etc.) they are often self-prescribed. After all, what is economics in the first place, but the study of how we as mere human beings interact to allocate limited resources among us. If the "economy" by its nature is something that happens because we have created it, surely our imperfect abilities and lack of infinite wisdom will cause us to make mistakes in its development. Once the economy has been developed and things seem to be humming along as they should, we often wonder how we can make it better and attempt to do so, which doesn't always turn out so good. On the other hand, external shocks outside of our control impact our local economies, more so in an increasingly integrated global economy. Our solutions don't always beget the perfect outcome. Just as there is no perfect economy, there is no perfect economic policy solution.

Knowing our imperfections will inevitably lead to crisis, we can only look out for the next one and be as prepared as we can be. Where might the next economic quake come from? Of course, that is also impossible to know, but we can reexamine some of the discussion brought up in the Introduction to have a better understanding of what might be on the horizon. Across the globe savings are down (especially in the United States, the world's largest and most influential economy), but debt (private and corporate, as well as at the country level) is on the rise. Could this be the trend that kicks off a debt-induced crisis? Or will the crisis more likely stem from an asset bubble burst like in the United States in 2007, or in Japan in 1989? Or perhaps a currency crisis like that which has been incessantly nipping at the heels of Argentina? Or will World War III break out, stalling worldwide economic growth, pushing countries with precarious budgets battles over the edge? Regardless of the ignition source for the next crisis, every examination of economic crises intersects in some manner with a nation's fiscal status, and oftentimes propels it into a fiscal crisis.

Being that debt is so intricately connected with the future, we should understand the global trends in public debt. The IMF's new Global Debt Database[1] provides some new insight into just how much debt is building and where. As of 2017, total global debt has reached more than 225 percent debt-to-GDP. Before you get too excited wondering how we are all surviving at levels consistent with the Japanese government's total debt burden, the IMF database's figures also include private debt. Combining public and private debt, every person on earth now owes more than double the average income per capita of the world.

Considering only the public side of the debt, it's also interesting to note that the economic powerhouses of the world are also the most indebted . . . by far. The United States (the largest economy with approximately 21 trillion dollars of government-owned debt), China (second largest economy with around 10 trillion dollars of debt), and Japan (the third largest economy with debt equal to the Chinese) combine to own more than half of the total global liabilities (including privately held). If any of these countries' fiscal situations become untenable, the economic ramifications will reverberate throughout the entire world.

Private debt by itself has tripled since 1950, again led by the rich countries such as China and the United States. Since the financial crisis led to the Great Recession in the United States, U.S. consumer credit has risen by more than 60 percent. That's a 1.5 trillion dollar increase from 2011 to 2018! Some have predicted that certain sectors are already bubbling. For example, automobile loans were on a tear since 2008, but defaults and repossessions have increased substantially in the last few years in the United States. Could this mean that the next recession will be powered by a financial crisis based on bad auto debt?

There are a number of hotspots around the world that give rise to concern and may continue to do so today. Argentina, since the end of the Kirchner reign and the beginning of the administration of Mauricio Macri, has had a debt boom, combined with high inflation, and is now putting harsh austerity measures in place. Will Macri be able to continue to control for the debt problem? Will he let the peso enter into overvaluation territory again, leading to another currency speculation and another peso crisis that shocks the country into a sudden stop? Or, maybe Japan will finally hit the end of its debt road and decide to take up MMT on its offer to throw away prudent fiscal policies of the past in light of the opportunity to print the yen and borrow from itself in perpetuity (is it already doing so?). If inflation turns ugly or a global economic crisis hits it hard, Japan's economic collapse will have a big influence on the rest of the developed world that it is intricately connected to.

Yes, new theories suggest that deficits can be sustained into eternity, under certain conditions, but should we let that happen? If your country's growth rate can be maintained above the interest rate you pay on your debts, then yes, you can keep borrowing money that you can afford to repay, in theory. But, that magic word is *if*. How many countries around the globe are trying to improve their growth rates as we speak? The answer is all of them. We are all trying to adjust economic growth rates to what we perceive as the optimum level under our country's given circumstances, but rarely are we able to maintain the growth path we desire. So, why should we believe that we can target a growth rate that will forever sit above a country's average interest rate on its debt outstanding? Even if a country is able to precisely control its own national economic output and growth, the problem is not that nation's skills, but the skills and interests of economically connected neighbors. If war breaks out because XYZ regime suddenly wants to become the dictator of East Asia, our economy will be affected. If mismanagement of Aldovia's finances leads to a contagion across Europe, we will all be impacted. Some say the lack of control over these external factors must lead to more prudent fiscal policy management within one's own borders, not because of a lack of faith in your own policymakers' abilities (though you should be wary) but, at a minimum, because you know for a fact that someone else is going to mess it up for the lot of us.

In this book I've presented the idea of a fiscal paradox. The paradox of austere fiscal policies, that is when faced with the choice to implement a fiscal consolidation that we think we know will hurt us economically (but we also realize is for our own, long-term good), it is possible to be surprised and counterintuitively receive an economic benefit from the fiscal consolidation. FCs are important and necessary in many cases, even in a recession, and in lots of those cases actually help an economy. This is especially true if the composition of the fiscal adjustment policy is such that it focuses more on controlling for government spending, than relying upon an increase in taxes. There is no one-size-fits-all FC; countries must select the most optimal policy mix given a country's economic, social, and debt characteristics. Whether Argentina, Germany, Greece, Ireland, or Puerto Rico,—FC policy success has relied less upon preceding economic conditions than it has that the particular form of austerity is based on what investors and consumers see as the best long-term fix. In general, private consumers—and especially private investors—seem to have a lot more faith in the long-term economy when policy shifts veer from a reliance upon higher tax hauls, but instead refrain from spending (which also ensures fewer future outlays via the tax channel), especially if those policies are also accompanied by certain structural reforms.

But, that's not the only paradox of the world's story. The perhaps more important paradox is that despite the insistence of technocrats, academics, and other experts that there is an optimal set of fiscal policies that we should all adhere to, we refuse to make those policy choices until we're in an economic crisis; when we are in the midst of a crisis and need to make the toughest decisions regarding a country's finances, we are inclined to implement those fiscal consolidation measures the least that we know will benefit us the most (e.g., spending cuts may be the most conducive to future growth, but have very real consequences, including the political kind, today). If our nation's policymakers were truly interested in making the best fiscal choices, they will do so now and not wait until we are in the face of national or international crisis. So that we don't face harsh fiscal crises and become forced to undergo reforms by the likes of the IMF or World Bank, policymakers in both the developed and developing worlds should prepare the country's finances today.

This is why government debts and deficits really matter. The choices a country makes within its border, how to spend its dollars, which social programs to finance, which taxes to implement, and so on are value-laden discussions that matter little outside of the broader discussion of how to maintain enough fiscal discipline—given your country's principals for prosperity that lead to a certain level of growth—in order to avoid fiscal crises. However, in the face of fiscal catastrophe it behooves us to understand the best practices and policies that will most align with our country's goals as well as its present conditions. Gaining an understanding of the entire economic policy toolbox takes a monumental effort that has been tried since long before Keynes walked the Earth, but is a debate that has continued through today. In the broader scope, it's good to have insight into the models that have been developed by Italian economists and IMF researchers alike, while the debate should include the Paul Krugman's and Art Laffer's of the world as well.

In the face of out-of-control deficits, our search for the ideal policy to rectify our problems can't stop with a look at researchers' results, but should also encompass an understanding that the debate concerns the *process* for finding those results. For example, whether our relied-upon model implements a CAPB approach or a narrative-based one can have a tremendous impact on whether a specific type of policy has a negative or positive return to GDP, in both the short and the long run. Knowing the slew of other variables that may also impact the resulting output—such as monetary policy, the types of fiscal plans, precise composition, initial fiscal position of the country, accompanying structural reforms, and so on—can help authorities to construct their own models with more precision and accuracy based not only on the current conditions within their own country, but on the tools available to them and how they will compose a final fiscal consolidation or fiscal stimuli package.

As much as it all matters, it matters more that we continue to think about what we don't know. Learning the research pillars that have been laid before us is important, but pushing ourselves to think outside of the boxes that this research has developed is probably equally important, as no one knows from where the next crisis will come, nor how and if existing models can be applied to any particular country at a given moment in time to obtain an outcome with a known precision. Pushing ourselves, or at least our policymakers and the experts they lean on, to learn how policies have interacted to create various economic outcomes is important, as the impact isn't just a boon or detriment to today's generation, but can drive economic development across the globe for generations.

NOTE

1. "Global Debt Database," International Monetary Fund (IMF), accessed July 22, 2019, from https://www.imf.org/external/datamapper/datasets/GDD.

Bibliography

Acharya, Viral V., Philipp Schnabl, and Gustavo Suarez, "Securitization without Risk Transfer." *Journal of Financial Economics* 107, no. 3 (2013): 515–536.

Afonso, Antonio. "Expansionary Fiscal Consolidations in Europe. New Evidence." *Applied Economics Letters* 17, no. 2 (2010): 105–109.

Alesina, Alberto and Allan Drazen. "Why Are Stabilizations Delayed?" *American Economic Review*, 81, no. 5 (1991): 1170–1188.

Alesina, Alberto and Roberto Perotti. "Fiscal Expansions and Fiscal Adjustments in OECD Countries," *Economic Policy* 10, no. 21, (1995): 205–248.

Alesina, Alberto and Silvia Ardagna. "Large Changes in Fiscal Policy: Taxes versus Spending." *Tax Policy and the Economy* 24, no. 1 (2010): 35–68.

Alesina, Alberto, Carlo Favero, and Francesco Giavazzi. *Austerity: When It Works and When It Doesn't*. Princeton: Princeton University Press, 2019.

Alesina, Alberto, Carlo Faverro, and Francesco Giavazzi. "What Do We Know About the Effects of Austerity?" *NBER Working Paper no. 24246*. Cambridge, MA: NBER, 2018.

Alesina, Alberto, Omar Barbiero, Carlo Faverro, Francesco Giavazzi, and Matteo Paradisi. "The Effects of Fiscal Consolidations: Theory and Evidence." *NBER Working Paper no. 22385*. Cambridge, MA: NBER, November 2017.

Alesina, Alberto, Roberto Perotti, and Jose Tavares. "The Political Economy of Fiscal Adjustments." *Brookings Papers on Economic Activity* no. 1 (1998): 197–266.

Ardagna, Sylvia and Francesco Caselli, "The Political Economy of the Greek Debt Crisis: A Tale of Two Bailouts." *American Economic Journal: Macroeconomics* 6, no. 4 (2014): 291–323.

Bank of Japan. "Statistics." Accessed March 10, 2019, from http://www.boj.or.jp/en/statistics/index.htm/.

Barrett, Philip. "Interest-Growth Differentials and Debt Limits in Advanced Economies." *IMF Working Paper No. 18/82*. Washington: IMF, April 2018.

Beetsma, Roel, Franc Klaassen, and Massimo Giuliodori. "The Effects of Public Spending Shocks on Trade Balances and Budget Deficits in the European Union." *Journal of the European Economic Association* 6, no. 2 (2008): 414.

Bénétrix, Augustin S. and Philip Lane. "The Impact of Fiscal Shocks on the Irish Economy." *Economic and Social Review* 40, no. 4 (2009): 407–434.

Bernake, Ben S. *Japanese Monetary Policy: A Case of Self-Induced Paralysis?* Princeton University, 1999. Accessed March 6, 2019, from https://www.princeton.edu /~pkrugman/bernanke_paralysis.pdf.

Blanchard, Olivier. "Public Debt and Low Interest Rates." Speech given January 4, 2019 to the American Economic Association. Atlanta, 2019.

Blanchard, Olivier. "Suggestions for a New Set of Fiscal Indicators." In *The New Political Economy of Government Debt*, edited by H.A.A. Verbon and F.A.A.M. van Winden. Amsterdam: Elsevier Science Publishers, 1993.

Blanchard, Olivier and Daniel Leigh, "Learning About Fiscal Multipliers from Growth Forecast Errors." *IMF Economic Review* 62, no. 2 (2014): 179–212.

Blyth, Mark. *Austerity: The History of a Dangerous Idea.* Oxford: Oxford University Press, 2013.

Brender, Adi and Allan Drazen, "How Do Budget Deficits and Economic Growth Affect Reelection Prospects? Evidence from a Large Panel of Countries." *American Economic Review*, no. 98 (2008): 2203–2220.

Brook, Anne-Marie, Frank Sedillot, and Patrice Ollivaud, "Channels for Narrowing the US Current Account Deficit and Implications for Other Economies." *OECD Economics Working Paper 390*, 2004.

Buchanan, James A. and Richard E. Wagner, *Democracy in Deficit: The Political Legacy of Lord Keynes.* New York: Academic Press, 1977.

Bureau of Labor Statistics (BLS). "Local Area Unemployment Statistics: Puerto Rico." Accessed July 22, 2019, from https://data.bls.gov/timeseries/LASST720 000000000003.

Calfas, Jennifer and Alex Langone. "All the Members of the British Royal Family, Ranked by Net Worth." *Time*, 2018. http://time.com/money/5178274/royal-fami ly-net-worth/.

Caribbean Business. "Studies Peg Cost of Jones Act on Puerto Rico at $1.5 Billion." *Caribbean Business*, February 21, 2019, https://caribbeanbusiness.com/studies-pe g-cost-of-jones-act-on-puerto-rico-at-1-5-billion/.

Castro, Francisco and Daniel Garrote. "The Effects of Fiscal Shocks on the Exchange Rate in the EMU and Differences with the USA." *Empirical Economics* 49, no. 4 (2015): 1341–1365.

CBO. *Social Security.* Accessed on February 19, 2019, from https://www.cbo.gov/ topics/social-security.

Census Bureau. "Households and Families: 2010." *U.S. Census Bureau.* Retrieved February 5, 2019, from https://www.census.gov/prod/cen2010/briefs/c2010br-14.pdf.

Chazen, Guy. "Germany's Record Budget Surplus Triggers Calls for Tax Cuts." *Financial Times*, August 24, 2018, https://www.ft.com/content/ce744c1e-a784 -11e8-8ecf-a7ae1beff35b.

Cochrane, John. "Shocks," *Carnegie-Rochester Conference Series on Public Policy* 41 (1994): 295–364.

Congdon, Tim. "Milton Friedman on the Ineffectiveness of Fiscal Policy." *Economic Affairs (Institute of Economic Affairs)* 31, no. 1 (2011): 62–65.

Congressional Budget Office (CBO). "Social Security." Accessed February 19, 2019, https://www.cbo.gov/topics/social-security.

Congressional Budget Office (CBO). *The Effects of Automatic Stabilizers on the Federal Budget as of 2013*. Washington: CBO, 2013.

Dellepiane-Avellaneda, Sebastian. "The Political Power of Economic Ideas: The Case of 'Expansionary Fiscal Contractions.'" *The British Journal of Politics and International Relations* no. 17 (2015): 391–418.

Devries, Pete, Jaime Guajardo, Daniel Leigh, and Andrea Pescatori. "A New Action-Based Dataset of Fiscal Consolidation." *IMF Working Paper No. 11/128*. Washington: International Monetary Fund, 2011.

European Commission. "General Government Debt." Accessed February 18, 2019, from https://ec.europa.eu/eurostat/web/products-datasets/-/sdg_17_40.

European Commission. "Public Finances in EMU 2000." *European Economy 3/2000*. Brussels: European Commission, 2000.

European Commission. "Public Finances in EMU 2007." *European Economy 3/2007*. Brussels: European Commission, 2007.

European Commission. "The Economic Adjustment Programme for Greece." *Occasional Paper no. 72*, European Commission, December 2010.

Federal Housing Finance Agency. "Single-Family Loan-to-Value Ratios." Accessed July 22, 2019, from https://www.fhfa.gov/DataTools/Downloads/Pages/Public-Use-Databases.aspx.

Franko, Patrice. *The Puzzle of Latin American Economic Development*. Lanham, MD: Rowman & Littlefield Publishers, 2007.

Friedman, Milton and Anna J. Schwartz. *A Monetary History of the United States, 1867–1960*. National Bureau of Economic Research. Studies in Business Cycles: 12. Princeton: Princeton University Press, 1963.

Friedman, Milton. "Government Revenue from Inflation." *Journal of Political Economy* 79, no. 4 (1971): 846–856.

Fukao, Kyoji. "Real GDP in Pre-War East Asia: A 1934-36 Benchmark Purchasing Power Parity Comparison with the U.S." *Institute of Economic Research Papers*. Hitotsubashi University, February 2007. Retrieved March 6, 2019, from http://gpih.ucdavis.edu/files/Fukao_Ma_Yuan.pdf.

Furman, Jason and Lawrence H. Summers. "'Who's Afraid of Budget Deficits?' How Washington Should End Its Obsession." *Foreign Affairs*, January 27, 2019.

Gallup. "Most Important Problem." Accessed February 18, 2019, from https://news.gallup.com/poll/1675/most-important-problem.aspx.

Gerow, Andrew E. "Shooting for the Stars (and Stripes): How Decades of Failed Corporate Tax Policy Contributed to Puerto Rico's Historic Vote in Favor of Statehood." *Tulane Law Review* 88, no. 3 (2014): 627–650.

Giavazzi, Francesco and Marco Pagano. "Can Severe Fiscal Contractions Be Expansionary? Tales of Two Small European Countries." *NBER Macroeconomics Annual*, 76 (1990): 76.

Giavazzi, Francesco. "The 'stimulus debate' and the Golden Rule of Mountain Climbing." *VoxEU*, July 22, 2010, https://voxeu.org/article/stimulus-debate-and-golden-rule-mountain-climbing

Gourinchas, Pierre-Olivier, Thomas Philippon, and Dimitri Vayanos. "The Analytics of the Greek Crisis." *NBER Macroeconomics Annual* 31, no. 1 (2017): 1–81.

Government Accountability Office (U.S. GAO). *PUERTO RICO: Information on How Statehood Would Potentially Affect Selected Federal Programs and Revenue Sources*. GAO, March 31, 2014.

Government Accountability Office (U.S. GAO). *Pharmaceutical Industry: Tax Benefits of Operating in Puerto Rico*. GAO, 1992.

Government Development Bank for Puerto Rico. "Monthly Indicators." Accessed February 14, 2018, from http://www.gdb-pur.com/economy/latest-information-monthly-indicators.html.

Gruen, David and Amanda Sayegh. "The Evolution of Fiscal Policy in Australia." *Treasury Working Paper 2004-5* (2005). The Treasury of the Australia.

Guajardo, Jaime, Daniel Leigh, and Andrea Pescatori. "Expansionary Austerity? International Evidence." *Journal of the European Economic Association* 12, no. 4 (2014): 949–968.

Hamilton, James D. "Historical Causes of Postwar Oil Shocks and Recessions." *Energy Journal* 6, no. 1 (January 1985): 97–116. doi:http://www.iaee.org.proxy-bc.researchport.umd.edu/en/publications/journal.aspx.

Herndon, Thomas, Michael Ash, and Robert Pollin. "Does High Public Debt Consistently Stifle Economic Growth? A Critique of Reinhart and Rogoff." *Cambridge Journal of Economics* 38, no. 2 (2014): 257–279.

House, Christopher L., Christian Proebsting, and Linda L. Tesar. "Austerity in the Aftermath of the Great Recession." *NBER Working Paper*. Cambridge, MA: NBER, 2017.

Ilzetzki, Ethan, Enrique G. Mendoza, and Carlos A. Véghc, "How Big (Small?) Are Fiscal Multipliers?" *Journal of Monetary Economics* 60, no. 2 (March 2013): 239–254.

International Monetary Fund (IMF). "Central Government Debt." Accessed July 22, 2019, https://www.imf.org/external/datamapper/CG_DEBT_GDP@GDD/.

International Monetary Fund (IMF). "Datasets." Accessed January 10, 2019, from https://www.imf.org/external/datamapper/datasets.

International Monetary Fund (IMF). *Global Debt Database*. Washington: IMF, 2019. https://www.imf.org/external/datamapper/datasets/GDD.

International Monetary Fund (IMF). "GPD Per Capita, Current Prices." Accessed July 22, 2019, from https://www.imf.org/external/datamapper/NGDPDPC@WEO/OEMDC/ADVEC/WEOWORLD.

International Monetary Fund (IMF). *IMF Recent Economic Developments*. Washington: International Monetary Fund, 1987, 36–37.

International Monetary Fund. "Report for Selected Countries and Subjects." *World Economic Outlook Database*, October 2018. Accessed February 18, 2019 from https://www.imf.org/external/pubs/ft/weo/2018/02/weodata/.

International Monetary Fund. *IMF Recent Economic Developments*. Washington: International Monetary Fund, 1980, 34.

International Monetary Fund. *IMF Staff Report for Article IV Consultations*. Washington: International Monetary Fund, 1997, 22.

Keynes, John M. *The Economic Consequences of the Peace*. New York: Harcourt, Brace and Howe, 1919.

Keynes, John M. *The General Theory of Employment, Interest, and Money*. New York: Palgrave Macmillan, 1936.

Krogstrup, Signe and Wyplosz, Charles. "Dealing with the Deficit Bias: Principles and Policies." In *Policy Instruments for Sound Fiscal Policies*, edited by J. Ayuso-i-Casals, S. Deroose, E. Flores, and L. Moulin. London: Palgrave Macmillan, 2009, 23–50.

Krugman, Paul. "Dubya's Double Dip?" *The New York Times*, August 2, 2002. Accessed March 6, 2019, from https://www.nytimes.com/2002/08/02/opinion/du bya-s-double-dip.html.

Krugman, Paul. "Myths of Austerity." *The New York Times*, July 1, 2010, https://ww w.nytimes.com/2010/07/02/opinion/02krugman.html.

Krugman, Paul. *The Return of Depression Economics and the Crisis of 2008*. New York: W.W. Norton Company Limited, 2009.

Kuismanen, Mika and Ville Kämppi. "The Effects of Fiscal Policy on Economic Activity in Finland." *Economic Modelling* 27, no. 5 (2010): 1315–1323.

Larch, Martin and Alessandro Turrini. "Received Wisdom and Beyond: Lessons from Fiscal Consolidations in the EU." *EC European Economy* 320 (2008): 1–31.

Laya, Patricia and Andrew Rosati. "Venezuela's 2018 Inflation to Hit 1.37 Million Percent, IMF Says." *Bloomberg*. October 8, 2018, https://www.bloomberg.com /news/articles/2018-10-09/venezuela-s-2018-inflation-to-hit-1-37-million-percent -imf-says.

Legorano, Giovanni and Marcus Walker. "Italy Says It Struck a Budget-Deficit Compromise With EU." *The Wall Street Journal*. Accessed December 18, 2018, from https://www.wsj.com/articles/italy-says-it-struck-a-budget-deficit-compromise-wi th-eu-11545169334.

Lopez, Pablo J. and Cecilia Nahon. "The Growth of Debt and the Debt of Growth: Lessons from the Case of Argentina." *Journal of Law and Society* 44, no. 1 (March 2017): 99–122.

Marxuach, Sergio. "The Puerto Rican Economy: Historical Perspectives and Current Challenges." *Center for the New Economy* (2007). Accessed February 18, 2019, from http://grupocne.org/wp-content/uploads/2012/02/FLMM.pdf.

McSpadden, Kevin. "You Now Have a Shorter Attention Span Than a Goldfish." *Time Magazine*, May 2015.

Monacelli, Tommaso and Roberto Perotti. "Fiscal Policy, the Real Exchange Rate and Traded Goods." *The Economic Journal*, 120, no. 544 (2010): 437–461.

Mueller, John and Marc Miles, "Section 936: No Loss to Puerto Rico." Econometric paper produced by Lehrman, Bell, Mueller, and Cannon (1997).

Mundell, Robert A. "A Theory of Optimum Currency Areas." *The American Economic Review* 51, no. 4 (September 1961): 657–665.

National Archives (UK). "United Kingdom Financial Statement and Budget Report (FSBR) of 1994–95." Accessed December 14, 2018, from https://webarchive. nationalarchives.gov.uk/20130105093314/http://www.official-documents.co.uk/d ocument/hmt/budget94/budget94.htm.

Neil, Dan. "The 50 Worst Cars of All Time." *Time* (2017). Accessed December 13, 2018, from http://time.com/4723114/50-worst-cars-of-all-time/.

Northrop Grumman. "Defense Systems." Accessed December 12, 2018, from http://www.northropgrumman.com/Capabilities/DefenseSystems/Pages/default.aspx.

Odishelidze, Alexander and Arthur Laffer. *Pay to the Order of Puerto Rico.* Fairfax, VA: Allegiance Press, 2004.

Organization for Economic Co-Operation and Development (OECD) National Accounts Statistics. "Government expenditure." Accessed January 15, 2019, from https://www.oecd-ilibrary.org/economics/data/oecd-national-accounts-statistics_n a-data-en.

Organization for Economic Co-Operation and Development (OECD). *OECD Economic Survey.* Paris: OECD, 2003, 15.

Oscar Jordà, Maritz Schularick, and Alan M. Taylor." Sovereigns Versus Banks: Credit, Crises, and Consequences." *Journal of the European Economic Association* 14, no. 1 (2016): 45.

Otake, Tomoko. "Japan's Population Projected to Plunge to 88 Million by 2065." *The Japan Times*, April 10, 2017. Accessed March 7, 2019, from https://www.japantim es.co.jp/news/2017/04/10/national/social-issues/japans-population-projected-plun ge-88-million-2065/#.XIFNDChKjD4.

Pardington, Richard. "Argentina Launches Fresh Austerity Measures to Stem Peso Crisis." *The Guardian*, September 3, 2018. Accessed March 8, 2019, from https ://www.theguardian.com/world/2018/sep/03/argentina-austerity-peso-crisis-macri.

Perotti, Roberto. "The 'Austerity Myth': Gain without Pain?" In *Fiscal Policy After the Financial Crisis*, edited by Alberto Alesina and Francesco Giavazzi, 307–354. National Bureau of Economic Research Conference Report. Chicago and London: University of Chicago Press, 2013.

Philippopoulos, Apostolis, Petros Varthalitis, and Vanghelis Vassilatos, "Fiscal Consolidation and Its Cross-Country Effects." *Journal of Economic Dynamics and Control* 8355 (2017): 106.

Posner, Paul L. "The Politics of Fiscal Austerity: Democracies and Foresight." *Indiana Journal of Global Legal Studies* no. 2 (2015): 433–485.

Poterba, James M. "Explaining the Yield Spread Between Taxable and Tax-Exempt Bonds: The Role of Expected Tax Policy." In *Studies in State and Local Public Finance*, edited by Harvey S. Rosen, 5–49. Chicago: University of Chicago Press, 1986.

Ramey, Valerie, and Matthew D. Shapiro. "Costly Capital Reallocation and the Effects of Government Spending." *Carnegie-Rochester Conference Series on Public Policy*, 48 (June 1998): 145–94.

Ramey, Valerie. "Identifying Government Spending Shocks: It's All in the Timing." *Quarterly Journal of Economics* 126, no. 1 (2011): 1–50.

Ramey, Valerie. "Macroeconomic Shocks and Their Propagation." In *Handbook of Macroeconomics, Volume 2*, edited by John B. Taylor and Michael Woodford, 71–162. Amsterdam: Elsevier, 2016.

Ravn, Morten O., Stephanie Schmitt-Grohé, and Martin Uribe. "Consumption, Government Spending, and the Real Exchange Rate." *Journal of Monetary Economics* 59, no. 3 (2012): 215–234.

Reinhart, Carmen and Kenneth Rogoff. "Growth in a Time of Debt." *American Economic Review* 100, no. 2 (2010): 573–578.

Reinhart, Carmen, Vincent Reinhart, and Kenneth Rogoff. "Public Debt Overhangs: Advanced Economy Episodes Since 1800." *Journal of Economic Perspectives* 26, no. 3 (2012): 69–86.

Reuters. "Spain Raises Deficit Targets for 2018, 2019." *Reuters Business News*, July 12, 2018. https://www.reuters.com/article/us-spain-economy-deficit/spain-raises-deficit-targets-for-2018-2019-idUSKBN1K22VA.

Romer, Christina D. and David H. Romer, "Does Monetary Policy Matter? A New Test in the Spirit of Friedman and Schwartz." *NBER Macroeconomic Annual* 4 (1989): 121. doi:10.2307/3584969.

Romer, Christina D. and David H. Romer, "The Macroeconomic Effects of Tax Changes: Estimates Based on a New Measure of Fiscal Shocks." *American Economic Review*, (June 2010): 763.

Romer, David. *Advanced Macroeconomics*. New York: McGraw-Hill, 2012.

Rotemberg, Julio and Michael Woodford. "Oligopolistic Pricing and the Effects of Aggregate Demand on Economic Activity." *Journal of Political Economy* 100, no. 6 (1992): 1153–1207.

Sánchez-Alonso, Blanca. "Making Sense of Immigration Policy: Argentina, 1870–1930." *The Economic History Review* 66, no. 2 (November 2010): 601–627.

Santurno, James, Bill Heniff, and Megan Lynch. *The Congressional Appropriations Process: An Introduction*. Washington: Congressional Research Service, 2016, https://www.senate.gov/CRSpubs/8013e37d-4a09-46f0-b1e2-c14915d498a6.pdf.

Slavin, Robert. "Puerto Rico Plan Aims to Reboot Economy." *The Bond Buyer*. Accessed May 10, 2014, from http://www.bondbuyer.com/issues/123_90/puerto-rico-plan-aims-to-reboot-islands-economy-1062350-1.html.

Smith, Adam. *An Inquiry Into the Nature and Causes of the Wealth of Nations*. London: Printed for A. Strahan and T. Cadell, 1784.

Solow, Robert. "Building a Science of Economics for the Real World." *Prepared Statement*, presented to the House Committee on Science and Technology Subcommittee on Investigations and Oversight, July 20, 2010.

Summers, D. 2009. "David Cameron Warns of 'new age of austerity.'" *The Guardian*.

Tax Policy Center. "Tax Units with Zero or Negative Income Tax Under Current Law, 2011–2028." Accessed January 1, 2019, https://www.taxpolicycenter.org/model-estimates/tax-units-zero-or-negative-income-tax-liability-september-2018/t18-0128-tax-units.

The Local Switzerland. "Anger as Switzerland Records 'surprise' 2.8 Billion-Franc Budget Surplus." *The Local*. https://www.thelocal.ch/20180214/anger-as-switzerl and-records-surprise-28-billion-franc-budget-surplus.

Treasury Direct (U.S. Department of the Treasury). "Interest Expense on Debt Outstanding." Accessed February 1, 2019, from https://www.treasurydirect.gov/govt/reports/ir/ir_expense.htm.

U.S. Census Bureau. "Trade in Goods with South and Central America." Accessed June 10, 2019, from https://www.census.gov/foreign-trade/balance/c0009.html.

Vélez, Gustavo. *Reinvención boricua: Propuestas de reactivación económica para los individuos, las empresas y el gobierno*. San Juan, PR: Inteligencia Económica, 2011.

Vélez-Hagan, J. 2015. *The Common Sense Behind Basic Economics: A Guide for Budding Economists, Students, and Voters.* Lanham, MD: Lexington Books.

Weingast, Barry, Kenneth Shepsle, and Christopher Johnsen. "The Political Economy of Benefits And Costs: A Neoclassical Approach to Distributive Politics." *Journal of Political Economy* no. 89 (1981): 642–664.

Wiese, Rasmus, Richard Jong-A-Pin, and Jakob de Haan. "Can Successful Fiscal Adjustments Only Be Achieved by Spending Cuts?" *European Journal of Political Economy* 54 (2018): 145–166.

Wolswijk, Guido. "Short- and Long-Run Tax Elasticities – The Case of the Netherlands." *European Central Bank Working Paper Series No. 763.* Frankfurt: European Central Bank, 2007.

Wooldridge, Jeffrey M. *Introductory Econometrics: A Modern Approach.* 6th ed. Mason, OH: South-Western Cengage Learning, 2016.

World Bank. *Poverty.* Washington: World Bank. Accessed February 13, 2019, from https://www.worldbank.org/en/topic/poverty/overview.

World Bank. "What Is an International Dollar?" Accessed March 20, 2019, from https://datahelpdesk.worldbank.org/knowledgebase/articles/114944-what-is-an-international-dollar.

Index

Page references for figures are italicized.

211

About the Author

Justin Vélez-Hagan is an economic policy analyst in Washington, D.C., where he currently serves as the executive director and chief economist of the National Puerto Rican Chamber of Commerce. His work has been featured in a number of national publications, and he is also a frequent guest on national and international television news outlets.

He is also the author of *The Common Sense behind Basic Economics: A Guide for Budding Economists, Students, and Voters* (Lexington Books, 2015).

Vélez-Hagan received his MBA from the W. P. Carey School of Business at Arizona State University and his PhD in economic policy from the University of Maryland, Baltimore County. He currently resides in Virginia with his wife and three children.

Lightning Source UK Ltd.
Milton Keynes UK
UKHW021335010322
399398UK00004B/186